"*Living in a Mindful Universe* goes beyond Dr. Alexander's previous books in showing how science and spirituality are coming together to give us a more complete understanding of consciousness, meaning, and purpose in the universe—and in describing how we can realize our role in it."

–Bruce Greyson, MD, Carlson professor emeritus of Psychiatry and Neurobehavioral Sciences at the University of Virginia Health System

"In this third book, Eben Alexander provides new information about the coma and its aftermath . . . then goes on with his partner Karen Newell to survey a variety of practices and technologies that may enable others to access these expanded states of consciousness and the normally latent human potentials associated with them. An exciting new journey of scientific self-discovery is certainly underway."

–Edward F. Kelly, PhD, author of *Irreducible Mind* and *Beyond Physicalism*

"In *Living in a Mindful Universe*, Eben Alexander and Karen Newell explore the worlds of both science and spirit. They offer clear explanations of findings that challenge the Supreme Illusion of everyday physical reality, along with frank accounts of their own efforts to connect more with the Collective Mind. The result is a work filled with wisdom and compassion."

–Jim B. Tucker, MD, *New York Times* bestselling author of the *Return to Life*

"With a background in neurosurgery and having had direct experience of nonordinary aspects of reality, Eben Alexander is a unique and valuable cultural asset in our efforts to develop a more mature understanding of the nature of self and world. In this delightful and mind-opening book, Eben and Karen take us with them on their journey of exploration. They show that their insights are accessible to any one of us and that sane, coherent, nonmaterialist views of reality not only exist but are no longer fringe."

–Bernardo Kastrup, PhD, author of *More Than Allegory* and *Brief Peeks Beyond*

"In this impressive book, Eben Alexander gives us a frank and very personal account of the life-changing transformation following his deep-coma experience. This clearly written book will bring deeper understanding of the nature of the human spirit and gives us all a greater knowledge about the nature of reality. Highly recommended."

–Pim van Lommel, cardiologist and author of *Consciousness Beyond Life*

"Eben Alexander and Karen Newell skillfully and beautifully drive home a timely and important message: You are not just part of a self-aware and ever-evolving universe, you are the one that gives it awareness and is evolving it! The future of our world is directly in our hands through the choices we make."

–Rudolph E. Tanzi, PhD, professor of neurology, Harvard Medical School, and *New York Times* bestselling coauthor of *Super Brain* and *Super Genes*

"Dr. Alexander couldn't ignore something that science cannot (currently) explain—namely, a detailed NDE when his brain was clinically incapacitated. Highly recommended for anyone looking to harness the power of the human mind!"

–Kelly Turner, PhD, *New York Times* bestselling author of *Radical Remission*

ademic neurosurgeon for ..
years. He was educated at Duke Medical School and has worked at Duke University Medical School and Harvard Medical School. He has a passionate interest in physics and cosmology, and is the author of the #1 *New York Times* bestseller *Proof of Heaven* and *The Map of Heaven*. To find out more visit ebanalexander.com

Karen Newell is a lifelong seeker of esoteric wisdom and has amassed a wealth of firsthand experience exploring realms of consciousness. Cofounder of Sacred Acoustics, she teaches how to enter and engage with expanded awareness in order to connect to inner guidance, achieve inspiration, improve wellness and enhance intuition. To find out more visit sacredacoustics.com

Praise for *Living in a Mindful Universe*

"*Living in a Mindful Universe* is a compelling introduction to a vitally important and rapidly unfolding paradigm shift in science, providing a far more comprehensive worldview where consciousness is the fundamental 'glue' that defines reality itself."

–Dean Radin, PhD, chief scientist, IONS, and author of *Entangled Minds* and *Supernormal*

"Eben, a man of science, delves into the Spiritual Oneness. He realizes that there are many paths up the mountain and they end up in the same place. As a result of understandings that Eben encountered during his coma, he succinctly conveys familiarity with many planes of consciousness, and the way he demonstrates this awareness is fascinating."

–Ram Dass, author of *Be Here Now*

LIVING IN A
MINDFUL
UNIVERSE

A NEUROSURGEON'S JOURNEY
INTO THE HEART OF CONSCIOUSNESS

EBEN ALEXANDER, MD,
AND KAREN NEWELL

PIATKUS

PIATKUS

First published in the US in 2017 by Rodale Inc.
First published in Great Britain in 2017 by Piatkus
This paperback edition published in 2021 by Piatkus

1 3 5 7 9 10 8 6 4 2

Copyright © 2017 Dr Eben Alexander and Karen Newell

A CIP catalogue record for this book
is available from the British Library.

ISBN 978-0-349-41742-4

Designed by Carol Angstadt
Printed and bound in Great Britain by
Clays Ltd, Elcograf S.p.A.

Papers used by Piatkus are from well-managed forests
and other responsible sources.

MIX
Paper from
responsible sources
FSC® C104740

Piatkus
An imprint of
Little, Brown Book Group
Carmelite House
50 Victoria Embankment
London EC4Y 0DZ

An Hachette UK Company
www.hachette.co.uk

www.littlebrown.co.uk

To our children,
Eben IV, Bond, and Jamie,
whose generation we trust will make
this world a far better place

CONTENTS

PREFACE

This book is an ambitious effort to unite science and spirituality, two topics that are typically seen as opposites and are rarely so thoroughly addressed in the same book. We aim to reach a broad reading audience: those with both scientific and spiritual leanings—and everyone in between. This is a message for *all* of humanity.

We wish to engage the modern, informed reader with a sincere interest in further understanding the nature of our world, and their relationship to it. The first five chapters generally clarify the problems facing our prevalent Western worldview and confront many ingrained conventional scientific and philosophical assumptions. We then outline a broadened paradigm supported by both human experience and the empirical evidence of scientific research.

Some of the content in those opening chapters may be of less interest to a nonscientific reader, but full comprehension of these concepts before moving on to the remainder of the book is not required. Some may find it useful to read the early chapters *after* the rest of the book. Chapters 6 through 16 relate examples and information involving actual tools and techniques of value to individuals wanting to learn more about their connection with the universe and their capacities for fully manifesting their free will.

The text is written in my first-person voice because it is my narrative. But my coauthor, Karen Newell, understands my voice better than anyone and significantly added to, clarified, and refined what is truly *our* message—I could not possibly have come up with this on my own. Karen's lifetime spent in pursuit of deeper understanding of the nature of all existence has offered a treasure trove of insight and understanding, and this book is far more informative (and friendly to the less scientific reader) through her sage wisdom.

INTRODUCTION

Discovery consists of seeing what everybody has
seen and thinking what nobody has thought.

—ALBERT SZENT-GYÖRGYI (1893–1986),
NOBEL PRIZE IN PHYSIOLOGY OR MEDICINE, 1937

What is the relationship between the mind and the brain? Most people do not dwell on this question. It's best to leave such musings up to neuroscientists and philosophers—why spend time thinking about such scholarly matters? Brain and mind are clearly related, and that's enough for most of us to know, right? We have more important things to focus on in our lives.

As a practicing neurosurgeon, I was exposed daily to the mind-brain relationship due to the fact that my patients would often have alterations in their level of consciousness. While this phenomenon was interesting, my focus was pragmatic. I was trained to evaluate those alterations in consciousness in order to diagnose and treat various tumors, injuries, infections, or strokes affecting the brain. We have the tools and, hopefully, the talent to benefit our patients by restoring them to more "normal" levels of conscious awareness. I closely followed developments in physics and knew there were theories about how it all works, but I had patients to care for, and more important things to consider.

My complacency with that arrangement of casual "understanding" came crashing to a halt on November 10, 2008. I collapsed on my bed and fell into a deep coma, after which I was admitted to Lynchburg General Hospital—the same hospital where I had worked as a neurosurgeon. While in coma, I experienced things that, in the weeks after awakening, baffled me and cried out for an explanation within the bounds of science as I knew it.

According to conventional neuroscience, due to the severe damage to my brain caused by an overwhelming bacterial meningoencephalitis, I should not have experienced anything—at all! But while my brain was besieged and swollen with infection, I went on a fantastic odyssey during which I remembered nothing of my life on earth. This odyssey seemed to have lasted for months or years, an elaborate journey into many layers of higher dimensions, at times viewed from the perspective of infinity and eternity, outside of space and time. Such a complete inactivation of my neocortex, the outer surface of the brain, should have disabled all but the most rudimentary experiences and memory—yet I was haunted by the persistence of so many ultrareal memories, vivid and complex. At first I simply trusted my doctors and their advice that "the dying brain can play all kinds of tricks." After all, I had sometimes given my own patients the same "advice."

My final follow-up visit with the main neurologist involved in my care came in early January 2010, fourteen months after awakening from my treacherous weeklong coma. Dr. Charlie Joseph had been a friend and close associate before my coma, and had struggled with the rest of my medical colleagues through the brunt of my horrific meningoencephalitis, recording the details of the neurological devastation along the way. We caught up on the specifics of my recovery (all of which were quite surprising and unexpected, given the severity of my illness during that fateful week), reviewing some of the neurological exams and MRI and CT scan results from my time in coma, and performing a complete neurological examination.

As tempting as it was to simply accept my extraordinary healing and current well-being as an inexplicable miracle, I couldn't do that. Instead, I was driven to find an explanation for the journey I took during the coma—a sensory experience that completely defied our conventional neuroscientific concepts of the role of the neocortex in detailed conscious awareness. The unsettling prospect that fundamental tenets of neuroscience were incorrect led me into deeper territory in my final discussion with Dr. Joseph that blustery winter afternoon.

"I am left with no explanation whatsoever as to how my mental experiences deep in coma, so vibrant, complex, and alive, could have possibly occurred," I said to him. "It *seemed* more real than anything I had ever experienced." I recounted for him how numerous details clearly placed the vast majority of my coma experience as occurring between days one and five of my seven-day coma, and yet the neurological examinations, lab values, and imaging results all confirmed that my neocortex was too damaged by the severe meningoencephalitis to have supported any such conscious experience. "How am I to make any sense of all this?" I asked my friend.

I'll never forget Charlie's smile, as he looked at me with a sense of *knowing*, and said, "There is plenty of room in our understanding of the brain, and mind, and consciousness to allow for this mystery of your remarkable recovery to indicate something of great importance. As you well know, we encounter copious evidence in clinical neurology that we have a far way to go before we can start claiming any kind of 'complete' understanding. I am inclined to accept your personal mystery as another lovely piece of the puzzle, one that greatly raises the ante in approaching any understanding of the nature of our existence. Just enjoy!"

I found it most reassuring that a highly trained and capable neurologist, one who had carefully followed the details of my illness, was open to the grand possibilities implied by my memories from deep in coma. Charlie helped open wide the door that has led to my transformation from a materialist scientist, proud of his academic skepticism, into someone who now knows his true nature and has also been offered a glimpse into levels of reality that is most refreshing, indeed.

Of course, it was not an easy journey in those initial months of exploration and confusion. I knew that I was entertaining concepts that many in my field would consider beyond the pale, if not outright heretical. Some might even suggest that I let go of my inquiry rather than commit professional suicide by sharing such a radical tale.

As Dr. Joseph and I had come to agree, my brain was severely damaged by a near-fatal case of bacterial meningoencephalitis. The neocortex—the part modern neuroscience tells us must be at least partially active for conscious experience—was incapable of creating or processing anything even remotely close to what I experienced. And yet I did experience it. To quote Sherlock Holmes, "When you have excluded the impossible, whatever remains, however improbable, must be the truth." Thus, I had to accept the improbable: This very real experience happened, and I was conscious of it—and my consciousness did not depend on having an intact brain. Only by allowing my mind (and my heart) to open as widely as possible was I able to see the cracks in the conventional consensus view of the brain and consciousness. It was by the light allowed in by those cracks that I began to glimpse the true depths of the mind-body debate.

That debate is of extreme importance to us all because many of our foundational assumptions about the nature of reality hinge on the directions in which that debate flows. Any notion of meaning and purpose in our existence, of connection with others and the universe, of our very sense of free will, and even of such concepts as an afterlife and reincarnation—all of these deep issues depend directly on the outcome of the mind-body debate. The relationship between mind and brain is thus one of the most profound and important mysteries in all of human thought. And the picture emerging from the most advanced reaches of scientific investigation is quite contrary to our conventional scientific viewpoint. A revolution in understanding appears imminent.

This pathway of discovery continues to unfold, and will no doubt occupy me for the rest of my life. Along the way I have encountered some of the most expansive experiences and intriguing people I could possibly imagine. I have learned not to be seduced by simplistic falsehoods about an assumed world, but to strive to assess and deal with the world *as it truly is*. As human beings seeking a deeper understanding of our existence, we are all well served to take that approach to heart.

DURING THE DEEPEST AND most perplexing phases in the nine years since I first awakened from coma, my mantra has often been, "Believe in it all, at least for now." My advice to you, dear reader, is to do the same—suspend disbelief for now, and open your mind as broadly as possible. Deeper understanding demands this liberation, just as trapeze artists must release the trapeze to tumble through the air, trusting that their partner will be there to catch them.

Think of this book as my outstretched hands, ready to support you as you take the greatest leap of all—into the glorious reality of who we truly are!

CHAPTER 1

MAKING SENSE
OF IT ALL

The Universe is not only queerer than we suppose,
but queerer than we *can* suppose.

—J. B. S. HALDANE (1892–1964),
BRITISH EVOLUTIONARY BIOLOGIST

Morbidity and mortality (M&M) conferences are the medical community's way of sharing the stories of hapless patients who end up maimed or dead from various illnesses and injuries. It is not, perhaps, the happiest of topics, but they are held in an effort to learn and teach so as to protect future patients from suffering the same fate. It is vanishingly rare for such a patient to be present at their own M&M conference, but that is exactly the situation I encountered a few months after my coma. The physicians who had cared for me were astounded by the high level of my ongoing recovery, and they took advantage of that apparent miracle to invite me to participate in a discussion of my unexpected escape from death.

My recovery defied any explanation in medical science. On the morning that I appeared at the conference, several colleagues shared with me what a shock it was that I had not only survived (which they had estimated to be a 2 percent probability by the end of my week in coma), but that I had seemingly recovered all of my mental function over a few months—that aspect was truly stunning. No one would have predicted such a recovery, given the extent of my illness. My neurological examinations, CT and MRI scans, and laboratory values revealed that my meningoencephalitis was one of radical—and very lethal—severity. My initial treatment was confounded by a relatively constant state of epileptic seizures that proved difficult to stop.

The neurological examination is one of the most important factors in determining the severity of coma, and can offer some of the best clues as to the prognosis. By assessing eye movements and pupillary responses to light, as well as the nature of arm and leg movements in response to painful stimuli, my doctors determined, as I would have, that my neocortex, the human part of the brain, was badly damaged even when I was first brought into the emergency room.

Another crucial factor concerns the quality of verbalization, but I had none—my only vocalizations were occasional grunts and groans, or nothing at all. The only exception was when I unexpectedly called out, "God help me!" while still in the emergency room (I have no memory of this, but it was reported to me later). Having heard nothing intelligible from me for hours, close family and friends thought those words might offer a glimmer of hope—that I might be returning to this world. But they were the last words uttered before I lapsed into deep coma.

The Glasgow Coma Scale (GCS)—which assesses vocalization, movement of the arms and legs (especially in response to painful stimuli in obtunded or comatose patients), and eye movements—is used to evaluate and follow patients with altered levels of awareness, including coma. The GCS is an assessment of one's level of alertness, and ranges from 15 in a normal healthy patient, down to 3, which is the score for a corpse, or a patient in very deep coma. My highest GCS score in the ER was 8, and it ranged as low as 5 at times during the week. I was clearly suffering from a deadly meningoencephalitis.

In the discussion around the level of damage to my neocortex, people often inquire about the electroencephalogram, or EEG. An EEG is a fairly cumbersome and finicky test to set up, and one would do so only if it were going to provide useful information for diagnosis or to assist in guiding therapy. Some studies have demonstrated a correlation between the degree of EEG abnormalities and neurological outcome in cases of bacterial meningitis. In addition, I had presented to the ER in status epilepticus (epileptic seizures resistant to medical control). There were good reasons to perform an EEG.

The sad truth was that I was so ill, with such a dismal prognosis based mainly on my neurologic examinations and laboratory values, that my doctors decided an EEG was not warranted. My EEG, as in other cases of severe meningoencephalitis, would have likely shown diffuse slow-wave activity, burst suppression patterns, or a flatline, indicative of incapacitating damage to the neocortex. This is clear from my neurologic exams and what they revealed about the severity of my illness, especially in the setting of similar cases.

In fact, an EEG recording goes silent (flatlines) within 15 to 20 seconds of cardiac arrest due to cessation of blood flow to the brain. The EEG is thus not a very demanding test in terms of revealing the extent of global neocortical damage. My neurologic examinations, and my CT and MRI scans that revealed the damage to be extensive (affecting all eight lobes of my brain), painted a plenty gloomy picture. I had been deathly ill, with significant brain damage, based on all of the available clinical facts alone.

Given such a rapid descent into coma due to severe gram-negative bacterial meningoencephalitis, by day three of such an illness virtually all patients are either beginning to awaken, or they're dead. My ongoing existence somewhere in between those definitive states vexed my doctors.

On day seven of coma, my doctors held a family conference in which they reiterated that I had been assigned approximately a 10 percent chance of survival on my initial arrival in the ER, but that that probability had dwindled to a pathetic 2 percent chance of survival after a week spent in coma. Much worse than the measly 2 percent probability for survival was the harsh reality they attached to it, and that was the likelihood of my actually awakening and having some return of quality to my life. Their estimate for that possibility was a most disappointing zero— no chance of recovery to any sort of normal daily routine. A nursing home was the best-case scenario, albeit a remote possibility.

Of course, my family and friends were devastated by this bleak depiction of the future. Due to my rapid descent into coma, and the extent of neocortical damage reflected in my neurological exams and the extreme lab values (such as the glucose level of 1 mg/dl in my cerebrospinal fluid, compared to the normal range of 60 to 80 mg/dl), any physician realizes the basic impossibility of a complete medical recovery, and yet that is what happened. I have discovered no cases of any other patients with my particular diagnosis who then went on to benefit from a complete recovery.

Toward the end of that morning conference, I was asked if I had any thoughts to share.

"All of this discussion about my case, and the rarity of my recovery, pales in comparison to what I see as a much deeper question that has plagued me ever since I opened my eyes in that ICU bed. With such well-documented decimation of my neocortex, how did I have any experience at all? Especially such a vibrant and ultrareal odyssey? How did that possibly happen?"

As I scanned the faces of my colleagues that day, I saw no more than a dim reflection of my own wonderment. Some might default to the simplistic assumption that what I had experienced had been nothing more than a feverish dream or hallucination. But those who had taken care of me, and those who knew enough neuroscience to understand the impossibility that such an impaired brain could have even remotely offered up that extraordinary and detailed complexity of experience, shared that much deeper sense of mystery. I knew that, ultimately, I would be responsible for seeking any satisfactory answers. A ready explanation of my experience wasn't lining up neatly, and I felt compelled to make better sense of it all.

I considered writing a paper for the neuroscience literature to demonstrate the fatal flaws in our scientific understanding of the role of the neocortex in detailed conscious awareness. I hoped to progress toward deeper understanding of the mind-body question, and maybe even glimpse some facet of how the mechanism of consciousness could be explained. I struggled with somehow framing it within my pre-coma worldview of scientific materialism, believing that my beleaguered brain during coma could somehow have had enough capacity to fully explain the origins of my experience.

Some of the greatest assistance in comprehending my experience has come from colleagues whom I trust and respect as truly open-minded and intelligent. The majority of physicians who have discussed my experience with me in depth have been intrigued and, for the most part, supportive. We considered many theories, all of which were attempts to somehow explain my experience as brain-based. These explanations attempted to place the origin of my perceptual experience in parts of the brain other than the neocortex (i.e., the thalamus, basal ganglia, brainstem, etc.) or by postulating that the awareness occurred outside of the interval of time during which my neocortex was clearly inactivated.

In essence, we tried to explain my memories during coma based on the common assumption that the brain is required for any type of conscious awareness. Over almost three decades of my life spent working daily with neurosurgical patients, frequently challenged by those with alterations in their consciousness, I had come to believe I had some understanding of the relationship between brain and mind—the nature of consciousness. Modern neuroscience has come to believe that all of our human qualities of language, reason, thought, auditory and visual perceptions, emotional forces, etc.—essentially all of the qualities of mental experience that become part of our human awareness—are directly derived from the most powerful calculator in the human brain: the neocortex. Although other more primitive (and deeper) structures, like those mentioned above, might play some role in consciousness, all of the grand details of conscious experience demand the high-quality neural calculator of the neocortex.

I accepted the conventional neuroscientific party line that the physical brain creates consciousness out of physical matter. The implications of that are clear: Our existence is "birth to death" and nothing more, and this is what I firmly believed in the decades preceding my coma. That's where a disease such as mine (bacterial meningoencephalitis) becomes a perfect model for human death by preferentially destroying that part of the brain that most contributes to our human mental experience.

Several months after coma, I returned to work and attended the annual meeting of the Society for Thermal Medicine in Tucson to help support the fledgling research for the Focused Ultrasound Surgery Foundation. What excited me most as I flew from Charlotte, North Carolina, to Phoenix that sunny Friday afternoon was that I would be able to reconnect with Dr. Allan Hamilton, my longtime friend and neurosurgical colleague.

Allan and I had become fast friends while working together in the neurosurgical laboratory at the Massachusetts General Hospital in Boston from 1983 through 1985. We had spent countless hours together, sometimes long into the evening, discussing various lab protocols, techniques, and projects, and commiserating over the endless stream of imperfections involved in such scientific efforts as experienced by those in the trenches who are actually doing the work.

Our friendship had overflowed the boundaries of our formal neurosurgical training, which is how, in the mid-1980s, I found myself trekking with "Old Mountain Hamilton" (as I used to call him when out in the wilderness) through ascents of some of the most storied peaks of the northeastern United States. These included Gothics and Marcy (two of the highest peaks in the Adirondack Mountains of upstate New York) and Mount Monadnock in New Hampshire, where we shared an overnight winter bivouac during a blizzard. That evening, the last thing we saw in the early fading twilight was an overflying Red Cross Huey helicopter evacuating a more hapless hiker off the mountain above us. And, of course, Mount Washington, home to some of the worst weather conditions on earth, which we had experienced together firsthand.

As an accomplished hiker who had led US Army missions on such peaks as Mount McKinley in Alaska (at 20,310 feet, the highest peak in North America, and now known as Denali), Allan excelled in preaching the importance of preparation and knowledge required to safely ascend such peaks. As part of my homework prior to our ascent to the summit of Mount Washington in October 1984, Allan had had me review decades of fatality reports. We had begun our ascent an hour before sunrise. Wind gusts up to 70 mph and thickening snowfall obscured our view to the point where we could barely see the next cairn (the rock piles that mark the trail over such lifeless landscapes). This came as no surprise. Wind speed has been measured here up to 231 mph, the highest sustained anemometer reading ever recorded on earth.

An immense sense of relief blanketed me as we entered the Lakes of the Clouds Hut, the highest of eight stone fortresses in the Presidential Range built to provide temporary shelter for hikers in this potentially deadly terrain. The fact that the heavy stone hut was chained to the rockscape seemed perfectly appropriate, given the extreme and steady force of such unearthly winds.

As my mentor in this situation, Allan challenged me to make a choice. "Shall we continue our ascent?" he asked.

Allan had asked me to read those Mount Washington fatality reports for a reason, and this was my final exam. The weather here can shift unexpectedly and he wanted me to decide whether or not we should continue our ascent in spite of the increasingly impressive blizzard.

From my time spent in extreme sports, beginning with a four-year skydiving career in college at the University of North Carolina at Chapel Hill, I knew that the real currency between participants in these potentially deadly adventures was the demonstration of professional and responsible decisions based on the situation, not some display of wild bravado. The only way to being invited onto and organizing those larger freefall star formations back in my skydiving days was through demonstrating a very cool head no matter how intense the challenges—no place for wild cowboys. Similarly, here on "the place of the Great Spirit," Allan deserved the best I could muster in making this decision.

"Maybe we should head back down," I finally said, reluctant to relinquish our treasured goal, but knowing in my heart that it was the right decision based on all of those fatality reports.

"Good choice," Allan muttered, as we started packing our gear to depart the safety and comfort of the massive stone fortress. He pushed the door out into the raging winds, as we started the arduous trek back down the mountain.

The fates were smiling down on us, though; soon after we stepped below the tree line on our descent, the weather changed abruptly. The clouds cleared, the temperature climbed into the forties, and we were able to turn back to ascending the peak in brilliant sunshine, stripped down to T-shirts, with breathtaking views for hundreds of miles all around. One of the final sections on the hike out was through a giant birch forest. I'll never forget the crystal blue skies beyond the intricate interwoven beauty of their white bark. Scattered bright golden leaves still clung on some branches in colorful defiance of the brutal winter that was fast approaching. The subtlety of the lesson of that day, and the glory we were rewarded by trusting our highest instincts and our connection with nature, is analogous to the life-changing shift in understanding I have reckoned with through the nine years since my coma.

Good choice, indeed!

I had come to respect Allan's deep intellect, rich insight, and refreshing sense of humor. He was a consummate scientist, which became abundantly clear as his career blossomed over the next few years. He went on to graduate from the top-notch neurosurgical residency program at Massachusetts General Hospital and ascended through the academic ranks at the University of Arizona, Tucson, not only to become the chairman of neurosurgery, but also to an appointment as chairman of the department of surgery. Allan was truly a star in the highest constellation of academic neurosurgery.

So as I flew out to Tucson for the Society for Thermal Medicine meeting mere months after my coma, I anticipated my reunion with Allan as the high point of the trip—and I was not to be disappointed! He picked me up in his shining blue Smart car and drove me to his home, a horse ranch on the outskirts of Tucson. All the while, our conversation allowed us to catch up on much that had happened since our previous visit together a few years earlier.

Allan listened in rapt attention as we sat in his study, richly adorned with books and memorabilia, the desert twilight fading in the large windows. I recounted for him a fairly complete summary, not only of my deep coma memories, but of the medical details that were so confounding, that had so far seemingly eliminated any chance of explaining it all as some feverish dream or hallucination. Like many of my medical colleagues, Allan shared my sense of mystery over interpreting my case, greatly enlivened by the extreme rarity of such a recovery. I knew I could count on him to help me assess the mystery of how I could have had such vivid experiences and memories during a time when my neocortex was being devoured.

Fortuitously, it was in the week preceding my trip to Tucson that I had encountered the crowning blow in my recent attempts to explain my experience. I had just received the picture of the birth sister whom I had never known, a week earlier, and the shock of understanding it had provided me about the reality of my coma memories was still fresh in my mind. As those who have read *Proof of Heaven* realize, connecting that picture of my lost birth sister with my beautiful companion deep in coma had been an earth-shattering recognition for me. Allan sensed the same astonishment, as I recounted that recent discovery.

"This is pure gold," he said, after a minute or so of thoughtful reflection at the end of my long sharing. Allan was already way ahead of me.

"Pure gold," he repeated, to which his wife, Janey, who sat in during parts of my recap, agreed wholeheartedly. "It's hard not to feel a bit jealous—I want to have your experience, too!" Janey added.

Allan explained that in his view, my story had provided a much richer and deeper understanding of the mind-body connection. If we viewed it with an open mind, rather than through the limited lens of the scientific view that I had, my experience could help us transcend our flimsy understanding of consciousness, of the relationship of mind and brain—indeed, of the very nature of reality.

"You might enjoy this," Allan said, smiling, personalizing and handing me a copy of his recently released book, *The Scalpel and the Soul: Encounters with Surgery, the Supernatural and the Healing Power of Hope.* Up to this point, we had not discussed anything strongly supernatural, so it was quite a surprise to learn he harbored such an interest—enough to write a book about it. Looking back, it occurred to me that many scientific-minded folks intentionally avoid bringing up such subjects to their colleagues and peers. Such frivolous sharing might induce raised eyebrows and rolling eyes. Given his prestigious academic appointments, it seemed he had gained the courage that so many others lacked.

I had recently allowed myself to read books on such subjects, and I devoured all 272 pages of Allan's book on the night flight back east. It contained a compelling collection of anecdotes from Allan's life experiences as a thoughtful neurosurgeon that opened the door wide to the reality of our spiritual nature. His reflective personal stories about deathbed visions, premonitions, angels, and the astonishing power of faith and love to achieve the deepest healing of the soul moved me to tears at several places in the book.

One example is a heartwarming story about a grandmother—who had been charged with taking care of her daughter's handicapped son—who now was struggling with her own diagnosis of advanced ovarian cancer, and was expected to die in just months. Who would care for this poor child when the grandmother succumbed to illness? The grandmother's faith allowed her to defy her doctors' predictions. She ended up outliving her own doctor and attending the wedding of her grandson, who also seemingly benefited from his grandmother's strong faith: Despite his disabilities, he became a skilled craftsman. Allan's blend of scientific insight combined with a deep and advanced awareness of the reality of soul, garnished with an appropriate sense of humor, greatly energized my personal quest.

Another excellent sounding board arrived in the form of Michael Sullivan, who had been at my bedside during the week of my illness. Michael was the rector at the Episcopal church I had attended for the previous two years since moving to Lynchburg, Virginia. I had not sought spiritual advice from him in the past—I had never felt the need before my coma.

Michael had become a good friend through the close connection of his son, Jack, with my youngest son, Bond. They had met while Bond was in third grade at the James River Day School, and we had shared many good family times together attending their Little League baseball games. While he happened to be a minister, he was more my fun neighbor and close friend than anything else. Given my spotty attendance in church, our conversations tended to be more secular than spiritual. Like many more evolved church leaders, he excelled at delivering spiritual grace to me, even though I had no idea he was doing so at the time.

Michael was grateful I had managed to defy my doctors' dire predictions. He had been preparing to perform my funeral (which seemed inevitable throughout the week of my coma), and offer solace to my family. Instead, he found himself becoming fascinated with the "miracle" aspects of my recovery. As a child, he had poked fun at the concept of miracles, especially as presented through televised evangelical faith healings when, for example, someone in a wheelchair might suddenly walk again after being touched on the head by an enthusiastic pastor. He assumed these were staged events believed only by gullible viewers, yet he watched with rapt curiosity. After many years of pondering the veracity of so-called miracles, his firsthand witnessing of my recovery had caused quite a stir in his own beliefs. It's one thing simply to read about such an occurrence or view it from afar on TV; it is quite another to be front and center at the bedside of a trusted friend who directly experienced such an inexplicable recovery.

In the early months after awakening from coma, I encountered Michael in our neighborhood Starbucks. We sat together to talk, and soon found the conversation delving into the memories of my coma experience. Each of our perspectives were better understood through this candid sharing.

I told him that I had been in a seemingly idyllic paradise with many earthlike features—a fertile, lush verdant valley filled with life and creation, such as plants growing, flowers and buds blossoming—all in a world much like Plato's world of forms (from his writings in *Timaeus*), in that the contents of that world are more ideal than what they represent from the earthly realm. What I came to call the Gateway Valley was only a stepping-stone to the Core, which I encountered by ascending through higher dimensions of space and time. The Core itself was the source of *all*, the ultimate nonduality of pure oneness. I was aware of the entire higher-dimensional universe as indescribably complex and holding all of existence, there as a model for the entire construct—all space, time, mass, energy, interrelationships, causality, and much more for which I have no words to express. Just beyond all of that, I encountered the power of infinite unconditional love, the very *feeling* of that ineffable love. I was awash in the source of all that is. That feeling is beyond description, yet so shockingly concrete and real that I've never lost the memory of it. Human words, developed to help us describe earthly events, obviously fall far short of conveying the astonishing majesty of the complete acceptance of that love without judgment or expectations.

"Your description of the experience reminds me of the writings of some of the early Christian mystics," Michael said to me. "I have a book that might help you even more than your neuroscience books. I'll drop it off this afternoon."

Later that day, I returned to find on the front step of my home, *Light from Light: An Anthology of Christian Mysticism*. It contained the fascinating writings of those who wrote about profound and life-changing spiritual experiences, some dating back almost two thousand years. I was in for a mind-opening read.

My knowledge of Christianity was then confined to the very limited popular variety one might expect from my conventional religious upbringing in a Methodist church in North Carolina. Mysticism was not a quality that I had yet come to associate with Christianity. This book was my first introduction to the mystics, those who actively traverse unseen realms and live a life knowing that the physical realm is but a small part of a much grander reality, most of which remains obscure from our normal waking awareness. I was surprised to learn the power and diversity of such writings from a Christian perspective. From Origen in the early 3rd century through Bernard of Clairvaux (12th century), Francis of Assisi (early 13th century), Meister Eckhart, Julian of Norwich (14th century), and Teresa of Avila (16th century), all the way up to Thérèse of Lisieux in the 19th century, the journeys sounded hauntingly familiar.

Profound mystical accounts had led the way in humanity's understanding of the full nature of the universe. Such extraordinary experiences deep in the spiritual realm were the basis for all religions. Personal experience is the greatest teacher, and Michael's recommended anthology of Christian mysticism helped me to gain a richer understanding of my own seemingly inexplicable experience. Most importantly, they began to reveal that all pathways to such knowing involve a journey into consciousness.

After several months of discussing my experience with trusted friends and colleagues, I found I had to greatly broaden my inquiries into territory quite distant from my familiar and comfortable knowledge base. The general approach to a case such as mine had been to sweep it under the rug, out of the way, and simply accept it as unexplainable. But my confidants understood my dilemma and supported my quest to more properly comprehend it. There was something much greater going on here, and I was driven to seek deeper understanding.

CHAPTER 2

A HARD PROBLEM, INDEED

Science's biggest mystery is the nature of consciousness. It is not that we possess bad or imperfect theories of human awareness; we simply have no such theories at all. About all we know about consciousness is that it has something to do with the head, rather than the foot.

—NICK HERBERT (1936–), PHYSICIST

As I first regained conscious awareness in Medical ICU bed ten, I had no memories whatsoever of my life before coma. In fact, I had no personal memories of having ever lived on planet earth. All I knew was the fantastic odyssey from which I had just returned—the astonishing deep coma journey that seemed to last for months or years, even though it all had to have happened within the seven earth days of my coma. All recollections I had up until then, including religious beliefs, personal memories, and the scientific knowledge gained through more than twenty years spent as an academic neurosurgeon, had vanished without a trace.

When I returned to this world that Sunday morning, my brain was wrecked. Even words and language had been wiped out, although they began to return rapidly in the first hours of my awakening. I initially explained the amnesia for my prior life as a result of the extensive neocortical damage my doctors insisted had occurred based on my neurological exams, scans, and laboratory values. My conventional neurosurgical training had postulated that memories were somehow stored in the brain, and particularly in the neocortex, so that was my default explanation.

My language came back over hours and days, followed by many personal life memories that returned, gently and spontaneously, over the next few weeks. The nurses were kind enough to allow two of my sisters, Betsy and Phyllis, to sleep on cots by my hospital bed to maintain that constant family vigil they had mounted during my week in coma. In my brain's beleaguered state, I found it very difficult to sleep, night or day. My sisters found my insomnia and restlessness quite annoying, and would attempt to lull me to sleep by recounting stories of our childhood vacation trips.

I was fascinated by their exotic-sounding anecdotes, of which I had no personal memories. But over a few days, vague fragments began to surface—memories that actually aligned with the fascinating stories shared by my sisters during those bizarre days (and nights) as my damaged brain attempted to right itself. Most personal life memories returned by three weeks after awakening from coma. All prior knowledge of physics, chemistry, and neuroscience (semantic memory) returned progressively over about two months or so. The completeness of my memory return was quite astonishing, especially as I thoroughly reviewed my medical records and held discussions with colleagues who had cared for me, and I realized just how ill I had actually been. Such patients do not survive, much less have extraordinary spiritual experiences and live to tell the tale, followed by a more-than-complete recovery—how to fathom it all?

The initial problem I faced concerning the nature of memory was the fact that I had *any memories whatsoever* from deep within coma. If details of my case had been presented to me before my coma, I would have very confidently told you that a patient as ill as I had been would have experienced nothing more than the most basic rudiments of conscious experience and would certainly have had no memory of it. I would have been dead wrong.

In neuroscience, we generally consider new memory formation to be a demanding process that is only incomplete and fragmented in a significantly impaired brain. This is why so many brain maladies result in partial to complete amnesia for the period of illness. Even after patients awaken from coma and interact with those around them, the capacity to remember those new experiences can take hours, days, or even longer to return, if at all. Note that recall of already formed long-term memories is not as demanding, which is why demented patients initially have their greatest problems recalling new short-term memories—for example, what they had for breakfast (even whether or not they have had breakfast)—yet their remembrance of childhood events and other distant episodes of life experience remain accessible.

Yet notably, my deep coma memories have not faded with time. After awakening from coma, I experienced roughly 36 hours of a paranoid delusional psychotic nightmare, distinctly different from the subjective sense of ultrareality that took place during the deep coma experience. I expected all of the memories (both deep coma ultrareal spiritual and postcoma delusional paranoia) to represent hallucinations of my beleaguered brain, somehow enabled through the damage to my entire neocortex and anticipated they would become less vivid over time. To my surprise, a fundamental difference between the two sets of memories has been the rock-hard resilience of the ultrareal deep coma memories compared to the ephemeral transience of the psychotic nightmare memories (which essentially disappeared over weeks). In fact, my memories of the deep coma experience have remained stable and clear even to this day.

I came to realize my ordeal could be termed a near-death experience (NDE) and was eager to learn more about similar reports to compare them with mine. But prior to reading any other accounts, during the first six weeks after awakening, I carefully wrote down everything I could remember about all of those memories from deep coma and early recovery. I then began an earnest search for records of similar experiences.

One of the first resources I encountered was *Life after Life,* Dr. Raymond Moody's world-changing 1975 book that first popularized the term "near-death experience." The loving comfort encountered by most of the hundred or so patients discussed in Dr. Moody's book resonated deeply and truly with what I recalled from my experience. The words he chose to relate from the various subjects, as well as the general sense that they were all confounded by the limitations of earthly language in trying to describe such nonearthly journeys, enlivened in me the vivid yet ineffable memories of my own experience.

The varied descriptions of that spiritual realm as a reality that was more fundamental than our earthly realm made eminent sense to me. I was blown away that other people could have had these kinds of extraordinary experiences when they were supposed to be dead. If it all worked the way materialist neuroscience imagined, where consciousness is completely shut down when the brain no longer functions, they should have had no memories at all. I was driven to explain how these experiences could be possible.

Having paid scant attention to the NDE literature before my coma, I had no idea that a hallmark of NDE memories is that they are very persistent and stable over long periods of time, unlike memories of most events, dreams, and hallucinations. Researchers have studied the remarkable stability of such memories, demonstrating that the detailed contents of NDE memories remain consistent over decades, compared to most other types of memory that seem to change somewhat every time we revisit them.

The other main quality of NDE descriptions concerns the sense of ultrareality. I was absolutely astonished by the "way too real to be real" quality of my deep coma memories, especially in the Gateway Valley and ascending to the Core realm of pure oneness. My reading revealed that more than half of NDEers are astonished by such a sense of heightened reality. I would agree with many of them who report that this normal waking reality is more dreamlike than the richness of transcendental NDEs. NDE memories are distinctly different from dreams or hallucinations. They suggest that our sense of a consensus reality in this material world is but one mode of possible realities we share.

Steven Laureys, a Belgian neurologist, and other colleagues who shared a keen interest in NDEs reported in March 2013 a fascinating study of memories in coma patients.[1] Their study evaluated three groups of coma survivors (eight patients with NDE as defined by the Greyson NDE scale, six patients without NDE but with memories of their coma, and seven patients without memories of their coma). These were compared with a group of eighteen age-matched healthy volunteers. Five types of memories were assessed using a memory characteristics questionnaire: target memories (NDE for NDE memory group, coma memory for coma memory group, and first childhood memory for no memory and control groups), old and recent real-event memories, and old and recent imagined-event memories. Since NDEs are known to have high emotional content, participants were requested to choose the most emotionally salient memories for both real and imagined recent and old event memories.

They concluded that NDE memories have more features than any other kind, from both real and imagined events, as well as compared to memories from an unconscious state, such as coma. In fact, they interpreted their findings as demonstrating that NDEs could *not* be considered as imagined events at all. They were faced with the realization that such recalled events had actually taken place. Their ultrareal nature is truly remarkable and sets them apart from any other type of memory.

Arianna Palmieri and her colleagues at the University of Padova in Italy published an interesting study in 2014 of the extraordinary quality of NDE memories. They used hypnosis to increase the amount of detail recalled from the exceptional experiences and found that the degree of detail, emotional power, and self-referentiality were more similar to memories of real events than they were to dreams and similar imagined events.[2]

Initially, my attempts to understand were dominated by my pre-coma assumptions about the nature of brain and mind. But the ultrareality itself was most difficult to explain from within my old paradigm. If the brain produces conscious awareness, and the neocortex (as the most powerful calculator in the information processing system of the brain) is essential in constructing any such detailed conscious awareness, then why would the progressive dismantling of my neocortex allow for such an astronomical enhancement in the detailed, multilayered quality and meaning of conscious awareness? I struggled for months with that conundrum before I finally started to rework my worldview from square one.

The more I read about the scientific study of NDEs, the more I felt like I was tumbling over the edge of a gargantuan precipice. This was becoming much more serious than my initial forays, in which I had first sensed a fly in the ointment—it now seemed much more like an asteroid destroying the home planet! All of my pre-coma assumptions about the nature of reality were now up for grabs. Something must be fundamentally wrong with our conventional scientific worldview, something revealed by these extraordinary human experiences—but what? How far down into my fundamental beliefs did I have to go in order to make changes that would allow for deeper understanding?

In essence, I was seeking a new scientific framework that could explain such experiences in a way that was more accurate and comprehensive than what conventional science allowed. To my great delight, I found that serious scientists had been studying these phenomena for decades, if not for more than a century. And, as fate would have it, one of the most prominent and renowned of such scientists worked right up the road.

Dr. Bruce Greyson, a remarkably mild-mannered psychiatrist at the University of Virginia (UVA) in Charlottesville, began researching NDEs in the early 1970s. He became fascinated with reported aftereffects of individuals who claimed to have vivid, transcendental memories of events that occurred while their bodies were in physical distress, leading him to develop the Greyson Scale to determine common features of near-death experiences. He created a questionnaire with questions such as "Were your senses more vivid than usual?" and quantified the results in order to classify the intensity of the experience as compared to others.

As a practicing psychiatrist, he was well suited to contrasting differences of such experiences with common mental disorders, such as psychosis and schizophrenia. Among many such distinctions is the often long-lasting beneficial transformation of beliefs, attitudes, and values that occurs following a near-death experience. Long-term follow-up reveals such effects continue for years, even permanently, a feature not typically found in other mental disorders.

Dr. Greyson has authored more than 100 publications in peer-reviewed medical journals and was editor in chief of the *Journal of Near-Death Studies* for more than twenty years. Naturally, he was interested in hearing the details of my experience, and I realized he possessed a gold mine of information on the phenomenon that might contribute usefully to my ongoing investigation. Among other prestigious appointments at the time, Dr. Greyson was the director of the Division of Perceptual Studies (DOPS) at UVA. After establishing an email correspondence over several months, he invited me to speak at one of their regular meetings. What was the subject of their weekly gatherings? Consciousness!

As I drove to Charlottesville for my presentation, I realized that I would be speaking at exactly the second anniversary (to the hour) of my emergence from coma—a worthy celebration, I reflected. I had reviewed the DOPS Web site and had been amazed by their world-leading efforts in the exploration of all matters of consciousness and, in particular, nonlocal consciousness (that is, that we can know things independently of our physical senses and beyond the constraints of space and time). The entire DOPS group was driven by a common goal: to establish an alternate theory describing our perceptions of the world, given the failures of the common physicalist (or materialist) paradigm to explain the mind-body relationship. Their mission was defined by the relative lack of scientific understanding about the brain and mind that had emerged, in spite of enormous research funding and effort (most of that funding devoted to brain studies, in particular, with the equally relevant field of parapsychology left woefully short of funding). The doctrine of physicalism, the notion that only physical stuff exists, had so far failed to offer up any meaningful understanding of the mind-brain relationship.

This scholarship began with the work of Dr. Ian Stevenson in the 1960s, who researched past-life memories in children using scientific protocols, and is continued today by Dr. Jim Tucker, the current director of DOPS. This focus led to the general study of nonlocal consciousness— i.e., aspects of mind occurring beyond the ken of our physical senses, such as near-death experiences, after-death communications, telepathy, psychokinesis, precognition, presentiment, out-of-body experiences, remote viewing, past-life memories in children indicative of reincarnation, and other types of altered states of consciousness. Their special interest is in using scientific methodology to study evidence for survival of the soul beyond death. I had no idea there was such research going on just 90 minutes up US Highway 29.

During my hourlong presentation to the thirty or so scientists and their colleagues, rather than disbelief, skepticism, or surprise, this group exchanged meaningful nods of understanding as my story unfolded. Our discussion spilled over into lunch at a local restaurant on the Downtown Mall, where I learned much more about the volumes of research being performed at DOPS.

Among these intrepid scientists was Dr. Edward Kelly, who had earned a PhD in psycholinguistics and cognitive science at Harvard in 1971 and later spent more than fifteen years studying psi (or "paranormal") phenomena at JB Rhine's Institute for Parapsychology in Durham, North Carolina. He had also worked at the department of electrical engineering at Duke University, where I attended medical school. We seemed to have crossed paths at several institutions, albeit at different times and with contrasting interests.

Dr. Kelly gave me a copy of their revolutionary book *Irreducible Mind: Toward a Psychology for the 21st Century.* I had never heard of the book prior to this. Upon reading it, I realized I had missed a giant body of existing research on the phenomena of NDEs, past-life memories in children, mystical experiences, and other examples of nonlocal consciousness. Shocking! I recognized that the DOPS team was far along the trail I was just beginning to follow. Surprisingly, I began to realize there are many scientists and physicians around the world who have already come to appreciate that conventional scientific materialism is hopelessly lost about any understanding of consciousness.

The past century has witnessed astonishing progress in our understanding of the human brain. After millennia of guessing what was happening in our heads during any human activity, we developed exciting new tools for exploring the physical actions within the brain. Starting in the 1970s, CT scans allowed us to create three-dimensional images of brain structure using x-rays; soon after, MRI gave us unprecedented detail in the normal and abnormal anatomy in people's brains, and soon fMRI ("functional" MRI) allowed a structural assessment of brain activity when a person perceives, thinks, or moves. Especially over the past few decades, neuroscientists have enjoyed unprecedented access to what is going on in the brain in magnificent detail.

As a neurosurgeon, I have been privileged to be part of that race toward mapping and understanding the human brain. I helped develop advanced neurosurgical techniques such as stereotactic radiosurgery (which utilizes precisely directed beams of radiation to treat various brain anomalies), image-guided operations (notably, a complete redesign of MRI systems to allow us to operate on people's brains while imaging in the MRI scanner, enabling far safer and more efficacious operations), and the use of focused ultrasound energy to treat (not simply image, as in the classical use of ultrasound) movement disorders (such as tremor), brain tumors, strokes, and Alzheimer's. Suffice it to say that by now, we know vast amounts about the brain's physiology and function. And yet we neuroscientists and researchers still can't answer the single most important question: What is consciousness and where does it come from?

In the world of neuroscience and philosophy of mind, this question is known as the hard problem of consciousness (HPC), a term coined by the eccentric Australian philosopher David Chalmers in his 1996 book, *The Conscious Mind*. Many scientists believe it to be the most profound mystery in the history of human thought. We know lots about the mechanics of the brain, right down to the molecular level, but when it comes to consciousness, we simply haven't got a clue. How might the physical matter of the brain give rise to the conscious mind? What is its relationship to the observer within that witnesses all that we experience and remember, the part of us that not only processes stimuli, but has thoughts and can even reflect on them? It's a crucial question, and it gets to the heart of what makes us us. But despite all of the advances in evolutionary biology and brain research, we don't know how our essential beingness gets formed—or even where it comes from.

Some scientists are ready to give up on the question. They arrive at a point where they abandon all hope of ever explaining how consciousness might arise from the physical workings of the brain. Others decide to sidestep the issue by declaring that consciousness does not even exist, or by claiming that one day we will discover exactly how consciousness arises from physical matter. It's unfashionable to point out that the most logical explanations are the ones that completely contradict the current brain-creates-consciousness (materialist) model of neuroscience. Believe it or not, when faced with the fact that there aren't even any inklings of a theory to explain how the brain *might* create consciousness, many scientists simply shrug and move on. For them, the hard problem is just too, well, hard.

Chalmers was onto something back in 1996, but he wasn't the first or last person to glimpse the profound mystery of this subject. The father of quantum physics, and winner of the Nobel Prize in Physics in 1918, German Max Planck, said, "I regard consciousness as fundamental. I regard matter as derivative from consciousness. We cannot get behind consciousness. Everything that we talk about, everything that we regard as existing, postulates consciousness." Another founding father of quantum physics, Austrian Erwin Schrödinger (Nobel Prize in Physics, 1933), said, "Although I think that life may be the result of an accident, I do not think that of consciousness. Consciousness cannot be accounted for in physical terms. For consciousness is absolutely fundamental. It cannot be accounted for in terms of anything else." And as Rutgers University philosopher Jerry A. Fodor has more recently stated, "Nobody has the slightest idea how anything material could be conscious. Nobody even knows what it would be like to have the slightest idea about how anything material could be conscious. So much for the philosophy of consciousness."

Scientists outside the formal bounds of neuroscience, especially physicists, also seem to grasp the enormity of the HPC. Edward Witten, a globally acknowledged leader in the advanced mathematical attempt to reconcile quantum physics with relativity through what is known as string theory, has said, "I have a much easier time imagining how we understand the big bang than I have imagining how we can understand consciousness." Clearly, the HPC has become something of a white whale—an endless quest for explanation by the most accomplished thinkers in their fields.

As students of science and reason, we are trained to study the world with the scientific tools in our possession: those CT scans, MRIs, and all the other modalities and techniques of modern medicine. But some scientists fall victim to the idea that everything must be quantifiable using those tools. What if we're using the wrong tools because we're not quite sure what we're looking for? What if, instead of a white whale, deeper understanding around human consciousness and its origins comes instead in the form of a black swan—something so completely unknown and unimaginable to our current mind-set that it does not exist until it is experienced firsthand?

What I've experienced—and what has been experienced by millions of other people who have had NDEs and other spiritually transformative experiences—is the black swan we didn't know to look for. We can't identify or analyze it with a spectral EEG or fMRI or any of the tools scientists have been using, but it's hidden in plain sight.

Some of the more modern scientific thinking now sweeping the field of consciousness studies concerns a wholly different concept of the mind-brain relationship: that the brain is a reducing valve, or filter, that reduces *primordial* consciousness down to a trickle—our very limited human awareness of the apparent "here and now." The physical brain only permits certain patterns of awareness to emerge from a broad group of possible mental states. This conscious awareness can be liberated to a much higher level when freed up from the shackles of the physical brain, as happened while I was in coma.

The scientific implications are stunning, and provide powerfully for the reality of the afterlife. But this is only the beginning. As we come to realize that examples of exceptional human potential (as in genius-level creativity, telepathy, psychokinesis, precognition, and past-life memories) really occur in some people, we begin to realize that the latent ability is there in all humans. In other words, these are skills that one can cultivate and enhance. I was elated by the potential for tremendous enhancement in human activity that is possible due to this grander view of consciousness. If abilities such as these are achievable, the implications for human potential are breathtaking!

This idea was new to me, but not to the world. Late-19th- and early-20th-century luminaries including William James,[3] Frederic W.H. Myers, Henri Bergson, F.C.S Schiller, and Aldous Huxley advocated for more serious consideration of this filter theory. The Canadian epilepsy specialist Dr. Wilder Penfield, one of the most prominent neurosurgeons of the 20th century, wrote a book in 1975 (*The Mystery of the Mind*) summarizing his life's work, especially evidence that consciousness (including free will) is not created by the brain. The filter theory doesn't mean we have to throw out all of our recent discoveries about the brain— far from it. Rather, it opens the door to better explanations of human experiences, both mundane and exotic. I began to realize our minds are much more than mere electrical signals; we are not, as some argue, just "fleshy robots."

The more I studied, the more I realized that on some level, humans already know this is true. Nearly all religious and philosophical traditions have a sense that some part of our essential selves exists separately from our physical brains and bodies. Even those few without a clear vision of an afterlife include some ritual or practice focused on connecting humans with the divine and with their own enlarged, unfettered consciousness. Practices of Kabbalah, Christian mysticism, Sufi meditation, Buddhist mindfulness, and devotional prayer, among others—these are all ways people have accessed this larger sense of consciousness and connection with a world just beyond their sight.

The kind of sensing and thinking encountered in mystical experiences confirms that, at some level, most of us are aware that there is more to this life than we can see. We might seek it in a deeper connection with God through prayer or meditation, or we may simply be visited by the sense, stronger at certain moments, that we are connected to something larger than ourselves. Have you ever paused alone in a beautiful place and found yourself feeling a powerful sense of safety and connectedness that seemed to fill you from the outside in? That's what I'm talking about. What I came to see—and what has been viewed by so many others who have had near-death and similar spiritually transformative experiences— was a full awareness, like finally being able to look straight at something that's been lurking just outside my peripheral vision. The truth is all around us and, at times, we catch glimpses of it—but how can we make better sense of it all?

CHAPTER 3

SCIENCE MEETS SPIRITUALITY

Science is not only compatible with spirituality; it is
a profound source of spirituality.

—CARL SAGAN (1934–1996),
AMERICAN ASTRONOMER

There's no question that my world was rocked to the core. It seemed as though I had stumbled upon a crucial factor that might contribute to the advancement of science. More than that, I realized this ultimately offered the potential for a fuller understanding of the true nature of human existence. I was drawn to share my message with all who would listen in hopes they could offer further insights into these matters.

Word of my experience began to spread in my local community, and through my personal network I began to connect with grieving parents whose children had died. This led to my first formal presentation in 2010 at a fund-raising dinner for Kid's Haven, a support group for children who have lost parents or siblings. I shared how my experience supported the notion that one's soul continues to exist after the physical body has died. The audience was comforted by this—it seemed to help many with their grieving process. Next, I spoke to a small group of twenty-five healers focused on helping people deal with grief at a Stephen Ministries group hosted by the Peakland United Methodist Church. One week later, I spoke at St. John's Episcopal Church, where Michael Sullivan was the rector, and where I was a member. This was the first big public event that ignited more widespread interest, and was followed by invitations from several other churches and organizations in the surrounding area.

Prior to being in coma, I had delivered approximately 200 presentations to medical groups concerning my research interests in neurosurgery, so public speaking was comfortable for me. But speaking to audiences about my personal experience was brand-new, shockingly different, and strange. People approached me afterward to tell me that my story resonated with them: a reassuring, positive message that left them feeling more complete. Many would be moved to tears. I was unaccustomed to emotional responses, yet amazed at this giant sense of evolving and reaching an aha moment with whole groups.

The audiences seemed to fully embrace the concept that our souls are eternal. This helped me to firm up the integration of everything I was coming to understand. Never is any part of this only one soul's journey: This is about a massive evolution of consciousness in which everyone partakes. It became clear that the process of telling my story helped others tremendously, but it also helped me to realize the universal aspects of the message I shared. I was absolutely bound to share with the world that our conventional understanding of reality as explained by materialist science was completely false and misleading. This was far too important to bury.

The risks to my career in academic neurosurgery were quite real—I was rocking the boat in a major way, and the end result could have been a forced separation from my tribe, that of neurosurgery and neuroscience. I was thus pleased to receive an invitation by the Lynchburg Academy of Medicine to speak to 150 fellow doctors (including some who had cared for me, and many who had attended my morbidity and mortality conference a few months after I awakened) and their spouses. As much as I had expected strong recoil and pushback from medical and scientific audiences, what I encountered was a generally open-minded group, with very pertinent questions appropriate to the deep nature of the subject matter. It seemed as if there was general agreement that my experience could not be explained by traditional models (that my spiritual journey had to be a hallucination) and we had to seriously question the reigning paradigm we'd all learned in medical school.

Through my connection with Bruce Greyson, I was invited to give a keynote presentation at the national conference of the International Association for Near-Death Studies (IANDS) in September 2011 in Durham, North Carolina. IANDS had been founded in 1978 to provide support and resources to early researchers in the field. Their annual conferences include presentations of the latest research and reports from those who have had a near-death experience.

Presenting to a room of more than 300 people, the majority of whom were near-death experiencers themselves, I was astonished how my story flowed even more fluidly. I had already sensed that the message of communication of a deep, true knowing conveyed in these talks often went beyond the summary of words into something more, and here is where I felt that fully for the first time. It struck me that it was no longer "I'll tell my story to other people and wait for their response"; these people were among the countless others who had reported an experience similar to mine. With this group, there was a greater depth and understanding of the journey and a shared sense of mystery around it all that was driving these people's lives.

It was at this conference that I met Dr. Raymond Moody (who had founded the modern era of the scientific investigation of near-death experiences). He had recently become a legendary figure in my mind, but from the moment I was introduced to him, I found Raymond to be one of the most open and personable souls I had ever encountered. He was refreshingly available, and I thoroughly enjoyed talking to him, together with John Audette (also present as a founding father of IANDS).

Raymond told me of his early interests that led him into his initial study of NDEs. Before he entered medical school, Raymond had earned his PhD in ancient Greek philosophy, where he became most enamored with the writings of Plato. In *The Republic,* Plato discussed the fascinating case of Er, an Armenian soldier killed in battle who was placed upon a funeral pyre. Just before its ignition he returned to life, to the amazement of his fellow soldiers. He went on to tell them that when one dies, they proceed through a review of the most crucial aspects of their life as a lesson of sorts (the "life review"), and that the most important quality by which they are judged concerns the love they have managed to manifest while here on earth.

That story had piqued Raymond's interest in the concept of an after-life. When, as a medical student, he then started encountering stories of strange memories in his patients who had come close to death, the stage was set for him to begin collecting such stories in a systematic manner. The first hundred or so patients were the subject material for his world-changing book, *Life after Life*. I was most impressed by his demonstration that these experiences have been occurring in similar fashion for at least 2,400 years, and seem to provide universal lessons that are untainted by one's prior belief systems (although one's beliefs can influence how they interpret and communicate their experience). His approach is more philosophical than scientific; he believes the solution to the afterlife question is not going to come initially from science, but rather from critical thinking and logic.

One of the crucial events in Raymond's journey was encountering Dr. George Ritchie, a Virginia psychiatrist who had shared a profound near-death experience he had had as a 20-year-old Army private. Raymond had been an undergraduate philosophy major in 1965 when he first heard George tell the story of his NDE. His book, *Return from Tomorrow*, remains a favorite, especially given the innocence of the environment in which it all transpired, since no one had yet discussed NDEs as a concept. The illness that induced his NDE began late in the evening of December 11, 1943. Thus, George's experience, eventually published in 1978, emerged out of a fairly pristine origin. As he witnessed his body lying dead in the military hospital at Camp Barkeley in west Texas, Ritchie's soul took a nocturnal journey, flying east across the southern United States, then back west to encounter a Being of Light and to harvest the rich lessons of the experience. It was a beautifully wrought journey that stands as one of the classics of the NDE literature.

"Did you ever meet George?" Raymond asked me.

"No, I never had the opportunity. Wish I had . . ."

"You remind me so much of George," Raymond smiled. "You share his boundless enthusiasm, and zest for existence. So similar . . . Amazing!"

My journey of discovery postcoma has been profoundly enriched by many other such enlightened minds I have encountered along the way, including many steeped in modern science and medicine. Members of the general public often assume that my journey and my sharing of it represent an anomaly that is antithetical to our modern science, whereas the exact opposite has been my experience. A number of the most advanced scientific minds in this world, especially those deeply involved in some understanding of consciousness, are not only on board with my central message, but serve as mentors. They *get it*.

It was exciting to meet more of those enlightened physicians at the conferences to which I was now being invited to speak. Another momentous opportunity occurred at the International Conference on After Death Communication, hosted by Anne and Herbert Puryear in Phoenix in April 2012. It was there that I met fellow physicians Pim van Lommel and Larry Dossey, two extraordinary and generous thought leaders whose work inspired me deeply.

NDEs have been reported for millennia, but a major ramp-up has taken place ever since the late 1960s, when doctors first developed techniques to resuscitate patients who had suffered cardiac arrest. Before that time, almost all such patients went on to die. The result is that we have now populated this world with a huge number of souls who have been to the other side and come back—and some doctors are paying attention.

Dr. van Lommel is a Dutch cardiologist who authored the landmark 2001 paper published in the highly esteemed medical journal the *Lancet*.[1] His widely acclaimed paper assessed 344 consecutive patients successfully resuscitated after cardiac arrest in ten Dutch hospitals, including follow-up for up to eight years after the events. Sixty-two patients (18 percent) reported an NDE, including 41 (12 percent) who had what they called a core (or exceptionally deep) experience (note that the use of the word *core* here is not the same as in my NDE, in which I identified the Core as the most profound level of the spiritual realm, at the origins of all existence). Such profound experiences were especially correlated with those who subsequently died within 30 days of their initial event ($p < 0.0001$, or 0.01 percent probability that this finding is due to chance alone).

He followed up the *Lancet* study with his landmark book *Consciousness Beyond Life: The Science of the Near-Death Experience,* an extensive examination of the burgeoning global occurrence of near-death experiences, analysis of current medical knowledge concerning the mind-brain relationship, and an overview of the implications from the viewpoint of quantum physics, especially as it relates to the nature of consciousness.

On first meeting Pim in Phoenix, I found him to be the epitome of the stately, wise, and experienced physician who would engender the highest trust and confidence among his patients. Yet I found his most striking quality to be his exuberant zeal for life. This was bundled with an enthusiastic pursuit of a much deeper interpretation of the available evidence than that which might have satisfied a more casual physician. In short, he was not the type to simply accept a conventional explanation for such exotic experiences when the evidence suggested otherwise—truly the consummate skeptical scientist.

Likewise, Dr. Dossey is a highly regarded physician who has written influential books related to nonlocal consciousness and the value of spiritual wellness, including *One Mind, The Power of Premonitions, Reinventing Medicine,* and *Healing Words.* Tall and fit, Larry also stands out as a "physician's physician"—one who is clearly so knowledgeable, insightful, and experienced that he instills in his patients and colleagues a deep trust and confidence. He was originally drawn to the concept of all minds being connected due to the deep connection he had felt throughout his life with his identical twin brother. In *One Mind,* he reveals extraordinary evidence, such as coordinated movement patterns of flocks of birds and schools of fish, communication between humans and animals, group behavior, premonitions, remote viewing, NDEs, and twin studies, showing how we are all bound together through consciousness. Familiar with the advanced understanding so evident in his books, I'll never forget the comfortable kinship I felt on first witnessing his exceptional warmth and humanity in person.

By acknowledging and investigating the potential of our spiritual essence, both Pim and Larry had been instrumental in ushering the world of medicine from the dark ignorance of pure materialism into a more enlightened age in the healing arts. I felt them to be such kindred spirits that it seemed as if I had known them forever. They had worked for decades in the wild and unknown frontiers of consciousness, and I was the new kid on the block. I found it most refreshing to interact with other scientists who fully appreciated the seemingly bottomless mystery of consciousness.

I don't recall all the details of what we discussed that day, but it was by far the most in-depth discussion about the fundamental nature of consciousness I had ever had with fellow physicians. Larry must have shared this sense, for his parting comment was "My gosh—I wish we had recorded this little conversation!" Although I wasn't sure how to put my perceptions of Pim and Larry into words at the time, I now know that what I sensed was that they were both very advanced souls, indeed.

I began to interact with scientists outside of the world of medicine who were also walking that tightrope between the domains of science and spirituality. John Audette, whom I initially met at the IANDS conference, had been a close friend for decades with *Apollo 14* astronaut Edgar Mitchell, who had had a profound personal transformation on his return from the moon in 1971. I was beyond thrilled when John made arrangements for me to stay with Edgar during a visit to Florida in July 2012.

As far back as I can remember, part of me always seemed to be more at home above this world than on it. My most vivid memory of the first grade occurred on May 5, 1961. The school brought a television set (limited to black and white, it was still a rarity in those days) into Mrs. Allen's classroom so that we could watch live as Alan Shepard rode a *Mercury-Redstone 3* rocket 116 miles up into space. Though it was but a 15-minute suborbital flight, I was hooked. Space was in my blood! I followed every *Mercury, Gemini,* and *Apollo* mission over the next fifteen years, getting to know as much about the men and the missions as I could, and following them live as if I were just another member of the crew.

My attraction almost diverted my neurosurgical career. After an inspiring dinner with Rhea Seddon, a mission specialist on the space shuttle who had previously trained as a surgeon, I applied for that program to fly on the space shuttle in 1983, when NASA was gearing up for another astronaut recruiting effort. I was only partly through my neurosurgical residency at the time, and my father urged me to finish my medical training before pursuing a career in the astronaut corps. History intervened with the *Challenger* tragedy in January 1986, which led to a 2½-year halt in our manned space program. I finished my neurosurgical training during that lull, and thus went straight into neurosurgical practice, as opposed to following my dream of flying into space.

My fascination with space flight led to my personally meeting four of the *Apollo* astronauts: Neil Armstrong (the first man to walk on the moon, during the *Apollo 11* moon-landing mission in July 1969), Jim Lovell (commander of the heroic *Apollo 13* mission, NASA's finest hour, when their spacecraft service module was damaged by an explosion en route to the moon and, through extraordinary human effort, they made it safely back to earth), Frank Borman (who had accompanied Jim Lovell on the December 1968 *Apollo 8* mission in which they broadcast a Christmas Eve message of peace to earth from lunar orbit), and Edgar Mitchell (the Lunar Excursion Module, or LEM, pilot for *Apollo 14* in February 1971).

Although I thoroughly enjoyed meeting and talking with all of them, I have been most grateful for developing a friendship with Edgar, who I believe will go down in history as one of the truly great explorers of the ages. I enjoyed talking with him about his childhood, growing up on a New Mexico ranch next door to one owned by Robert Goddard, the "father of American rocketry" (a fascinating synchronicity!), and how he, like me, had soloed an aircraft at the young age of 14. To have such an extraordinary experience at that tender age of discovery weds one's soul forever to the realms beyond earth.

During the third successful moon-landing mission, Edgar became the sixth man (of twelve total, to date) to walk on the moon. On February 5, 1971, he was piloting *Antares,* the LEM for the *Apollo 14* lunar landing mission, to alight in the hills of the Fra Mauro highlands on the moon. His partner in the LEM was Shepard. Although I had followed his original journey as a teenager fascinated with space travel, hearing him share it with me directly was one of the highlights of my life.

Edgar told me about his grand epiphany, or *savikalpa samadhi* experience (as he called it), an "ecstasy of unity," while returning from his "sacred journey" to the moon. This extraordinary revelation completely shifted all aspects of his life.

"I had piloted *Antares* down to the Fra Mauro highlands, and taken the longest walks ever taken on the moon through those dusty lunar hills with Alan," he explained over breakfast in his home. "Most people heard about his driving two golf balls on the moon, but few realize that I bested his distance for those two drives when I threw a javelin even farther! That lunar gravity one-sixth of earth's allowed for Olympian gold-medal performances. I then piloted the ascent module with Alan back up to rejoin Stu in *Kitty Hawk* [the command module]. As we left lunar orbit to head home, my work was done. So I had three days to relax and enjoy the view.

"We were in barbecue mode, with the spacecraft rotating every couple of minutes to avoid any area overheating in the intense sunlight. I could see ten times as many stars as you can ever see from earth, so the view was spectacular. With the rotation, I would see the earth, moon, and sun pass by the window every few minutes. The immensity and serenity of the universe struck me in an entirely new way, out there, suspended between the great blue jewel of earth and the dusky moon we were leaving behind. The setting was perfect. I suddenly sensed the profound consciousness of the universe—how it is completely interconnected and aware—an absolutely indescribable awareness. My life was changed forever."

His epiphany led him to pursue the deep study of scientific aspects of consciousness, and to help humanity awaken to a grander recognition of the unity of conscious awareness in oneness with the universe. During my coma journey, I experienced this same sense of oneness with the universe as a completely unified self-awareness of all that is—a truly mindful universe. Edgar's intuition that science and spirituality greatly strengthen each other, that their natural synthesis is an inevitable aspect of human history, is one that I share deeply. He wrote several wonderful books about his trip to the moon and resultant life journey, which I have found to be most inspiring (*The Way of the Explorer* and *Psychic Exploration*). I consider such enlightened individuals to be paradigm-shifting pioneers, heralding the next stage of humanity's evolving existence and leading us out of a world that many feel is void of meaning or purpose.

Dr. Mitchell pursued with tireless enthusiasm a passionate interest in deepening our understanding of reality, and of humanity's place in it, that I believe history will revere. In 1973, he created the Institute of Noetic Sciences, or IONS, that to this day carries on Dr. Mitchell's world-changing scientific work around the fundamental nature of consciousness and the universe. Their goal is to advance the concept that we can develop ways of knowing that we are all part of an interconnected whole. IONS conducts original research to broaden our understanding of reality and our human capacity to apply enhanced conscious awareness in our lives. I was heartened to learn about such efforts to bridge science and spirituality; this is not a choice to be made between one or the other. In fact, neither science nor spirituality is able to move forward without acknowledging the crucial role the other has to offer as humanity awakens into wholeness.

Despite my profound shift in view and my thorough academic education, I soon came to realize I was still quite near the bottom of an ever-steepening learning curve. As I continued to study and research the phenomena of nonlocal consciousness, I learned about various methods used by people to consciously access realms similar to what I had experienced during coma. I was curious to see what might be possible so I enrolled in a seminar on how to achieve different states of consciousness. This is where I encountered Karen Newell in November 2011. Since our meeting came prior to the publication of *Proof of Heaven*, she knew no details of my story. Already familiar with NDEs, she inquired about my spiritual journey during coma.

"Tell me one important thing you learned from your near-death experience," she asked.

"The brain does *not* create consciousness," I quickly answered with adamant enthusiasm.

"Why would anyone think that it *does*?" she replied, confused. "I have always accepted that our consciousness existed before we were born and will continue to exist after we die. How could we *not* have a soul?" she added.

She had never entertained the worldview I had embraced for the 54 years of my life before coma, that of scientific materialism. In fact, she had spent her life very comfortably embedded in a worldview very much the opposite of materialism—that is, believing that mind and mental experience are the fundamental essence of all existence, that mind has complete power over matter, and that our free will has tremendous capacity to change the world. I was drawn to her passion and knowing of that idealism because it was a worldview I was just beginning to assess in my arduous trek toward understanding my NDE. One thing was clear: Karen was an astute and fast thinker and quickly became a valuable sounding board. With her frank and authentic nature, I could always count on her to cut straight to the heart of a matter. I had an immediate sense that we shared a similar mission.

Karen felt very familiar to me, as if I were reencountering a long-lost family member or old friend, and I trusted her immediately. I sensed in her a childlike innocence, open to all possibility, but combined with a powerful sense of presence. Karen's depth of spiritual composure was not apparent only to me. When she met one of my new friends in the medical NDE arena, Dutch cardiologist Pim van Lommel, he almost immediately asked her, "Have you had a near-death experience?"

"No, I haven't," she replied. But he seemed quite certain, and he trusted his intuition. He seemed to sense the same potent energy resonating from her that I had originally felt.

"I wonder if you might have had an NDE as a child," he continued. "Did you have any illnesses or accidents?"

"None that I recall," she responded. "I did have childhood seizures, though. I grew out of them around age 5. But I don't remember anything that might have caused an NDE."

"Sometimes people don't remember, especially if it occurred at a very young age. But I can feel your energy. I'm familiar with the energy in people who've had an NDE, and you definitely emanate that same kind of energy."

As we discussed the common aftereffects of NDEs, it turned out that Karen had experienced several of them, such as a profound appreciation for nature, heightened intuition and sense of knowing, being spiritual but not necessarily religious, and a strong sense of pursuing a higher truth and meaning to life. Karen had developed a passion early in life for exploring deep questions, such as "Why are we here?" and "What is our purpose?" She deduced at a young age that her Methodist church teachings could not answer such questions to her satisfaction. Secular school was likewise lacking. As she grew older, she sought alternative resources for explaining our past and began to read esoteric writings such as the Kabbalah, Theosophical texts, the Dead Sea Scrolls, and other esoteric and mythical writings, such as Plato's discourse on Atlantis (from his *Timaeus* and *Critias*).

While much of it was challenging to fully comprehend and there were many contradictions, she began to note commonalities among different schools of thought. Rather than finding one approach that held all the answers, she was intrigued to find that some concepts were often repeated, such as the incredible value that comes from truly knowing one's inner nature by going within through a practice such as meditation. She avoided strict adherence to any specific discipline, favoring a blend of what she came to call "universal truths."

Karen was quite naive about the science I had spent so much of my life pursuing; I found myself, by comparison, at least as naive about so many spiritual matters that she seemed to know so well. I was just beginning to dive deeply into those uncharted waters, and this required me to develop new skills in discrimination to help fathom new sensations and concepts in a useful fashion. Although I was quite open to exploring every bit of this new experience of conscious awareness, Karen showed me the necessity for a very high level of discernment in order to separate the wheat from the chaff.

Along with her knowledge base, Karen had been cultivating her forays into consciousness consistently and tenaciously for many years. She had realized that experience is key to full understanding; it's not enough simply to read about certain topics. This was certainly true in my case—it had taken a seven-day coma and miraculous recovery to get my attention. Karen was intrigued by accounts of ancient mystery schools, where initiates would be led through a series of trials to learn the secrets of the universe. With no modern mystery school to attend, she had taken hands-on courses to investigate and develop such skills as lucid dreaming, astral travel, telepathy, remote viewing, self-hypnosis, and different forms of energy healing—many of the practices I had been reading about in my recent scientific research. She found this direct method of learning quite effective at contributing to her depth of knowledge.

Just as I had achieved my greatest lesson from the ordeal of my coma, Karen had learned from a long series of personal experiences. She tried out different theories and techniques by experimenting with and testing them in her daily life. She trusted her own body of personal evidence, which bolstered her strong sense of inner knowing. In this way, she formed a rather unique worldview, much broader than the scientific materialist view I had come to depend on during the years before coma.

There is a considerable difference between *believing* something, and *knowing* it. It is crucial not to simply believe what others say and then adopt those beliefs, including everything stated in this book. It is most beneficial to learn firsthand, to cultivate and trust personal experience in order to develop an inner capacity of knowing. Each of us will proceed on a slightly different path, according to unique motivations and goals. Letting go of ingrained beliefs can be extremely valuable in order to comprehend a situation from a fresh perspective. In fact, this is what science is all about. A truly open-minded scientist considers all available evidence before making any judgment.

CHAPTER 4

MOVING BEYOND MATERIALIST SCIENCE

If you thought that science was certain—well, that is just an error on your part.

—RICHARD FEYNMAN (1918–1988),
NOBEL PRIZE IN PHYSICS, 1965

I'm a surgeon, a skeptic, and a rationalist. I'm the last person to tell you to reject science. But, ideally, the scientific method involves questioning everything, so I *will* encourage you to examine some of the myths and beliefs that mainstream scientists cling to as articles of faith without proper foundation. To function properly, science must be held to a high standard and subjected to regular review. But the construct of scientific understanding of the world is only as strong as its foundational assumptions, and any errors in them will lead to major problems with the conclusions. One such metaphysical assumption (referred to as metaphysical because it is at the foundation of our thinking) is that only the physical world exists, a position known in science as materialism (also called physicalism). Under this theory, such things as thoughts, feelings, emotions, concepts, and consciousness are merely the results of some physical processes and have no real existence in their own right.

Materialist science thus posits that the brain creates consciousness out of purely physical matter—that there is nothing else. It asserts that everything we have ever experienced—every beautiful sunset, every gorgeous symphony, every hug from our child, every experience of falling in love—is merely the electrochemical flickering of around a hundred billion neurons in a three-pound gelatinous mass, sitting in a warm dark bath inside of our head. This school of thought holds that our choices, too, are not made of our own free will; rather, they are merely electrical and chemical reactions throughout the complex anatomy of the brain. And, it says, we are no more than our physical bodies; when they die, we cease to exist.

The problem with that model, the materialist brain-creates-consciousness model, is that not even the world's top experts on the brain have even the remotest idea *how* the brain could create consciousness. It's the modern equivalent of scientists thinking, Well, it sure looks like the sun rises and sets around the earth, so the sun probably revolves around the earth. Mainstream neuroscience just hasn't been doing its homework.

A few years after my quest began, I was invited to confront my pre-coma scientific worldview in a public debate on the question "Is death final?" hosted by Intelligence Squared on National Public Radio in New York City on May 7, 2014. Intelligence Squared is a nonpartisan, nonprofit organization founded in 2006 to "restore civility, reasoned analysis, and constructive public discourse to today's often biased media landscape." I very much looked forward to discussing the more than 2,400-year-old mind-body debate.

Dr. Raymond Moody served as my partner on the "for" position, arguing that, from a perspective of critical thinking and logic, the available evidence suggests the afterlife is real. On the other side were Sean Carroll, a physicist from the California Institute of Technology in Pasadena, and Dr. Steven Novella, a neurologist from Yale, who took the opposing atheistic tack, that death of the physical body is the end of any consciousness or soul. Novella is founder and editor of *Science-Based Medicine*, with a mission to evaluate both traditional and alternative medical care from a scientific perspective. He prides himself on being a professional skeptic so I was hoping he would acknowledge the lack of scientific consensus around consciousness.

Any in-depth review on the current status of materialist neuroscience's ability to explain the mechanism of consciousness arising from the physical brain will yield absolutely zero—there is no theoretical framework linking the brain and consciousness at all! Admittedly, there are vague propositions that might be useful for certain types of modeling. However, such proposals attempting to relate consciousness and the brain take no steps whatsoever toward addressing the hard problem of consciousness—that is, the explicit mechanisms by which any brain activity results in mental experience.

But Novella's bold opening statement immediately demonstrated his materialist-minded certainty that consciousness arises from the brain.

"How confident are we as a scientific conclusion, which is what we're here to talk about, that the mind is essentially the brain?" Novella began. "Well, we're very certain about that, and we're as confident of that as we are of anything in science. We have a mountain of neuroscience, countless experiments, that look for the neuroanatomical correlates of consciousness, of the brain functioning, of the mind. Everything that you think, feel, believe is something that's happening inside the brain, demonstrably.

"Every element of a near-death experience can be duplicated, can be replicated with drugs, with anoxia, with lack of blood flow, by turning off circuits in the brain. Every single component is a brain experience that we could now reproduce. And we're zeroing in on the exact circuits in the brain which reproduce them."

I doubt that many would question that the brain is somehow linked to mental experience. The problem in Novella's (and other materialists') analysis is the assertion that thoughts, feelings, and beliefs—even consciousness itself—are *caused* by physical brain activity alone.

Neuroscientists today have many fascinating tools and technologies with which to observe, document, and measure physical changes in the brain. There is so much observable data that it is easy to jump to the conclusion that a physical change *causes* the phenomenal experience, when in fact the opposite might actually be the case: the phenomenal experience might cause the enhanced physical activity seen in the brain. This is where they are blindsided by their underlying assumptions. In a lovely analogy (which I borrow from IONS's chief scientist, Dr. Dean Radin), just because sunflowers follow the sun does not mean that their turning causes the sun to move across the sky.

Dr. Wilder Penfield of Montreal is probably in a better position than most to comment on the linkage between the physical brain and the phenomenology of experience. His professional career involved stimulating the neocortex, the outer surface of the brain, in awake (i.e., not generally anesthetized) patients as part of his surgical treatment of their epilepsy.

Penfield would use an electrode to stimulate the surface of the brain. One such case involved a 16-year-old girl (Case M.G., a violinist since age 5) who presented with seizures and underwent an operation to expose her right temporal lobe.[1] Stimulation of her superior temporal lobe produced a response: "I hear people coming in. I hear music now, a funny little piece." Stimulation was in the posterior aspect, in what is often acknowledged to be the primary acoustic cortex, that is, a main region of sound perception. She went on to explain that the music was a theme song of a children's program she had heard over the radio (an actual memory of a real event). A second stimulation to the same location produced a sensation unrelated to any memory: "People were coming in and out and I heard boom, boom, boom," followed by yet another stimulation: "It's a dream. There are a lot of people. I don't seem to see them, I hear them. I don't hear their talking, I just hear their feet."

Such was the detailed nature of perceptions and memories he encountered through specific electrical point stimulation over the surface of the brain. This stimulation analysis was most useful in defining the crucial functional anatomy of the brain (especially sensory and motor cortex), and was combined with electrocorticography to select damaged brain tissue for removal to eliminate seizures. His daily work for over three decades involved careful recording of experience, perceptions, and memories brought to conscious awareness in his patients through electrical mapping of the neocortex, all in the process of identifying and safely removing abnormal parts of the brain that caused their seizures.

Given my own experience as a specialist in such procedures (brain stimulation during resections in locally anesthetized but awake patients), I know the powers and the pitfalls of the techniques involved. In these fascinating scientific experiments, Penfield came to know more than most neurosurgeons about the relationship of electrode stimulation of small brain regions with the associated phenomenal patient experiences. He adopted the dualistic position (termed "interactionist dualism") that honored human beings as having both a physical brain and a distinctly separate mind and that the brain alone does not explain the mind.

In *Mystery of the Mind,* Penfield said: "I worked as a scientist trying to prove that the brain accounted for the mind and demonstrating as many brain-mechanisms as possible hoping to show how the brain did so. . . . In the end I conclude that there is no good evidence, in spite of new methods, such as the employment of stimulating electrodes, the study of conscious patients and the analysis of epileptic attacks that the brain alone can carry out the work that the mind does. I conclude that it is easier to rationalize man's being on the basis of two elements [mind and brain] than on the basis of one [brain produces mind]."[2]

Sadly, Penfield's observations at that time were marginalized, or mis-interpreted, because they didn't fit the pervasive materialist model. And in spite of the gargantuan leaps in our understanding of the workings of the physical brain in recent decades, this notion of "brain creates mind" has not budged in the materialist mind-set. They don't seem to care that they can't find the mechanism—the central issue of the hard problem of consciousness. Novella seemed satisfied merely to declare that one day actual evidence would be found to support their assumptions (known as "promissory materialism").

"We don't have to know how the brain creates consciousness," Novella claimed. "That it creates consciousness, we absolutely know, just like we don't have to know how the earth generates gravity to know that it generates gravity. There's no question we have gravity even though we haven't untangled the deepest understanding of every possible thing. So yes, we don't know exactly how the brain creates consciousness, but the evidence can only lead to one interpretation, that it is consciousness. The consciousness is what the brain does, no question."

"No neuroscientist on earth can give the first sentence to explain a mechanism by which the physical brain gives rise to consciousness," I challenged Novella.

"Is that—is that true?" our seemingly shocked moderator asked Novella.

"It's not a black or white thing," Novella answered. "We have some knowledge. We don't have complete knowledge about it. It's like saying, 'Do we understand everything about genetics?' No. But we know that DNA is the molecule of inheritance. That's not questionable."

"But not one sentence. Give the first sentence of how you would trace from the physical brain that it gives rise to consciousness," I pressed on.

Novella was at a loss for words.

As a former believer of scientific materialism, I can certainly understand how one becomes addicted to the kind of simplistic thinking that links the brain and consciousness in the materialists' way. And I have come to see that *true* open-minded skepticism is one of the most powerful commodities in this enterprise. However, most of those in our culture who proudly claim to be skeptics are actually just the opposite—I call them pseudoskeptics. They have already made up their minds on the issue based on prejudices that often involve adherence to a particular belief system, such as scientific materialism. Their mind-set is the antithesis of what many hold to be the ideal of scientific thinking—approaching such deep questions with the most open mind possible, untainted by premature conclusions.

I hoped to have a richer exchange with the other speaker in the debate, Sean Carroll, who wrote *From Eternity to Here,* a deeply intellectual examination of the extreme challenges of understanding the nature of time in modern physics. He seemed a worthy opponent, given his impressive background in physics and a special interest in how quantum mechanics affects cosmology. I had come to see the crucial role that quantum physics played in understanding the mind-brain relationship, given that such experiments examine the very interface of the physical world (especially represented by the brain), and our knowledge of it (represented by the mind). Thus, I eagerly anticipated his deeper thoughts on the matter.

"I think it's important to point out, from my point of view, what drove the founding fathers of [quantum mechanics] into mysticism was the fact that getting at the very depths of trying to understand subatomic reality, they were led to believe that consciousness, *the observing mind,* actually played a role in the unfolding of what was being observed. And I think that that mystery, to my satisfaction, has not really been solved," I asserted.

I would have been supported by many in the global physics community in pointing out the very deep mystery of the measurement paradox in quantum physics. What greatly impressed the brilliant minds trying to make sense of it all in the first half of the 20th century (notably, the Hungarian American mathematician John von Neumann and theoretical physicist Eugene Wigner) was that the conscious *choice* of the observer was absolutely crucial in determining the measured outcome.

Any such subatomic observation thus depended on its perception by a sentient being. Even the insertion of a robot operating a random number generator failed to bypass the necessity of the mind of the observer in the interpretation of such results. There is no way to get behind the absolute requirement of the observing mind in interpreting the results of quantum experiments, leading some to the startling conclusion that *consciousness paints reality.*

Those founding fathers of quantum physics would be even more mystified today by ever more refined experiments. The physics community has only become more befuddled by recent experimental results suggesting that there is no objective external reality and that consciousness (the observer) is at the very core of all of emergent reality. The results are most insistent that we acknowledge that consciousness plays a significant role in the universe, but this has been a tough pill for the scientific community at large to swallow.

Carroll's answer to my question summarily dismissed the wonder of this finding: "The thing about Einstein, Bohr, de Broglie, etc., the founders of quantum mechanics, is that they're all dead, and they have been dead for many decades. And we know what's going on much better now than we did back then. They were inventing quantum mechanics, and occasionally they toyed with the idea that somehow consciousness had something to do with the fundamental laws of quantum mechanics. Now we know better."

Recent scientists have not "figured it all out," as Carroll claimed. In fact, recent studies are even more mystifying. Yet he, and like-minded thinkers, refuse even to consider that consciousness could be playing a significant role in our unfolding reality. He maintained that one can simply ignore the findings that led to such a deep sense of mystery those earlier brilliant physicists had in recognizing the key role of consciousness. In my view, however, that is shortsighted.

Admittedly, I had paid no attention to the scientific research on NDEs prior to my coma, but once I began reviewing it with a newly opened mind, I was stunned at the depth of its revelations. In fact, the evidence that we can access realms beyond the local here and now of the physical brain and its attached senses is quite strong. NDE reports by the tens of thousands—and similarly numerous reports of deathbed visions, after-death communications, shared-death experiences, and past-life memories in children indicative of reincarnation—represent data that demand explanation if one has any interest in understanding the world as it is, and not just as they think it should be.

The oft-heard cry from the skeptical community concerning the bolder claims from those investigating paranormal or psi phenomena is "extraordinary claims demand extraordinary evidence." Supporting data are actually abundant once you bypass the simplistic outright denial of it, but not only did Carroll completely ignore existing evidence, he expected any "new" evidence to be unmistakable.

"So, what are we actually being asked to accept?" Carroll asked. "What should we expect the world to be like if death were not actually final? For one thing, I would expect that the existence of souls persisting in the afterlife should be perfectly obvious. It should be just as clear that heaven exists as it is clear that Canada exists. But, in fact, it seems that the souls persisting in the afterlife are kind of shy. They don't talk to us, except sometimes they do talk to us."

I was struck by his statement that "souls persisting in the afterlife should be perfectly obvious," as if every scientific observation is "perfectly obvious." I wondered if, as a physicist, he had heard of neutrinos because they are very subtle (more so than Canada, at least), with those originating in the sun passing through the earth by the quadrillion quadrillions every second, hardly even noticing the planet as they zip through it as if through empty space. The existence of neutrinos is not in doubt to most physicists, neutrinos being a very subtle form of matter, yet their existence is crucial to evolving models of subatomic physics. The fact that they are not as obvious as Canada does not mean they do not exist.

Applying such a double standard makes it next to impossible for such studies ever to demonstrate "significance." Examination of the statistical threshold used to separate a real finding from one due to chance alone clarifies this prejudice.

In a controversial 2011 report entitled "Feeling the Future,"[3] psychologist Daryl Bem of Cornell University presented compelling evidence of precognition—that is, that people demonstrate conscious cognitive awareness of impending stimuli seconds *before* the computer has randomly selected the stimulus to present (!). A follow-up meta-analysis,[4] rigorously constructed from ninety experiments in thirty-three different laboratories spread across fourteen countries, confirmed this experimental violation of the most fundamental notions of materialist science and our commonsense ideas about cause and effect and the nature of time itself. Bem's work ignited a firestorm of fierce criticism among conventional materialist scientists.

The widely accepted standard p value (the probability that a given relationship could be due to chance alone) for most biomedical studies is placed at $p < 0.05$ (meaning that the statistical likelihood of the observations would be expected by chance to occur less than 5 percent of the time, or less than one time in 20). By comparison, Bem concluded that the probability that the observations in his meta-analysis could occur by chance alone to be 0.000000012 percent, an astronomically robust finding of significance, and yet it is not enough to persuade the hard-core "skeptic." They are basically setting the bar at a level impossible to meet.

I came away from the debate disappointed in Carroll's and Novella's refusal to apply the same scientific standard—the openness of mind, the pursuit of honest results—to the question of consciousness, rather than trying to fit evidence into a predetermined conclusion. Unlike them, many scientists and physicians are quite aware of the deep nature of this recent turn in the mind-body discussion, and are wide open to the novel possibilities for human potential. Unfortunately, some do remain stuck in the conventional paradigm.

Occasionally, one encounters what can best be described as an irrational fear of this grander view of consciousness among supporters of the materialist position. Such prejudicial commitment to worldviews hardly seems scientific, suggesting a deep cause for such a bias in otherwise well-meaning and intelligent people. I believe such posturing is an echo from four centuries ago, when the scientific revolution was born of the ravages of the Dark Ages, by intellectual giants such as Galileo Galilei, Sir Francis Bacon, Sir Isaac Newton, and Giordano Bruno. They were seeking the laws governing the natural world, yet if they strayed remotely into the territory of mind or consciousness, they were likely to be burned at the stake by the far more powerful church (as Bruno indeed was). Science began to replace mysticism, shamanism, and spirituality as a source of truth for many. In reality, pure science and spirituality together have always provided rich sources of truth, but the vague, impure shadows of science and religion (as a proxy for spirituality) have often been pitted against each other, to their mutual detriment.

The worldview postulating man to be separate from nature in this dance of discovery was perpetuated by those studying the natural sciences. Naturalism proposes that everything arises from natural properties and causes, completely excluding or discounting supernatural or spiritual explanations. Even with the advent of quantum physics in the early 20th century, that sense of separation has become ingrained to the point where it is now inherent in the very structure of our thought. Our foundational assumptions are crucial to our understanding—but what a source of mischief! As the great German philosopher Arthur Schopenhauer said, "The discovery of truth is prevented more effectively, not by the false appearance of things present and which mislead into error, not directly by weakness of the reasoning powers, but by preconceived opinion, by prejudice."

As Western science has delved ever more deeply into investigating the workings of the brain through more refined tools and techniques, some scientists have become increasingly shocked by the seemingly bottomless depths around the phenomenon of consciousness itself. Those who took on the challenge have confessed, after various periods of struggle, that the evidence suggests *mind* is much more than can be explained by *brain*. These more advanced thinkers (including Roger Penrose, Henry Stapp, Brian Josephson, Amit Goswami, Bernard Carr, Dean Radin, and Menas Kafatos, among others) suggest that one cannot explain conscious experience as arising totally from the physical brain.

The evidence that the brain is not the producer of consciousness emerges from clinically reported phenomena, including (1) terminal lucidity, in which elderly demented patients surprisingly demonstrate episodes of great reflection, interaction, and communication with those around them that completely defy the ability of such a badly damaged brain to muster such memories and insightful sharing;[5] (2) acquired savant syndromes, in which some form of brain damage, such as a stroke, head injury, or autism, unmasks some superhuman mental capacity, e.g., the ability to calculate pi to thousands of digits in one's head, or the ability to have perfect memory of every name and number in a phone book where the subject only glanced at any given page for seconds; (3) numerous recent experiments during extraordinary psychedelic drug experiences, assessing that the greatest mental experiences involved a significant *decrease* in regional brain activity found in especially crucial junctional regions of massive interconnection between major brain areas (see Chapter 8).

Another crucial piece of evidence worthy of more extensive review is the assumption of materialist science that memories are stored in the brain. This idea is so ingrained in our culture that it seems to have become a popular "fact" for many. My coma experience proved especially difficult to understand given my prior notion that memory must somehow be stored in the physical brain. For example, with my brain so damaged, how did my memories of pre-coma knowledge and personal events return in the months after awakening in the ICU? Where did they come from? Was it simply that, as the physical brain recovered, memories stored there were refreshed? Given the severity and duration of my illness, such high-level recovery should have been impossible. Eventually, I came to realize through subtle evidence over the next few years that, in fact, my memories had come back even more complete than they had been before my coma.

One instance of this phenomenon concerns a man named Will who used to perform odd jobs in our home in the early 1960s, when I was approximately 10 years old. I reminisced about him with my father in the early 1990s, when the most sophisticated information I could retrieve about Will concerned a certain limp in his walk (after a mild stroke), but precious little else in the way of any specific memories.

Fast-forward two decades (to a time *after* my coma) to a conversation I shared with my mother concerning the same man. I recalled specific memories of driving with Dad in his 1957 Thunderbird to pick Will up at the Greystone Hotel, across Fourth Street from the Winston Theater, to bring him home to help with some tasks. I even remembered how Will had cut his right index finger while repairing part of our basement oil furnace, and that Dad then drove him over to his office at the Baptist Hospital to place five sutures in the laceration. *None* of those details had been part of my earlier reminiscences with Dad in the early '90s.

How could memories become *more* vivid and detailed after such a devastating brain malady? Here was another mystery to address. Conventional neuroscience teaches that memories are stored in some form in the neural networks of the physical brain. However, the neuroscientific community has been seeking such a site for the physical storage of memories in the brain for more than a century, to no avail. Although scientific reports in recent years have made various claims about mechanisms of memory storage in the physical brain, the supposed mechanisms and structures vary considerably—there is nothing remotely approaching a consensus. Especially as to the actual *location* of memory storage, the brain has proven absolutely mute on offering any possible answers.

Recall a memory from your childhood, say, from 3 or 4 years of age. Most people can pretty readily summon a few back to age 2 or so, and some can actively reminisce scenes going back even closer to birth. Close your eyes and let that recollection return fully to repaint the experience for you. Think of any other people involved in the memory, and associated sights, sounds, and, especially, feelings. Strong emotions enhance our ability to commit certain experiences to long-term memory, and can aid in their recovery. Our sense of smell can also provide a strong stimulus for evoking certain memories—a specific perfume may bring back recall of one's grandmother, or a whiff of tobacco smoke might awaken thoughts of a grandfather. Let your mind wander to any other memories that might be lurking right at the edge of awareness from similar early years, and marvel at the mind's ability to revive such moments.

The materialist model attempts to encode such memories in the molecular details of synaptic connections of neurons with one another. Whatever atoms and molecules were involved in the initial encoding of a given memory more than half a century ago, they have since been replaced numerous times, yet the memory has been retained. Although one might argue that the original synaptic constituents have been replaced faithfully with similar atoms and molecules over time, the fact remains that the memory is recalled from different material than that in which it was (allegedly) originally stored.

Since the 1940s, neurosurgeons have realized that small regions of the medial temporal lobes (including the hippocampi) seem to be crucial in the general conversion of short-term to long-term memory, but that does not seem to be the actual locale of memory storage. Damage here has no impact on the retrieval of old memories, only on the formation of new ones. This evidence supports the notion of the brain as a receiver or filter for primordial consciousness, but not the producer of it nor the location of memory storage.

One rarely discussed mystery in the world of clinical neurosurgery involves brain resections (removing a part of the brain tissue) and memory storage. If one assumes that memories are based in the neocortex, then one would expect to see some definable patterns of memory loss following major brain resections, yet that is not the case. This failure to locate physical storage of memory within the brain provides some of the strongest evidence against the materialist position that somehow the brain must be the source of memory, and of conscious awareness.

In fact, over three productive decades, Dr. Wilder Penfield achieved major revelations that suggest memories are not actually stored in the brain at all (see Appendix A). Although Penfield's work initially led him to believe that he was hot on the trail of the locale of memory itself, he soon came to realize that the picture was not nearly so simple. Electrical stimulation over the temporal lobes elicited interesting and often reproducible reports from his patients, but not in any consistent way that demonstrated anything more than that the physical brain provided some interface that allowed for the retrieval of memories. He even reported situations in which a cortical region associated with a reproducible memory had been entirely removed, and yet the patients reported the same memories perfectly! The reigning materialist assumption that memories are stored in the brain was not borne out by his decades of intensive study.

The inability to identify any physical location of memory in the brain is one of the greatest clues that materialism is a failed worldview. The more we learn about the structure and biology of the brain, the clearer it becomes that the brain does *not* create consciousness, nor serve as the repository for memory. The brain doesn't produce consciousness any more than it produces sound waves when you hear music. In fact, the situation is just the opposite: We are conscious *in spite of* our brain.

Materialist science as a foundation for comprehending our reality is at a dead end. We are long overdue to rise above this facade, and this demands the robust incorporation of consciousness into our working model of the universe. A convergence of understanding about our approach to science, our universe, and ourselves is the only way forward. For those with the most open minds, this is where science finds itself now, in the early 21st century, as it finally comes closer to some understanding of the depths of the mind-body debate. This fascinating investigation into the fundamental nature of reality is directly relevant to us all.

CHAPTER 5

THE PRIMORDIAL MIND HYPOTHESIS

> The universe begins to look more like a great
> thought than a great machine.... We ... ought
> rather to hail [Mind] as the creator and governor of
> this realm.
>
> —SIR JAMES JEANS (1877–1946),
> BRITISH ASTROPHYSICIST

As I progressed in my search for answers, my challenge was to explain two profound mysteries: How could progressive infection of my neocortex have allowed for such a wildly expansive and ultrareal conscious awareness like the one that occurred deep in my coma? And what is the fundamental nature of that indescribably comforting force of knowing, trust, and pure unconditional love—that basic intelligence and creativity (that many have identified as God or Supreme Deity)—at the source of it all? My coma journey suggested that consciousness originated from that core essence of the universe. How might I connect it all?

I began to review the many different models that explained the relationship between mind and brain. The entire scope of possible answers to the mind-body discussion can be envisioned as a linear spectrum anchored by two opposite poles, with materialism at one end (brain creates mind) and metaphysical idealism (mind creates brain, and all physical matter) at the other. Between the two poles lie many options of "dualism" that accept some existence of mind that is not simply reducible or explained by the physical brain. Dualism allows for brain and mind to coexist in some parallel fashion (as Wilder Penfield and other researchers have surmised).

Along with its other limitations, materialism proposes that humans have no free will whatsoever, given the view that the illusion of consciousness simply follows the natural laws of physics and chemistry applied to the substance of the brain. But what about any free will that might be involved in our deciding whether or not we have free will? Is that process likewise simply the result of a chain of chemical reactions in the brain that predictably falls into "yes" for some minds and "no" for others? To fully accept the materialist explanation requires acknowledgment that humans have no free will. For me, this was the crowning blow that eliminated materialism from the list of possible positions vis-à-vis the mind-body question.

Such fundamental questions as mine demanded a broader search, but it was not obvious where to turn. Religions and mystical traditions certainly acknowledged the existence of a creative force in the universe and were consistent with my experience, but this alone was not enough; my scientific mind demanded further elucidation. And for this, I turned to quantum physics.

Quantum physics—that is, the behavior of molecules, atoms, and their constituents in the microscopic realm—is the most proven theory in the history of science. The success of the underlying math and physics supports roughly a third of the world's economy (in the form of microelectronics, notably cell phones, computers, televisions, and GPS systems). Yet in the roughly 115 years of its existence, the scientific community has made no real progress in interpreting what the experimental results in quantum physics actually imply about the nature of reality.

One reason for this difficulty has to do with the fact that quantum physics deals directly with the mind-body question at a most fundamental level. Quantum physics ultimately addresses the intersection of our minds (knowledge) with the matter being observed (the physical). When scratching deeply into the physical world around us, we find that it does not behave according to the commonsense principles of our daily lives or the physical laws that govern large objects, such as our bodies. Experiments in quantum mechanics reveal that the energetic tapestry of all of the stuff that makes up our physical world has a decidedly bizarre nature to it, one so strange as to call into question all of our notions of the nature of reality.

Much of the apparent confusion around consciousness and quantum physics results from the efforts of scientific materialists to prevent their union, generally by denying that consciousness even exists or failing to grasp the deeper lessons of quantum evidence about their relationship. With a fresher perspective, some vexing problems in science become more approachable.

An overarching lesson from the study of modern physics is that the world is not as it appears. All of the basic components of the physical world (including our human brains and bodies)—the molecules, atoms, electrons, protons, neutrons, and photons of light, among others—are best viewed as vibrating strings of energy in higher dimensional space. Atoms make up every bit of the material stuff around us, but most of an atom is actually empty space. The nucleus at the center of an atom (99.95 percent of its mass) is orbited by tiny electrons (only 0.05 percent or less of the overall atomic mass).

An often-used analogy is to think of the atomic nucleus as the size of a gnat inside the vastly spacious Notre-Dame Cathedral (representing the size of the entire atom). This vast "empty space" of the material world is not quite so empty because it also seems to contain huge amounts of energy, in what is known as the "zero-point field" that pervades throughout the universe. And for those keeping track of the "matter" in this exercise, remember that only 2 percent of the mass of that atomic nucleus is the mass of the constituent quarks—the other 98 percent is actually binding energy captured when those quarks were initially wed together at the beginning of time. There really is almost *nothing to it*! Niels Bohr (1885–1962), who won the Nobel Prize in Physics in 1922, was alluding to this situation when he said, "Everything we call real is made of things that cannot be regarded as real."

The ancient Vedic term *maya* speaks to this as well. It is often translated as "illusion," but this is not necessarily to say that the world is "not real." It is just not as it appears to be. This is what Karen Newell and I often refer to as the Supreme Illusion—that our perceptions of the world mask the foundational truth of it. Contrary to conventional materialist science's notion that consciousness is the unimportant and confusing epiphenomenon of the workings of the physical brain, consider the fact that you have *never* witnessed anything other than the inside of your own consciousness.

"But wait!" you might protest as you point out all of the material stuff around us, from the couch we're sitting on to the house in which we live; from the mountains, trees, and lakes surrounding us, the cities and buildings, to all those fellow beings out there and the lovely stars in the night sky—all of it. Paramount in any effort to comprehend reality at a deeper level is to understand that what you have been witnessing since before you were born—all of that stuff "out there"—has actually been an internal model: a construct within mind that we *presume* represents something that *should* be "out there."

In response to the results of quantum experiments suggesting otherwise, Albert Einstein famously quipped, "I like to think the moon is there even if I am not looking at it." Most of us would agree with Einstein, but let's review what we can truly know about this process. In your daily meanderings, your eyes absorb photons of light from objects around you, whether the trees and birds in the yard or the moon, stars, and galaxies in the night sky. Let us focus on the moon, in line with Einstein's lamentation. Those lunar photons stream through 240,000 miles of space (in 1.6 seconds) to interact with molecules of pigment in the retina of your eye, initiating a cascade of neuronal firing that follows pathways through several regions of the brain, until the information from those photons (the colors, shapes, relationships, and motion of objects being observed) finally reaches conscious perception.

Neuroscience has never identified any particular site in the brain where this final instant of conscious awareness occurs. Most of the evidence suggests there is no "consciousness center" anywhere in the brain. The causal chain reaches the interior of the brain, causing the brain to change in some way that corresponds with our conscious perception of some external object, as Dutch philosopher Baruch de Spinoza (1632–1677) pointed out "that [which] corresponds with our conscious perception which represents some external object as present to us."

The perception of the moon in the mind's eye is not the moon itself, nor any physical entity remotely resembling the moon. Conventional neuroscience would tell us that your perception of the moon is a pattern of electrochemical firing in a highly organized network of millions of neurons whose complex pattern represents the moon in the "mind's eye." The moon in your mind is pure information, presumably in the form of neuronal connections that have built up over your lifetime of being in this world and observing it, and correlating all of your perceptions into a working internal model of the presumed outside world. Note that this mental model also includes your brain and body, which themselves are part of the physical world "out there." In a very real sense, none of what we perceive is anything more than our coded interpretation of pure information.

The main stumbling block to this realization is the shockingly efficient trick of the human brain and mind in fooling us into believing that the physical world exists *out there,* as we perceive it, "independently" of us. An excellent metaphor for this situation is that of asking a fish what it's like to live in the water. "What water?" the fish might easily challenge. It has never known anything but the water, and thus is oblivious to its existence. Likewise for us, swimming in the sea of consciousness—it is the only thing we've ever known.

Deeply enmeshed in our evolving notions of consciousness and reality is the fact that time flow, from past through present into future, is very much part of the Supreme Illusion. We tend to presume that something as primordial as time is a given and well worked out in our conventional scientific worldview. Nothing could be further from the truth. Not only is physical matter not what it appears to be, but neither is time. Cornell psychologist Daryl Bem's bizarre yet irrefutable experimental evidence[1] (Chapter 4) demonstrating precognition (conscious cognitive awareness) and premonition (emotional apprehension) *before the computer has made the random selection (!)* is just the beginning of the puzzle. The existing body of evidence suggests time flow is built into earthly reality as part of our limited human awareness.

In some sense, in this *eternal now,* past and future are quite symmetrical. An extended form of John Wheeler's delayed-choice quantum eraser experiment (see Appendix B) makes the surprising point that the decision an astronomer makes tonight about how to observe a quasar a few billion light-years away actually causes the incoming photons, which left that quasar billions of years ago, to alter their behavior into the distant past, to appear as particles or waves. In essence, a choice we make now has causal influence on the past. It is all about the perception, and the knowledge we can gain of the world, in the now moment.

Other brilliant physicists have likewise glimpsed this peculiar wrinkle in our human concepts of the apparent flow of time. As Einstein stated after the death of his lifelong friend, Michele Besso, "Now he has departed from this strange world a little ahead of me. That means nothing. People like us, who believe in physics, know that the distinction between past, present, and future is only a stubbornly persistent illusion."

Major clues exist in the apparent passage of time, or *not,* in dreams, under general anesthesia, during near-death experiences (and especially during the life review), and in other altered states of awareness. Time flow in these states of altered conscious awareness can be very different: Time can seem to go forward and backward, can run faster or slower than "earth time," or our awareness can jump to regions remotely distant from a consensus "earth time."

Deep in coma, my experience of time flow in the physical universe was wrapped into a tight loop, or even a point. I became aware of a more fundamental form of causality, manifested in what I call "deep time." Deep time is primary, related to the evolution of all consciousness, and especially the myriad events in the lives of sentient beings. The steadily flowing river of earth time was shown to be an illusion promoted by our consciousness on "this side of the veil." Compared with deep time, apparent "earth time" is only a subset related to our shared "consensus reality," in which all of our collective consciousness is simultaneously witnessing the same group reality. Conscious awareness in alternate dimensions is not limited by earth time, and has access to regions outside of consensus reality with ease.

Clearly, the implications of the most sophisticated recent experiments in quantum physics only strengthen the sense that there is no underlying objective physical reality independent of the mind of the conscious observer.[2] And yet, the Supreme Illusion offers a most compelling sense of a consensus reality. The Supreme Illusion is "cunning, baffling, and powerful," to borrow a phrase from the addiction literature found in

12-step programs. Even given our cognitive acknowledgement of the Supreme Illusion, we are drawn into its seductive and irresistible power.

Many might wonder just *why* we have a shared awareness of a common world, since this shared reality seems to strongly support the independent existence of the physical world. This shared "reality" is, in fact, the basis of our earthly experience. The consensus reality of the physical realm serves as a convenient stage for the unfolding of the events of our lives, even though, like the old Western town facades that Hollywood used for filming, *it does not exist as such*. In many ways, our jointly perceived physical world serves the same role that our bodies play in providing a focus of our here-and-now experience.

Regarding that consensus reality, when David Chalmers defined the hard problem, he also mentioned the "easy" problem of consciousness. The easy problem is the question of assessing qualia. Simply put, qualia are the subjective or qualitative aspects of perception. The easy problem concerns, for example, an evaluation of the redness of an apple, and an attempt to compare one person's sensation of red with another's—are they the same perception or are there differences in quality or content that one might say are different from each other? Scientists interested in consciousness have estimated that the easy problem of consciousness might be solved within "a few centuries." You can imagine how long they'd estimate the hard problem might take, by comparison.

Given the great difficulties in even defining the nature of what we are comparing, the possible disparities between our individual qualia and whether they converge into any meaningful consensus should point out the tremendous difficulty in trying to compare our individual versions of reality in any given setting. Of course, we agree that our perceptions match similar perceptions we've had in the past because we agreed on these definitions and understandings as they evolved. Thus, our language is coded to mean certain things in certain situations, but we can only agree that those qualia remain stable to us in our ongoing perception of the world. We continue to face the problem of not knowing or being able to compare the contents and qualia of our perceptions with those of others. We are left merely to assume that we have some agreement in our perceptions.

Many view the objective scientific method as the only pathway to truth, and believe that subjective individual experience counts for nothing in the current era of evidence-based conclusions. In fact, all of human knowing is deeply rooted in personal experience (including that of the scientist performing the experiment), so that the *subjective* experience of the scientist, indeed of all of us, must be viewed as integral. In fact, anecdotes and subtle mental realizations known only to the subjective self have been involved in any scientific truths that have come to be known through the application of the scientific method.

Princeton University professor of philosophy Thomas Nagel wrote an interesting and often-quoted paper in 1974 that helps to demonstrate the fundamental value of subjective over objective knowledge. Nagel's provocative thought experiment considers what it is like "to be a bat." He chose this animal because it is a mammal, as are human beings, and thus similar enough to us to be considered as having subjective conscious experience. But he notes that the bat's main perceptive mechanism for constructing a model of the external world is echolocation, which involves emanating high-pitched shrieks as outgoing signals, then constructing a model of the three-dimensional world through the complex patterns of the sound echoes reflected off of all the myriad surrounding physical entities (mosquitoes, birds, trees, other bats, etc.) back to the bat's ears and subsequently processed by the bat's brain. This complex sonar system allows the bat to construct a high-resolution mental model of the distance, direction, size, texture, shape, and motion of all of its physical surroundings so it can effectively fly through the night sky and lap mosquitoes out of thin air for its dinner.

More recently at NYU, Nagel clarifies that this exercise is not one of assessing "what it would be like for *me* to behave as a bat behaves. . . . I want to know what it is like for a *bat* to be a bat." The subjective information inherent in the bat's experiencing of its world is indeed extensive, yet it is quite different and independent of the similar information available to humans. His thought experiment greatly elucidates the point that a tremendous amount of information conveyed through subjective experience surpasses the knowledge available through "objective" assessment alone—in fact, it is challenging to assert that unbiased objectivity can even exist.

Given our evolving notion of the Supreme Illusion, the only knowledge available to any human being is the subjective. In fact, we never have access to any "objective" reality. There seems to be a consensus reality that we assume to be the external world, including all humans and other beings in addition to ourselves, but we must be cautious not to assume too much about any objective reality outside of what is subjectively verifiable to us. Nagel saw all materialist explanations as guilty of just that.

The Australian analytical philosopher Frank Jackson enlivened this discussion in 1982 with his fable of Mary, a neurophysiologist who had spent her life studying the neural mechanisms of color vision, but who herself had gleaned all of her knowledge from a black-and-white computer screen, living in a black-and-white room from which she had never once in her life emerged. Although she studied all that neuroscience could offer about the mechanisms by which one could see the redness of a ripe tomato, the rich green of an early-spring grass lawn, or the blueness of the clear sky, she had never experienced seeing color with her own eyes. Her knowledge included all that is known in the psychophysical experiments of neuroscience around the neural processes of perception.

Jackson then liberates Mary from her bleak black-and-white world, by providing her with a color monitor, and allowing her to venture outside into the real world, rich with all the colors of the rainbow. Has Mary learned anything new by perceiving that ripe red tomato, seeing with her own eyes the rich green lawn and crystal blue sky? Most humans would argue that yes, she has gained new knowledge about the world that she never could have acquired through exhaustive scientific study (and the verbal descriptions of such information from others) of the physical mechanisms of color vision—she gained knowledge through the *experience* of color. Personally witnessing the brilliant colors of the natural world added information that was absolutely crucial in her comprehension of the world in general, and nothing short of that direct personal experience could have completed her knowing of the world.

Jackson concludes that the entirety of physical substance does not include all possible data—that there is crucial information in subjective experience that extends beyond an exhaustive physical description. That critical something is the subjective experience itself. Mary's tale also reveals a fatal flaw in the argument that the only information that is useful in our scientific era is that which is gleaned from the strictly controlled objective scientific method. On the contrary, reports from people around the world defy what materialist science claims to be fact, and such empirical evidence must be addressed if we have any serious interest in understanding the nature of our world.

My subjective experience during coma was certainly a powerful piece of evidence that showed me the reality of the spiritual realm. I had been used to dismissing personal experience as having any value at all, but I began to realize subjective experience was *the* critical piece to our comprehension of the world, despite its anecdotal nature. Thus, so-called "paranormal" phenomena become much more relevant. I came to realize that even accepting any dualist theory, where mind is accepted as a separate entity from brain, was not going far enough. What if quantum physics experiments are telling us that *mind* actually *creates* all of the events witnessed in the material world? What if our personal choices are integrally influencing our unfolding reality?

Bold new thinking is the way out of our current situation. Welsh philosopher H. H. Price said, "We may safely predict that it will be the timidity of our hypotheses, and not their extravagance, which will provoke the derision of posterity." And as Einstein pointed out, "We cannot solve our problems with the same thinking we used when we created them."

Here is where I began to seriously ponder the philosophical position called metaphysical idealism. Metaphysics concerns the most fundamental assumptions about existence, such as the notion that the universe is comprehensible, or that the only stuff that exists is physical or material matter. Idealism is the notion that reality (our entire universe) is fundamentally a form of thought in which the human mind participates. Existence thus emerges from the realm of ideas, or from the mental (out of consciousness itself). Metaphysical idealism can also be called ontological idealism—ontological simply refers to "all that is."

Metaphysical idealism exists at the other extreme from the conventional materialist position, that of "brain creates mind." From this opposite pole of idealism, one assumes that consciousness exists primarily, which generates all particular minds, brains, and bodies. There are rules that govern the stage setting (i.e., the facade of the physical world) for this drama (broadly, the laws of physics, or laws of the illusion), but the theme and plot of actual events (especially from a human perspective) are not so limited. There is still a powerful principle of sufficient reason—the notion that all effects must have sufficient causes or that nothing can occur simply as a chaotic or random event. This principle was developed from early Greek philosophers such as Plato and Aristotle, but its modern form is attributed to the 18th-century German philosopher Gottfried Leibniz. Hence, our attention to complex synchronicities, or our sensing some of the deep interconnections manifested through the events of our lives, often suggests an intelligent force guiding our lives and understanding.

An example of such a synchronicity concerns my life career path. During my neurosurgical residency, I spent two years (1985–87) investigating cerebral vasospasm, a particularly deadly complication of subarachnoid hemorrhage (SAH) from aneurysms that maims and kills approximately one-third of the patients who survive the actual hemorrhage. Following residency, in 1987 I pursued a fellowship in vascular neurosurgery, intensely studying the surgical management of aneurysms, before securing a position at Harvard Medical School heading up vascular neurosurgery at the Brigham and Women's Hospital.

I was adopted, and in the search for my birth parents, I later learned that this hereditary affliction was part of my biological family's medical history. It was this hereditary condition that motivated my birth sister to reach out to the adoption agency, a crucial step in our eventual reconnection. Information revealed to me in February 2000 indicated that my maternal grandfather had suffered an aneurysmal subarachnoid hemorrhage that left him badly impaired for a few months before he finally succumbed in 1966. My birth mother had two sisters, and in 1978, her youngest sister suffered an SAH and died within a day. Her other sister endured an SAH in 2004 at age 65, which seriously incapacitated her for about 3 years, although she has gone on to a miraculous recovery (to the point where she has won several local golf tournaments in recent years). I initially reacted with amazed shock at this seeming coincidence, but perhaps my career choice in the 1980s had some deeper connection with the discovery of my personal biological predisposition two decades later.

In metaphysical idealism, as also in quantum physics, all of the universe is deeply interconnected: Any separation of a part from the whole in our thinking leads to distortion and confusion. However, such sufficient reasons within the position of metaphysical idealism represent a grander repertoire of causes and effects extending far beyond the simplistic assumptions of materialist science and the laws of the illusion. They are what allow for the vast interconnectedness revealed through synchronicities or the broader implications of the placebo effect (mind over body to promote healing) and other phenomena to nudge us gently toward an awakening in understanding. Making sense of the vast swathes of human experience beyond those of our mundane daily conscious awareness thus becomes more accessible.

The laws of physics generally govern the rules of engagement, limiting what is actually possible in our observable physical universe. However, much hinges on what humans *believe* to be possible, and any limitations are largely "within the mind." Such beliefs have expanded dramatically in recent decades, with the overwhelming evidence for nonlocal consciousness, such as the reality of telepathy, precognition, presentiment, out-of-body experiences, remote viewing, and past-life memories in children indicative of reincarnation. Researchers of these subjects are leading the charge in eliminating the simplistic falsehoods of scientific materialism, and the self-imposed limitations of human capability that they imply.

A basic principle in science and philosophy, referred to as Occam's razor (named for the 14th-century English Franciscan friar, William of Ockham), is the notion that the simplest explanation, that which involves the least additional construction in trying to explain our world, is most likely to be true. As Einstein is often paraphrased to have said, "Explanations should be as simple as possible, but no simpler." William of Ockham might thus support metaphysical idealism as the most fitting model for the nature of reality, given the admission that we are always limited to our first-person experience in seeking our deepest understanding of existence. We simply need to overcome our addiction to the Supreme Illusion, and realize that the objective physical world is a construct within mind.

Metaphysical idealism is derived directly from such deep thinkers as Irish philosopher George Berkeley (1685–1753), who addressed the relationship between material objects and our perception of them through the following question: Is it possible to conceive of a sensible object existing independently of any perceiver? In other words, if a tree falls in the forest and no one is present to witness its fall, does it make a sound? More broadly, does the event of its falling actually occur, if unwitnessed by a conscious observer? Our common sense would lead us to answer in the affirmative, yet we would have to admit that it is impossible to know for sure. Such certainty would require an observer to be present to witness the tree actually falling, violating our requirement that "no one is present to witness its fall." Our common sense says that encountering a fallen tree in the forest is sufficient to warrant the belief that it actually fell at some time in the past—but "common sense" often leads to erroneous conclusions concerning the fundamental nature of reality.

Berkeley further explored the issue by noting that the only crucial elements involved in perceiving something like a fallen tree are the perceiver and the perception. Given those, he realized that the requirement that a physical object (the fallen tree) had to actually exist was an absurd notion only required by the minds of philosophers riddling over the question. Berkeley summarized his conclusion thus: "To be is to be perceived."

Thus, the perception in mind is sufficient to explain it all, without the external physical object, when we appreciate the purely informational nature of the described events and realize that a more inclusive substrate than the apparent physical world (i.e., the quantum hologram) would sufficiently support the entire process.

Of note, the version of metaphysical idealism we are promoting here acknowledges the oneness of the universe within consciousness beyond the more "atomistic" or "separatist" view promulgated by Berkeley (more aptly viewed as solipsism), who saw all souls as individual, and separate from God. Our view is more aligned with that of German philosopher Georg Wilhelm Friedrich Hegel (1770–1831), who followed Plato's lead in honoring the will of the soul, or of Dutch philosopher Baruch de Spinoza, who explicitly accepted Saint Paul's dictum: "in Him we live and move and have our being"—that all of our perceptions are within the one mind of a higher being. It is Spinoza's view in particular that best explains our experience of a shared consensus reality.

This view considers our conscious awareness to originate in the Collective Mind, which comprises all sentient consciousness throughout the universe. Our individual awareness is superficially split out into a sense of being separate, which allows for this vast dance of all of the elements in the evolution of consciousness. Some might label this one mind as "God," the ineffable force of pure love encountered by so many during all manner of spiritually transformative experiences. The apparent reality of such a deity tends to become lost in the weeds of conflicting contemporary religious dogma.

A more modern argument for metaphysical idealism comes from computer scientist Bernardo Kastrup, who notified me of a blog post he had written in response to neuroscientist Sam Harris's attack on my book *Proof of Heaven*. Harris had challenged my contention that brain damage could foster surprising enrichment and expansion of conscious awareness, and Bernardo took up my side in his blog, as well as in his book *Brief Peeks Beyond*.[3] He tackles just how our deep-seated collective beliefs might actually create physical matter in *More than Allegory*, a fresh and ambitious approach invoking metaphysical idealism at its core. Bernardo's diligence in pursuing the issue of enhanced consciousness in the setting of brain damage led to his guest entry on the *Scientific American* blog,[4] in which he opened the door to filter theory and metaphysical idealism (or at least a form of dualism) on the basis of brain damage enhancing mental function in many different settings. It is interesting that such insight into the mind-body problem originates from those studying computer science, especially as they deal with the fundamental principles of information and its role in emerging reality.

Recall that conscious awareness itself is the only information source available to any human being in existence. The objective physical world is projected as outside of and independent of our conscious awareness of it, yet our assumption that it exists as we perceive it is only an *interpretation* of our sensory experience, and not an established fact. The actual existence of the objective physical world is an extra step that is not necessary.

Metaphysical idealism fits well with filter theory, the framework emerging today in neuroscience and philosophy of mind promoting a more viable linkage between brain and consciousness. In filter theory, the physical brain serves as the reducing valve or filter through which universal consciousness, or the Collective Mind, is filtered, or allowed in, to our more restricted human perception of the world around us. Further, I suggest the filtering function is intimately associated with the neocortex, the outer surface (and human part) of the brain. In the conventional neuroscientific production model, where the brain produces consciousness out of physical matter, the neocortex represents the most powerful calculator in the human brain and is intimately involved in all of the details of our conscious awareness. I postulate that the neocortex is the dominant influ-ence on how much and what specific conscious awareness is allowed in from Collective Mind. Its filtering function is to limit and reduce, thus only allowing in the trickle of conscious awareness that becomes our perceptions of the world around us.

Filter theory takes us much further in explaining a wide variety of exotic human experiences, such as near-death and shared-death experi-ences, precognition, after-death communications, out-of-body experi-ences, and remote viewing. This hypothesis explains my own personal ultrareal NDE in coma, when my neocortex was so thoroughly disman-tled. Without a properly functioning filter, I experienced a much broader contact with universal consciousness, as have millions of others who have witnessed the ultrareality of such transcendent experiences in consciousness.

Experimental results in quantum physics serve as the smoking gun to indicate that consciousness is fundamental in creating the universe: All of the observable universe (and all of the rest of the cosmos that exist any-where or anytime) appears to emerge from consciousness itself. Quantum physics results are quite baffling when viewed from the purely materialist perspective. Richard Feynman (1918–1988), who won the Nobel Prize in Physics in 1965, is renowned for his statement, "If someone tells you they understand quantum mechanics, then all you've learned is that you've met a liar." One reason for this sense of profound mystery, and the decid-edly nonsensical behavior of the quantum world, is contained within what is known as the measurement problem. This concerns a phenome-non known as the "collapse of the wave function," that is, that the act of observation seems to influence the measured result of an experiment.

The hallmark of quantum mechanics (according to Feynman) is con-tained in the famous double-slit optical experiment, in which a light beam (a stream of photons) shined on two parallel slits in a metal sheet produces a wavelike interference pattern on the screen on the other side. The interference pattern appears as the dark and light bands that repre-sent the peaks and valleys of the two waves intersecting. Given our notions of wavelength and frequency, such as colors of visible light, it is important to recognize that in quantum experiments, light can behave as both wave and particle. Particles are all the subatomic constituents of physical matter, such as electrons or protons, and in this discussion also include atoms and molecules. Surprisingly, studies reveal that particles of matter also demonstrate wavelike behavior.

In the double-slit experiment, blocking one of the slits on the metal sheet causes the photons to behave like particles, which appears as two solid bands on the screen beyond. If one places detectors adjacent to the slits in order to gain some information as to which slit a photon traverses, then those photons behave like particles. The surprising aspect of the experiment is that if there is *any way* that information is available from the detector, even in principle, then the photons will show particle-like, and not wavelike, behavior. It is almost as if the photon is *aware of being observed,* and behaves accordingly by appearing as a particle when a detector could conceivably provide information about which slit it traversed. Very peculiar, indeed!

Improved experimental design and advances in technology have allowed progressively stronger support for the reality of quantum observer effects. Starting in 2012, Dean Radin and his colleagues reported on a fascinating series of experiments[5] evaluating the effect of distant human observers in double-slit experiments. Radin set it up so that a participant would focus their attention—purely in their mind's eye—on either one slit or the other. Remarkably, the participants' attention alone affected the behavior of photons so that they appeared more particle-like when mentally focusing on one slit, and more wavelike when mentally withdrawing their focus from the optical system. Seventeen iterations of this experiment, involving four different double-slit systems, generally confirmed and strengthened the findings from earlier experiments. The findings reveal the influence of a small but detectable effect of "mind over matter" in its most basic form, and suggest how our minds might have influence over the entire physical world.

The most shocking realization from these experiments is that the outcome of the measurement is crucially related to choices made by the mind of the observer. The commonsense assumption in classical physics that whatever is being objectively measured is separate from the observer, proves to be false when the physical world is examined in a more comprehensive quantum way. That an outcome would depend on the choices of the experimenter making the measurement is completely unexpected. And this deep relationship between the observer and the observed is not limited to quantum mechanical experiments set up in the modern physics laboratory—it suggests that this is true of all of our interactions with the physical world, as the observers of that world.

The general concept among many is that quantum physics is applicable only in the subatomic (very small) world at extremely low temperatures. Many also view that the behavior inherent in atomic-level particles disappears as you get larger assemblies of such particles (anything larger than molecules). Some physicists refer to this arbitrary boundary between the small and the large as the "Heisenberg cut." In reality, such a "cut" is only useful for discussion and modeling; there is no such boundary in the real world—every bit of it is quantum, not classical.

In quantum physics, subatomic particles generated together are said to be entangled. This occurs, for example, when photons of light are passed through a nonlinear crystal, allowing their polarization measurements to then be correlated with each other. Other correlated properties of entangled particles can include their position, momentum, and spin. Entangled objects can thus include not just photons of light, but also electrons, protons, neutrons, neutrinos, atoms, molecules, and even small diamonds. Before a measurement is made, the potential values for such particles are said to exist in a superposition state, where all possible measurements are associated with specific probabilities. Beginning with the report of Stuart Freedman and John Clauser concerning entangled photons in 1972, what an observer *chose* to measure about one of a pair of entangled subatomic objects instantaneously influenced the result obtained by a separate observer of its entangled partner, irregardless of the distance between the members of the entangled pair.

Freedman and Clauser's experiment was a direct response to Einstein, who was never satisfied that quantum physics was a complete theory. In a paper he wrote with colleagues Boris Podolsky and Nathan Rosen in 1935 (renowned as the "EPR paradox"), he complained that the quantum-wave function did not provide a complete picture of physical reality, and that there thus must exist "hidden variables" that could explain the results more satisfactorily. To illustrate his complaint, the Einstein-Podolsky-Rosen (EPR) paper elucidates the paradoxical behavior that ensues when one makes a measurement of one of the entangled photons. That measurement of the first particle forces a correlated measurement value to be obtained in the second particle, no matter how far apart the two might be at the time. At the moment of measurement, entangled particles seem to violate the principle of special relativity (which states that no information can travel faster than light). Einstein scoffed at this instantaneous collapse of the wave function, which he called "spooky action at a distance."

Such quantum experiments suggest that the act of measurement in the first particle instantaneously *causes* the correlated measurement to occur in the second particle. This shocking result suggests that the entangled particles are somehow acting as one particle that seems to be separated from itself in space. This is a most surprising finding, one that appears to be inexplicable given our everyday notions of space and time, and yet it has been confirmed many times in recent decades. Applying the principles of metaphysical idealism, such results seem to indicate that we are indeed connected on a fundamental level.

This is but the tip of the iceberg in conveying the fundamental role of consciousness in creating all of emergent reality. As the most successful and proven field in the four-century history of the scientific revolution, quantum physics would make better sense through the admission that the observing mind is absolutely crucial in the actuality that emerges as our perceived reality. This is simply another expression of metaphysical idealism.

Princeton physicist John Wheeler contributed much to our modern cultural appreciation of physics and cosmology, including popularization of the terms *black hole* and *wormhole*. Toward the end of his life, he became fascinated with the question of the role of life and consciousness in the universe, wondering whether they were accidental by-products, or central to the very existence of the universe. His deep knowledge of quantum physics led him to believe that reality is created by observers and that "no phenomenon is a real phenomenon until it is an observed phenomenon." This thinking evolved into what he called the Participatory Anthropic Principle. He saw the universe as a work in progress, one in which the past does not exist until it is observed in the present, and considered the "participatory" conscious observer to be crucial in all of unfolding reality. As Wheeler concluded, "To be is to be perceived," pointing out his agreement with idealist George Berkeley stated more than two centuries earlier. The most robust expression of such consciousness at the core of reality is, again, metaphysical idealism.

Although Wheeler might have considered some type of existence of the universe without observing minds, he clearly saw all of evolving reality as depending on the actions of conscious observers. As his delayed-choice quantum-eraser experiment reveals, the choice of an observer can even influence the past history of observed particles. "It begins to look as if we ourselves, by a last-minute decision, have an influence on what a photon will do when it has already accomplished most of its doing. . . . We have to say that we ourselves have an undeniable part in shaping what we have always called the past. The past is not really the past until it has been registered. Or put it another way, the past has no meaning or existence unless it exists as a record in the present," Wheeler concluded.

To truly resolve such curiosities, I began to view metaphysical idealism as a viable model to explain how my consciousness could have been so robust, despite the disruption of my neocortex. Recalling the spectrum of mind-body models, materialism is the only position that has absolutely no place for "mind" other than as something decidedly unreal, the very confusing illusion of the physical workings of the brain (epiphenomenalism) that we call "consciousness." Note that all dualistic positions accept that the mind has an existence and some relationship to the brain, but that metaphysical idealism is particularly pure in this sense, postulating that all of reality and existence emerge from the realm of mind alone.

A word of caution is in order about the position of panpsychism—the idea that elements of primitive consciousness naturally exist in every particle inhabiting the subatomic world. This remains a materialist position, one that attempts to acknowledge the dualistic stance that there must be more than just the physical to explain the mind. But panpsychism does not account for the more powerful ordering principles, such as the greater structure of the tapestry of all life, where our actions and thoughts link us very meaningfully with the universe, as addressed in later chapters. And to be complete, any theory must address this rich aspect of human experience.

Feeling somewhat satisfied with the concepts of metaphysical idealism as a useful starting point, my second question remained: What is the nature of the creative, loving force at the core of all existence that I had encountered during my coma? In musing over all possible universes, it is astonishing that ours appears to be as simple and orderly as it does. As Einstein said, "The most incomprehensible thing about the world is that it is comprehensible." The very fact that so much of the apparent structure and function of the universe can be so elegantly expressed through the formulations of mathematics (as revealed through the lens of physics) is a stunning realization, worthy of our deepest reflection.

Advanced forms of mathematics, widely used throughout the world of physics, represent an abstract world of ideals. Why should the real world be so completely definable within the logical formalism of mathematics? While philosophers of mathematics might ruminate over whether mathematics was discovered or invented, mathematicians themselves would widely acknowledge that mathematics is *discovered* in the underlying reality. One is justified in wondering if the intelligence underlying our universe, or "the Old One," as Einstein put it, fashioned its existence from an idealized and carefully balanced model. Amazingly, our physical universe seems to be completely beholden to such perfect mathematical formulation.

In addition to this surprising mathematical comprehensibility of the universe, the precise tuning of the values of physical constants that determine the behavior of all of the components of our universe is, likewise, shocking. There are currently twenty-six such parameters involved in the standard model of particle physics (plus the cosmological constant, concerning the accelerating expansion of all of space), including the speed of light in a vacuum c, the elementary charge of an electron e, Max Planck's constant h, the fine structure constant a, and the gravitational constant G. These basic parameters are currently believed to remain constant throughout the space of the observable physical universe, as well as over all of time (although this constancy across space and time is an assumption, not established fact).

If any of these twenty-six numbers varied by even a tiny fraction from their measured values (far less than 1 percent), the result would have prevented the formation of atoms, molecules, humans (and other life-forms), planets, stars, and galaxies—none of it would exist. This "fine-tuning," as it is known in the world of physics, is an astonishing realization not to be ignored in trying to fathom the deeper nature of reality. Both the mathematical precision of the universe and the fine-tuning of physical constants present a serious challenge to anyone trying to argue for a cold, chaotic, mechanistic—and purposeless—universe.

The mathematical precision of our world and the fine-tuning of physical parameters involved in its structure provide compelling evidence of a highly ordered consciousness underlying all of existence. I believe that this ordering intelligence, which many might see as a creative God, is actually the very source of our conscious awareness as sentient beings. There is no separation between this ultimate creative force and our conscious awareness of existing in this universe. The observer, the self-awareness of the universe for itself, *is us* at the deepest level.

It is this aware observer who is also behind the hard problem of consciousness and the measurement problem in quantum physics, two of the leading conundrums at the frontiers of modern science. Note that the "hard problem" is actually an impossible problem, at least if one is shackled within the limited mind-set of materialism. But it becomes less of a problem with broader views of the possibilities, such as those allowed through filter theory and metaphysical idealism. More expansive paradigms include concepts such as the "mind-at-large" (in the words of Aldous Huxley) or the "collective unconscious" (according to Carl Jung) as that omnipresent engine that underlies the entire self-aware universe. There is an information substrate (which might be referred to as the quantum hologram, or the Akashic record) that holds complete potentiality for all of conscious experience—for the universe to be aware of itself.

The great psychologist William James (1842–1910) offered up what he called "the More." His concept was simply that one could not fully explain the events of human lives through interactions defined in the physical realm alone. I view "the More" as a top-down organizational principle that sets the stage for true evolution on a grand scale—that is, evolution of information and understanding of the nature of the universe, aligned with a structure suggestive of meaning and purpose in human existence. In many ways, this grander evolution of consciousness is the reason the entire universe exists.

It is *all* about consciousness—literally and truly, *all* of it.

By consciousness, I mean that self-awareness, that knowing in this moment that you exist, that you are a human being alive in the here and now—the *observer* part of awareness—the *knower* of knowledge.

That spark of awareness that *experiences,* and that remembers experience—*that* is consciousness. That very awareness itself is the profound mystery at the heart of René Descartes's famous observation: "I think, therefore I am."

Recall the deep mystery of the observer's role within quantum physics.

Such mysteries used to be an isolated curiosity within the world of physics alone, but we've come to realize the principles are applicable not only in the field of chemistry, but also in biology. In recent decades, biologists have found robust evidence that quantum physics is crucial to any understanding of biological processes such as photosynthesis (plants' ability to convert the energy of sunlight into living matter), the human sense of smell, and bird migration (through their ability to see the earth's magnetic field). In reality, all of existence is quantum—even the classical (or Newtonian) elements that apply on the macroscopic level are operating within a quantum system, by quantum laws.

This astonishing "mindfulness" of the universe, its very self-awareness of existence, manifests at the smallest level through the conscious awareness of individual beings, and is tightly interwoven with the purpose of all of evolving consciousness. This identity with the oneness of the universe fully enlivened my NDE experience in the Core. That was the richest, most fundamental reality of my entire journey, and yet it was naturally also the experience most distant from our daily earthly lives. The beauty is the perfect oneness of it all—that these enormously separate perspectives are merely different facets of the same perfect diamond—the gem of our existence.

This general framework of understanding around the mind-body discussion allows for a more reasonable explanation for the vast scope of human experience. Such a model must be consistent with the deepest truths illuminated in the scientific community, but not a slave to incorrect assumptions underlying our conceptual framework. By honoring the profound nature of the Supreme Illusion wed to the concept of metaphysical idealism and the filter theory of mind, the proper interpretation of quantum physics then offers up meaningful ways of viewing consciousness as fundamental in generating all of the apparent physical universe.

To fully address the vast experience of sentient beings, we are postulating a very grand universe, indeed—one with wide-open possibilities for human potential, as we are all participants and cocreators in this grand evolution of consciousness itself. We are on a journey of experience, of the heart and soul, not accessible to the armchair philosopher through academic scholarship alone. Rising above the Supreme Illusion requires, first and foremost, paying attention to one's experience.

CHAPTER 6

TRUSTING PERSONAL EXPERIENCE

There are two ways to be fooled. One is to believe
what isn't true; the other is to refuse to believe
what is true.

—SØREN KIERKEGAARD (1813–1855),
DANISH PHILOSOPHER

His Holiness the fourteenth Dalai Lama has been in exile from his
country and his people since the Tibetan Uprising of 1959, when the
Chinese military took over Tibet. He currently lives as a political exile in
India. Through his support of the Tibetan people, he was awarded the
Nobel Peace Prize in 1989. Reincarnation is an accepted concept in
Buddhism—in fact, the individuals of the lineage of the Dalai Lamas
have been actively identified, since 1391, through acknowledgment that
the Dalai Lama's soul is perpetually reincarnated. Following a statement
from His Holiness in 2011 that he might complete his spiritual endeavors
on earth and choose *not* to reincarnate, the officially atheistic and anti-
religious government of China responded with a stern warning that he
must choose to reincarnate, or else! They made it clear they wanted to be
in charge of the reincarnation, and of the selection of the fifteenth Dalai

Lama. Their interest, of course, is not in providing safe passage to the bodhisattva of compassion through the spiritual realms, but in controlling and suppressing the Tibetan people.

While he has no formal training in any scientific discipline, nonetheless he is intrigued by what science can potentially offer. "As in science, so in Buddhism, understanding the nature of reality is pursued by means of critical investigation: If scientific analysis were conclusively to demonstrate certain claims in Buddhism to be false, then we must accept the findings of science and abandon those claims," he states in *The Universe in a Single Atom*. In 2013, after reading *Proof of Heaven*, the Dalai Lama invited me to join him for a public discussion of modern scientific views on reincarnation. The discussion was part of the graduation ceremony for Maitripa College, a Tibetan Buddhist school and meditation center in Portland, Oregon. The crowd of students, faculty, and community members was calm but excited.

His Holiness spoke last, and his topic of choice was different types of phenomena that influence our views. He explained that phenomena fit into one of three categories: (1) evident phenomena, which can be studied by direct observation; (2) hidden phenomena, which can be inferred based on observed phenomena; and (3) extremely hidden phenomena, which can be accessed only through our own first-person experience or inference based on the trustworthy testimony of someone else.

The first type (evident phenomena) is the hallmark of materialist science research and refers to observations that can be verified through direct perception via the five physical senses. The second type (hidden phenomena) refers to theories or inferences that can be drawn from such observations using cognitive analysis. One noteworthy case is the example of terminal lucidity I described in *Proof of Heaven*: A close colleague, chairman of one of the most respected neurosurgery programs in the country, witnessed his father having a profound spiritual connection with the soul of his own mother at the time of his passing over. The father had become progressively demented over months, with no expectation of any kind of higher-ordered thinking possible, given the decline in his mental faculties. My friend, an eminent neuroscientist, was shocked by the unexpected and inexplicable clarity, insight, and understanding he saw his father demonstrate minutes before his passing on. He was certain of the reality of the encounter for his own father, and that event forever changed his views on the reality of the spiritual world; witnessing his father's experience convinced him of the falsehood of the model "brain creates consciousness."

For me, of course, my NDE experience fell into the third category—extremely hidden phenomena—because I experienced it directly. But for others, they must choose to decide if my testimony is trustworthy. Unless you've had the experience yourself, you can't know with certainty that it actually took place.

"When we touch upon the third category of phenomena—which is really extremely hidden and obscure—then for the time being, for the other people, there's no real access, direct or inferential. So the only method that is left is to really rely on the testimony of the first-person experience of the person himself or herself," His Holiness explained, with the help of his translator. "With respect to science and its scope for discovering knowledge, we need to make a distinction about the fact that there might be certain types of phenomena which are beyond the scope of scientific inquiry."

Pointing at me, he finished, "At a deeper level, there [are] still more mysterious things."

His Holiness acknowledged that my experience (and others like it) are not possible to fully explain using traditional scientific methods. But firsthand experiences are vital to our personal understanding. We can trust the experiences of others, or we can cultivate and trust our own. And that is what I'm interested in: the mysteries of how consciousness interacts with the physical world and how each of us plays a role in that process. Mysterious phenomena are around every corner—we just need to pay attention to our experience. That sounds simple, but I've come to learn it's easier said than done.

I first met Michael Shermer, publisher of *Skeptic* magazine, when we were both guests on *Larry King Live* in December 2013. Shermer posed as the "token skeptic" on a panel discussing my NDE. The panel also included spiritual activist Marianne Williamson and Rabbi Marvin Hier. Shermer's main role was to present the materialist argument in which he stated that I must have had a dream or hallucination. At the end of the discussion, he said he hoped I was right about the afterlife, but still maintained his posture of disbelieving and denying the medical evidence in my case. As we parted after the taping, he kindly gave me a personalized copy of his book, *The Believing Brain*. In it, he attempts to explain how the brain forms beliefs by assigning meaning to patterns perceived in our surroundings.

Given his stance, I was impressed when a few months later, in October 2014, he wrote an article in his monthly column for *Scientific American* concerning a rather unusual and seemingly inexplicable personal story. He and his wife, Jennifer, had gotten married in June of that year. Jennifer seemed a bit sad in the days leading up to the wedding and expressed her wish that her grandfather, who had served as a father figure to her until his passing when she was 16, could be there on her most special day. All she had from him were a few inherited personal items, many of which had been damaged over the years. A few months before the wedding, Michael had tried to fix a broken radio, Jennifer's grandfather's prized 1978 Philips 070, with fresh batteries and some coaxing with a screwdriver, but alas, his efforts were to no avail—the radio refused to function at all and was relegated to the back of a desk drawer with other broken effects.

After exchanging vows at home in the presence of family members, the newlyweds stepped away for a private moment and soon realized there was unfamiliar music coming from their bedroom. Following the sounds of a romantic love song, they discovered to their shock that the music was coming from that abandoned broken radio in the back of the desk drawer. They were stunned to silence, until Jennifer, as much a skeptic as Michael about "paranormal and supernatural" phenomena, spoke up.

"My grandfather is here with us. I'm not alone," Jennifer claimed through tears.

The music was heard by other family members and continued playing into the night. But by the next morning, it stopped. They could never get the radio to work again. Shermer closed his article stating that the scientific credo is "to keep an open mind and remain agnostic when the evidence is indecisive or the riddle unsolved."

I admired Michael's courage in sharing a story of possible after-death communication in *Scientific American,* a bastion of materialist thinking. I was excited to talk to him about the article the next time we met, in August 2015, when we were interviewed together on the *Ask Dr. Nandi* television show. As he arrived with Jennifer, we greeted each other and I said, "That really took some courage. It showed you truly are an open-minded skeptic."

"Well, we ended up understanding it had a perfectly natural explanation," he replied, as Jennifer nodded in agreement.

"Oh, really? I'd love to hear about it," I responded. "What happened?"

"Well, it obviously wasn't a real communication from her grandfather's ghost. It has a perfectly rational explanation."

"Which is . . . ?" I queried, surprised by this turnaround.

"Well, it could not have been supernatural, so there must be some logical explanation."

I stared at them both, awaiting the "scientific" explanation.

"We don't really know, but it must have *some* rational explanation," Michael finished.

Hundreds have told me similar stories, many of whom had never considered after-death communication to be possible before their encounter. Most of them have been forever changed by such an event and awakened to the spiritual nature of the universe. When a door opens, our free will allows us to walk through it—or to close it and retreat. As I see it now, the rational explanation would be that Jennifer's grandfather's soul was offering his support and love from "the other side."

Before my coma, I had heard many tales from my patients suggestive of after-death communication, but I had always filed them away as fantasies or wishful thinking. I had even had my own quite stunning personal encounter in 1994, although, like Michael and Jennifer, I had convinced myself over time that it was just some inexplicable fluke.

Stuart Massich (not his real name) was a close friend and colleague who followed a life path eerily similar to mine. Common features included (though five years behind me throughout) all of the following: Stuart grew up in Winston-Salem, attended the University of North Carolina at Chapel Hill, attended Duke University School of Medicine, served his neurosurgical residency years based at Duke, but with two years spent in the laboratory at Harvard Medical School, then went on to join the neurosurgical staff at Brigham and Women's Hospital, a flagship among Harvard Medical School's teaching hospitals. We had clearly shared many similar life experiences, more than most people.

Stuart was a close friend and confidant from our first meeting, when he started his surgical internship in 1985, destined for the neurosurgical resident training program at Duke. We enjoyed several overlaps in our training, when we were on the same team. Stuart was my junior resident when I was chief resident at the Durham Veterans Administration hospital in late 1986.

I'll never forget when he taught me how to tie a bow tie, a skill I was advised to learn after I had secured a job offer from Harvard Medical School. I had worn bow ties as a child, but always the clip-on style. Stuart stood behind me, arms over my shoulders, as we stood in front of a mirror and he passed that sacred knowledge on to me, given that bow ties were considered signature items for many of the academic doctors at Harvard. Almost exclusively, I now prefer bow ties (or butterfly ties, as they are known in the Netherlands) to neckties.

When Stuart spent his two research years at Harvard, he was working closely with me in my research efforts evaluating receptor populations in the blood vessels that supply the brain, ultimately trying to treat a condition known as cerebral vasospasm, a very lethal and common complication of bleeding into the brain from aneurysms (discussed in Chapter 5). After he finished his Duke residency training in 1992, Stuart headed up to Boston to join our neurosurgical team at Brigham and Women's Hospital as the main spine surgeon.

Stuart's son was just a bit older than my oldest son, Eben IV, and we often spoke of the joys of fatherhood and shared some of the antics of our boys. Stuart had introduced me (for the benefit of Eben IV, obviously) to a computer game called Maelstrom that his son enjoyed. The player is a small cartoon spaceship shooting at passing rockets, asteroids, and comets. The space debris comes mostly in ones and twos, but the really fun part involves occasional small groups of comets that fly across the screen, briefly offering an opportunity for scoring significant points by shooting them out of the black sky. When this happens, the game sound effects let out a big "yippee!" Our young boys spent hours playing Maelstrom, and we spent hours together playing with them and catching up with each other. I can still hear that silly "yippee!"

Stuart took his oral neurosurgical board examination in November 1994. He and his wife, Wendy, had been planning a celebratory trip with their three young children to Florida in mid-November, immediately following that grueling trial by fire (as those examinations tend to be).

That's when our similar life paths tragically diverged.

The morning of November 18 found me deeply involved in one of my favorite kinds of neurosurgical cases. I was performing a retromastoid craniectomy for microvascular decompression of the trigeminal nerve, that is, opening a hole smaller than a 50 cent piece through the bone behind the patient's ear, then, using an operating microscope, very carefully working my way down to her brain stem and dissecting an errant artery from pulsating against the main cranial nerve carrying sensory information from the face. Such patients present with severe facial pain, or tic douloureux, which can often be so severe as to induce them to commit suicide—hence such aggressive and major surgical management is warranted in patients who fail to respond to appropriate pain medications.

The most challenging part of such cases occurs in the dark because the operating room lights are off when the surgeon is using the operating microscope (which has its own very bright light source), a 7-foot-tall behemoth weighing more than 800 pounds, but so delicately balanced that the surgeon can move it into any desired position with the light touch of a finger.

During that part of the operation, the room is usually filled with the quiet background whispers of the ten or so people supporting the surgeon in the OR. I was deeply focused on the arduous dissection of delicate blood vessels and nerves tangled around the brain stem when I noticed, just barely, the main OR door opening as someone stepped in and whispered to one of the nurses circulating in the room. The soft whispers spread through the room over the next minute or so, followed by a deafening silence. I remained so focused on the task at hand that I barely noticed the silence, although it did register at some deep level.

"Hmm. I wonder . . ." curiosity flitted through my mind, but I continued my delicate work under the microscope until the offending artery had been carefully moved away behind a Teflon sponge blanket, protecting the injured nerve from further pain-inducing damage. Ten minutes after the dome of silence had invaded the room, I was satisfied with my surgical efforts and pulled the scope away from the operative field, declaring, "Lights up. It's closing time."

Only then did the main pod nurse explain the mysterious silence.

"Wendy Massich is on the phone. She needs to talk with you."

I knew this had to be extremely important. I had never in my sixteen years spent in operating rooms been exposed to such a request in the middle of surgery.

"What in the world about?" I asked with some trepidation.

"It's Dr. Massich," she managed. Tears filled her eyes, and as I looked around the room, I saw that several other people were crying, too. They had heard the news while I was under the microscope, and they had wisely elected not to involve me until I had finished the toughest part of the operation.

I asked my resident to start closing the operative field as I removed my scrub gown and exited the OR for the adjacent head nurse's office. Another nurse, her eyes brimming with tears, handed me the telephone.

"I lost him," uttered Wendy's voice over the line. "Stuart's gone," she said, simply.

My head was swimming, trying to make any sense of it. She proceeded to explain how a hurricane had come through the Ft. Lauderdale area the day before, and how the weather had cleared that morning and they had taken the kids down to the beach. The water was still roiling after the passing storm, so there were red flags up to signal people away from the deceptively calm waters. Dangerous undercurrents still loomed.

Their 8-year-old son had picked up a boogie board from one of the unmanned stands at the beach and taken it down to jump in the ocean. By the time Stuart and Wendy noticed him, he was 50 feet out and being drawn seaward. Stuart raced down the beach and into the water to retrieve him. As he swam out, his son chucked the boogie board and hugged his arms around Stuart's head.

Wendy soon noticed that Stuart's head was no longer above the water. She cried out for help, at which point two men swam out 100 feet or so to where the son was crouched on the water, supported by his father's floating body. They rescued the son unharmed and brought Stuart's lifeless body back to the beach, where an unsuccessful attempt at resuscitation followed.

Our small neurosurgical family at Brigham and Women's and Children's Hospitals was crushed by the loss. Everyone loved Stuart. We arranged for the staff neurosurgeons and residents, all but a skeleton crew, to fly to Winston-Salem, North Carolina, for Stuart's funeral. Wendy and the kids would fly directly to North Carolina from Florida, and she asked me to go by their home just off Route 9 outside of Boston to pick up a few items to bring to the funeral.

My eyes were misting with tears as I pulled into their driveway and entered their home. Sadness overwhelmed me as I gathered the items Wendy had requested, and I thought back on the wonderful times I had shared with Stuart. It was such a tragic loss of a brilliant surgeon, colleague, and great friend.

As I was preparing to leave, I noticed that Stuart's desktop Macintosh computer was still on. There on the screen was the welcome to play Maelstrom. Somehow, it felt like an invitation. I sat down at his desk.

"Okay, Stuart. One last game. Just for you," I muttered softly.

I started to play, shooting at passing objects and racking up points. I was almost in a trance, overwhelmed by the ugly finality of Stuart's absence and the list of practical tasks I had to do to help Wendy get through the next few days. I was just mindlessly playing along, with some vague sense of honoring his memory and our wonderful times together.

Just as I was feeling the depths of tragedy around losing Stuart, a steadily growing storm of comets flew by on the computer screen. The accompanying "yippee!" sound of the comets grew rapidly into a cacophony of sounds far beyond anything I had ever experienced in previous games. The largest group of comets I had ever scored on before was around ten, yet what I saw on the screen now was a blizzard of thousands of comets, with their joint "yippee!" sounds coming out of the speakers in a storm of points that rapidly built to twenty times the highest score I had ever seen in the game.

What in the world just happened? The software seemed to have totally violated all its prior rules. What had changed? Why had it happened in this moment?

Some part of me—the same part that had felt a wordless invitation to sit down and play—knew the answer. I felt that such an extraordinary display must have been instigated by Stuart's still-present spirit. It gave me some sense of relief, feeling that somehow it was Stuart's spirit showing me he wasn't gone. But the rational neurosurgeon in me had no room for such thinking. I sternly admonished myself for feeling anything like comfort from the experience and refiled this event away under "unknown," mentioning it to no one. It was just too weird, and it made me feel too vulnerable. The professional side of me was not ready to admit the possible reality of communication from the spirit world.

This is a perfect example of how "the other side" can contact us through the world of microelectronics. From those who study after-death communications, it is quite common to hear about contact made through electronic devices. For example, the night that Karen's stepfather died, her mother reported that all the ceiling fans in the house came on by themselves. I've heard many similar stories about house lights or televisions turning on or off, or even inexplicable phone calls and text messages related to their communication with departed loved ones.

It is the very ephemeral nature of conscious awareness itself interacting with the physical world that allows for such obvious examples of physical effects due to spiritual influence. The 1987 book *Margins of Reality* by Robert Jahn and Brenda Dunne from the Princeton Engineering Anomalies Research (PEAR) laboratory reveals the commonality of psychic influence on microelectronics. They have amassed an extensive body of data correlating human influence of a specialized microelectronic random-number generator, a device that generates sequences of zeros and ones. In these experiments, participants have shown that their minds can significantly influence what numbers will appear. In a meta-analysis performed by Dean Radin, citing 490 studies, he identified odds against chance for such results were 3,050 to 1. These data clearly demonstrate the active participation of consciousness to be affecting the behavior of physical systems. Although this example is one of living minds influencing the quantum realm of microelectronics, the broader implications include interactions of minds who are no longer entangled with physical brains (i.e., the deceased) in our earthly realm.

Brilliant minds wrestling with some of the deepest mysteries of science are often challenged to reckon with unexpected anomalies in their personal lives. Nikola Tesla is widely regarded as one of the most brilliant scientific thinkers of the 20th century. Much of our modern electrically powered world is thanks to his brilliant scientific insights, and some of his more advanced ideas concerning the "harnessing of free cosmic energy" might still indicate ideas destined for fruition in the future.

Pulitzer Prize–winning biographer John J. O'Neill's beautifully wrought biography of Tesla[1] is all the more valuable owing to the very close personal relationship that O'Neill and Tesla shared. In that biography, O'Neill writes that Tesla professed to having endeavored to solve the enigma of death, but that he could claim only one event in his life that he interpreted as a supernatural experience. This event was deeply personal, and concerned an awareness that occurred around the time of his mother's death.

A few months before, Tesla had visited his friend Sir William Crookes, whose "epochal work on radiant matter" had engendered Tesla's embrace of a career steeped in the study of electricity. However, during that recent visit to London, it was Crookes's interest in spiritualism that had dominated their conversation. Those discussions were much on his mind when Tesla was called back to New York due to his mother's failing health. He was intermittently present at her bedside during her last days, but became so exhausted during the prolonged vigilance that he had to be physically carried to his home one particular evening. As much as he regretted having to be away from his mother during that critical phase in her potentially leaving this world, he sensed all would be okay.

Early the next morning he dreamed a fantastic vision in which he saw "a cloud carrying angelic figures of marvelous beauty, one of whom gazed upon me lovingly and gradually assumed the features of my mother. The apparition slowly floated across the room and vanished and I was awakened by an indescribably sweet song of many voices. In that instant a certitude, which no words can express, came upon me that my mother had just died. And that was true."

In the months after he recovered from that loss, Tesla tended to default to his "rational beliefs," in some effort to explain his extraordinary knowing of his mother's passing, and attributed his vision to a painting he had seen before her death. But his biographer calls him out on his most unscientific attempts to be "scientific" in his explanation, reminding us of the "certitude" that Tesla felt at the time, and the fact that his extraordinary vision occurred at the same time his mother actually died.

Personal experiences outside the "normal" range are often dismissed when they can't be fully integrated into our current understanding or belief system. I thought my experience with Stuart's computer would sound crazy to others and never shared it with anyone until after my coma. I have become much more open to accepting such after-death communication and other phenomena as being crucial clues to the nature of our existence, even though certain events remain challenging to understand.

PMH Atwater is a feisty and energized woman living life with ferocious intensity ever since 1977, when she suffered three NDEs in three months. Her pace in life has never slowed since. She has meticulously researched the full spectrum of NDEs, including the major life changes that occur in people following an NDE (aftereffects), and has thoroughly investigated the unique qualities of children experiencers. We met at the IANDS annual conference three years after my coma where I had met Raymond Moody. Her energy and enthusiasm were infectious, yet her final words to me at the end of the conference, in retrospect, fell on relatively deaf ears.

"Eben, you are still in that magic phase of integrating your experience when everything is *so* wonderful and exciting, confusing, and infused with spirit. I will email you a chart about the four phases of integration. Please take that to heart. It does take a while before you land and can balance out your life. . . . I will also send my special bulletin on the electrical component of storms and earthquakes, which affects many experiencers—maybe you, too. Be especially careful driving back to Virginia, and try to take some time for yourself. You are sitting on a maelstrom of energy!"

In those early days and weeks of recovery after my coma, I experienced a constant crackling energy, a hypersensing of my being alive, of being aware—a sizzling bodily sensation. That was perhaps what my older son, Eben IV, majoring in neuroscience in college at that time, sensed when he first saw me two days after discharge from the hospital.

"You are so clear, so focused . . . so much more present than ever before. It is as if there is a kind of light shining within you," he had confessed after we first hugged on his return home from college for Thanksgiving in 2008.

Street lights would blink off as I walked beneath them. My Macintosh laptop seemed especially prone to crashing. I went through three watches before I found one that would work. I initially had no idea such phenomena were commonplace among NDEers, and simply dismissed them as degraded urban infrastructure, Apple's outsourcing to China, and a declining level of quality in small segments of American manufacturing.

That crackling energy might have also been associated with the main side effect of my meningoencephalitis—that I had great difficulty sleeping. That diminished requirement for sleep slowly normalized over several years, but not before it had benefited me by allowing much time to read, study, and reflect.

Those kinds of aftereffects faded over a few years, although they would occasionally rear their heads again. Such a head rearing involved the extraordinary energy around the time of that 2011 IANDS conference, when I interacted with other near-death experiencers and researchers. As one begins to appreciate the notion of Collective Mind, that our consciousness is interconnected, such resonance of common experiences among such a spiritually seasoned group contributes to a collective *knowing* that transcends the simplistic verbal communications shared.

The roiling energy of discovery in which I had been immersed throughout that Labor Day weekend conference fueled an intense phase of creativity. My discussions with other experiencers and with the scientific thought leaders of the field at that meeting had thrown an exciting and energetic spin into my efforts to record all of my thoughts on the matter into the most definitive narrative I could provide. As soon as I arrived home, I dived deeply into continuing to write the manuscript that would later become *Proof of Heaven*. As midnight approached, I was immersed in a creative flow, soothed by the soft patter of a gentle autumn rainfall just outside my window . . .

Craaaaaccckkkkkkkk!

An earsplitting crash, the sound of thunder right outside the window, shocked me into heart-pounding alertness. It was so odd that there was absolutely no flash of lightning—none at all! I peered through the window into the backyard, but could make out precious little given the rain flowing down the pane in the pitch blackness just before midnight. Finally, I was able to make out some detail in the darkness—I saw tree leaves and surmised that a branch had fallen from a tree. On stepping into the backyard, however, I was shocked to see that half of an 80-foot-tall pin oak tree had fallen along the back (north-facing) wall of the house, just outside of my little second-story office window behind which I had been feverishly typing away. The fallen behemoth stretched along the entirety of the backyard, from one neighbor's edge to the other. I solicited my sons' help in chopping away some of the branches in an effort to rescue those smaller trees and bushes. We were at it until around 2:30 a.m., when I felt we had done as much as we could to salvage the yard plantings around the small backyard garden.

Examining the scene, I was bewildered that there seemed to be no sign of *why* the tree had fallen. There had been no actual lightning flashes at any time during the gentle, windless rainfall, although the terrific crack sound I had heard at the outset suggested that lightning might have been the culprit. I had seen trees freshly struck by lightning before, and had always noted bark blown off and scorch marks corresponding with the furious heating to five times the temperature of the sun's surface. Yet—nothing. The 2½-foot-diameter trunk was mute on any possible cause for the calamity.

"Have to wait for an expert opinion," I thought.

The tree, however, was not yet done with its antics. I was busily typing away in my corner office the next afternoon, when I was shocked by yet another "*craaaaack!*" sound, as another major trunk of the same pin oak tree fell 90 degrees from the first fall, bracketing the northwest corner of the house that contained my small upstairs office. This second major trunk, even broader than the first, fell along the western wall of the house, toward the front yard and street. It was so large that even lying flat on the ground, one major branch of it reached up over the roof of the two-story house beside the chimney.

I collected several estimates for the tree's removal, but never received any satisfactory explanation for its premature demise. The experts were all bewildered, as was I.

"I can usually explain why a tree came down," said one of my consultants, who had been a professional arborist for three decades, "but this one beats the hell out of me. No idea. The wood appears perfectly healthy, no sign of insect damage, rot, wind, or lightning as a cause. You're damn lucky, though—both of these two main trunks are so heavy, they would have cut through your house like a hot knife through butter, all the way down to the basement, if they had actually fallen *on* your house, as opposed to alongside its walls. Funny how they both *just missed* your home."

He surveyed the scene again. "Damn miracle!" he finished, walking back to his truck, slowly shaking his head.

"Perhaps I should've paid a little more attention to PMH's warning" ran through my mind.

For me, the jury is still out on this matter. Psychokinesis is the general term for the pure influence of mind over physical matter, and its role in the world of microelectronics has been discussed. However, larger objects have also been shown to be involved in such actions of mind (macro-PK). Of course, my rational mind would hesitate to entertain any connection between the enhanced energy I felt after the conference and the demise of a century-old pin oak tree. But I have encountered other stories like mine, especially the rich repertoire of synchronicities reported by many others, and seen the wisdom in not dismissing these potential connections so readily. Spiritual experiences (or extremely hidden phenomena) that seem so unreal in our modern culture are actually the blessing of our existence. As we come to realize the primacy of consciousness and adopt the power inherent in full-blown metaphysical idealism, many perceived limitations will disappear. The possibilities for extraordinary human potential are exhilarating!

CHAPTER 7

THE POWER OF PRAYER

Gratitude is not only the greatest of virtues, but the parent of all others.

—CICERO (106 BCE–43 BCE),
ROMAN STATESMAN

As our worldview evolves toward something closer to the truth of all existence, it provides refreshing liberation and insight—not just for humanity at large, but for each individual soul participating in this shared journey of discovery. As we proceed from the stark implications of pure scientific materialism into more expanded versions of understanding the role of consciousness in manifesting reality, we glimpse that being more aware of our inner world, whether through meditation, centering prayer or other means, offers vast potential to the individual soul to take charge of their lives through harnessing the power of love and compassion in the spiritual realm.

As a doctor, I was accustomed to prescribing symptom relief or treatment with medicine or recommending changes in behavior. Of course, surgery of the brain and spinal cord was my specialty, so my evaluations also considered the option of operating. But because there are risks in any surgical procedure, the goal is always to maximize the benefit to the patient while minimizing the risk, especially with any potential side effects. The brain and spinal cord are most unforgiving—their ability to heal from any damage, due to the complexity of their inherent structure, is much less than with other systems in the body.

As one of my main mentors repeatedly cautioned, "You can always do an operation, but you can never take it back." It was vital to exhaust all nonsurgical possibilities before taking that step. A tremendous amount of my work involved investigating new forms of treatment that were safer and more effective for the patient. For example, I helped to completely redesign MRI technology to enable its use while performing surgery, allowing more minimally invasive and more efficacious neurosurgical procedures, ultimately safer for the patients. Enhanced imaging combined with less invasion of the physical body meant, in general, a decrease in possible adverse effects.

Following my coma, I began to open to the possibility of more subtle forms of healing due to an experience I had in January 2011. I was invited to speak at a lecture and workshop event entitled "Scientific Reconciliation of Near-Death Experience," presented at the request of the Virginia Beach International Association for Near Death Studies, to Edgar Cayce's Association for Research and Enlightenment. I had been exposed to a fairly nasty respiratory virus the week before my talk and, as I was driving to Virginia Beach, I was hoping I had escaped infection. However, a short time into the afternoon workshop I felt the rapid progression of sinus congestion, sore throat, and muscle aches—all symptoms that seemed to herald an ugly bout with the virus.

The audience of 125 participants included many who were practitioners of alternative healing therapies, not to mention a sizable cadre of hospice workers (who, by and large, have quite advanced experience with the spiritual aspects of human health thanks to their daily work with dying patients). As I coughed a few times and tried to clear my throat of the rapidly accumulating mucus, a kindly dark-haired 50ish-year-old woman sitting in the second row raised her hand.

"Dr. Alexander—are you feeling all right?" she asked, softly.

"I think I'm coming down with the flu," I replied, coughing again, still trying to clear my throat.

The audience responded efficiently. Like a well-trained team, they quickly invited me to lie down on four chairs that they hastily arranged as an emergency gurney in the front row. I was a little embarrassed at first—I had gone there as a physician to discuss an extraordinary spiritual journey and its relevance to healing, and now I was becoming the patient.

"Lie down here," said the woman who had originally inquired as to my symptoms. "Close your eyes, and take a deep breath," she went on.

I sensed at least twenty members of the audience standing around me, some with their hands held up, palms facing me, ready to deliver healing energy. I closed my eyes and breathed slowly, following their advice. One of them was beating out a soft, steady rhythm on a small drum, others were chanting quietly, and I could hear some murmurings of what sounded like prayers, though I could not make out any of the words. I allowed myself to drift into the soft and welcoming reverie of the energy I sensed around me.

The next few minutes were quite a blur, and I do not have a very detailed memory of other activities that may have taken place. I had a strong awareness of all the well-meaning beings around me, and a sense that we were joining as one toward a common goal. They proceeded for the next 15 minutes or so. I soon started to feel my throat clear of mucus, and the sharp throat pain that had begun during the workshop started to dissipate. Likewise, the muscle aches that had begun just before our lunch break also evaporated. Before I knew it, I was feeling whole again, without any lingering viral symptoms.

The group did not seem so surprised at my rapid turnaround, but I was quite amazed by the encounter. I completed the last few hours of the workshop feeling perfectly well. That particular virus never bothered me again. Somehow, the group had worked with unseen forces to facilitate a change in my physical body, similar to the effects of prayer. I clearly still had a lot to learn about healing, and especially about the power of love and connectedness in nurturing our well-being.

Undoubtedly, I would have dismissed such an encounter as a mere coincidence prior to my coma. My personal knowledge and understanding of the possibilities of complementary healing are still quite rudimentary, but I am witnessing some of the benefits conferred by such training through my older son, Eben IV, who is currently in osteopathic medical school.

Osteopathic medicine encompasses not only traditional medical diagnosis and treatment that was included when I obtained my MD degree from Duke University School of Medicine in 1980, but also includes manual diagnosis and treatment and a more holistic approach to patient care. Osteopathic hands-on treatment serves to complement their use of pharmaceuticals, surgery, and other medical techniques commonly employed in Western medicine.

In the osteopathic field, a large emphasis is placed on hands-on diagnosis and treatment of the entire body. For example, the motion of cranial bones is closely connected to circulatory patterns of lymph and cerebrospinal fluid involved with the central nervous system (i.e., brain, spinal cord, and lymphatic system). Osteopathic physicians are trained to sense by palpation rhythmic motions and patterns present within the skull and distortions to the cranial bones and fascia. Skilled hands-on manipulation of the cranial bones and fascia within the skull is then used to correct the distortions. The intention of this type of treatment is to enhance the body's ability to heal on its own by removing any anatomical dysfunctions or distortions—a useful method when addressing the patient's overall vitality and state of health. This has opened my eyes to a whole new level of the potential use of such noninvasive techniques. Eben IV is more focused on wellness and fitness, an approach that will contribute to a much healthier world than the more problem-focused treatment-oriented medicine that I was taught.

While my son is a current inspiration, my father had been a profound influence throughout my life and served as a perfect role model to emulate. He was a consummate scientist who kept abreast of major developments in physics, chemistry, biology, and especially neuroscience, chairing the neurosurgical training program at what was then Baptist Hospital and Wake Forest University Medical School in Winston-Salem, North Carolina. Like other neurosurgical chairmen of the 1950s and 1960s, Dad had honed his craft on the battlefields of World War II—he was very confident, and extremely competent. I knew him not only as a father, but as a mentor in the field. My childhood had been peppered with visits by some of the top neurosurgical minds in the world—his close friends, who would often stay in our home and share colorful stories of their reminiscences and reflections about life.

Dad was also very religious, or, more correctly, spiritual. His deeply reflective practice of science—including the daily management of neurosurgical patients and the teaching of neurosurgical residents who would become leaders in the field—melded seamlessly with his deeply spiritual religious beliefs. He believed that his part in healing any patient was minuscule, and he trusted that the power of prayer and an omnipotent and omniscient God were the main means of healing. His exceptional sense of ethics and justice was a marvel to me, providing a constant polestar to aid in navigating my life.

My father's influence had instilled in me a habit of praying, in a form directly related to my childhood in the Methodist church and to my later Episcopalian traditions. I would sometimes apply my prayers to healing efforts when I might ask that a friend's flu be cured swiftly, or that a challenging operation I had to perform would go well. Or I would ask on my sons' behalf for help on an important test in school. Before mealtimes and bedtime, I repeated standard prayers by rote with my sons. This supplication form of prayer occurred all in my mind, which is how I assumed it worked. *Ask, and ye shall receive.*

I never received direct answers, even if I did notice that sometimes my prayers appeared to achieve the desired goals. Did my son pass the test because God helped, or only because he studied? Even as I prayed, part of me wondered if prayer really made a difference. I had no idea if it was actually working, but it seemed like a comforting habit. In 2000, a personal crisis led me to reject any thought of a loving personal God, and during the eight years leading up to my coma, I had stopped praying entirely.

Following my coma, praying felt completely different. In the earliest months, while my brain was still recovering from the damage of the meningitis, it was almost effortless to reconnect with that overwhelming sense of love and being loved that I felt during my spiritual journey. In blinding contrast to my prayers before coma, I felt a constant stream of affirmation and of knowing that ever-present loving force, and prayer flowed quite naturally. I seemed to have an ongoing connection to the other realm, most especially with that loving sense of oneness at the Core.

This completely changed the way I prayed. I learned of "centering prayer," popularized since the 1960s by such spiritual leaders as Father Thomas Keating and Thomas Merton, who described the process as a "return to the heart, finding one's deepest center, awakening the profound depths of our being." Such prayerful practice acknowledges silence at its focus, which serves as a temporary reprieve from the thoughts and chatter of the linguistic brain. For the first time, my prayers became simple but powerful expressions of gratitude for blessings that seemed to happen at every turn. They were much less a request for intervention, especially for a specific outcome, and much more a trust in knowing that "all is well."

One of the more remarkable memories I have from my deep coma experience in November 2008 concerns the multitude of beings I sensed surrounding me as I neared the end of my odyssey. These myriad figures were around me in partially circling arcs, receding out into the distant mists. Most were kneeling, many wore hoods, others held what appeared to be candles, and all had their hands folded over their chests and their heads bowed. I was aware of a very comforting emanation of what can best be described as a loving and healing energy that came from them, bundled with the subtle and indecipherable murmurings they uttered. The most striking and memorable aspect of the whole experience was the tremendous sense of relief their murmurings engendered in me. The emotional bliss that resulted from basking in that energy—that, in fact, matched the most transcendental and extreme bliss and oneness I had encountered through the unconditional love in the Gateway Valley and the Core—is something I will never forget. I often wondered if such prayers contributed to my remarkable healing.

Studies on prayer reportedly began in 1872, when Sir Francis Galton— a pioneering scientist with varied interests such as meteorology, genetics, and psychology—compared the longevity of religious leaders with nonreligious professionals. Assumedly, clergy prayed more often than the others and would thus live a longer life. Results were inconclusive, much like other studies that have taken place in the ensuing years, but challenges in proper experimental design have been difficult to overcome. How exactly does one conclusively demonstrate that a divine entity has intervened on one's behalf? The elaborate process of setting up a scientific assessment of prayer in a controlled setting often strips much of the spiritual energy out of the entire endeavor. One wonders if such an artificial form of prayer is even valid, compared with spontaneous heartfelt prayers for a loved one. It is difficult to prove beyond doubt, yet there is a great deal of experiential evidence to support its value.

On April 25, 1999, Alison Leigh Sugg (a reader who shared her story) gave birth to her second child at a birthing center in Dallas, Texas. The pregnancy was healthy and markedly uneventful, which boded well for her commitment to give birth completely naturally. Immediately following the birth of Alison's daughter, the midwife did not lay the baby on her chest to snuggle and root for the breast, as she had with her son. Instead, she whisked the distressed newborn away immediately to receive oxygen. Alison was confused about why she had not felt a great wave of relief after the baby appeared; she was still in just as much pain as she had been during this abbreviated laboring—unlike her first delivery, when the pain of labor was replaced all in a rush with the joy of birth the moment her son emerged.

As she lay hemorrhaging uncontrollably on the delivery bed with a massive tear in her uterus, she knew something was gravely wrong. Her uterus refused to clamp down as it should have, in order to stop the extensive flow of blood caused by an abnormal tetanic contraction during labor. She had loss of peripheral vision and was looking, as through the mouth of a straw, up at her husband and the doula who had just arrived on the scene. She couldn't lift her head, and felt herself drifting away, melting into the atmosphere around her. The midwife wheeled the Pitocin drip to Alison's bedside to help stop the bleeding. She tried every vein she could access to start the IV flow, but no needle would hit the mark; all of Alison's veins were already collapsed. The midwife ordered the doula to call 911 for an ambulance. Alison was going to be the first-ever postpartum emergency transport from the birth center to the associated hospital nearby, and there was not enough time for the hospital ambulance to get there.

As the paramedics entered the room, Alison filled with a wave of sympathetic love for the youngest, who was obviously frightened out of his mind to see a woman so close to death. He told her, "Everything will be okay and we are here to take care of you." She knew he was lying to make her feel better and that activated a massive swelling of love for him, as a fellow human, that felt as though it came not from her, but from another presence that had begun to emerge from below and emanate through her. This presence was shimmering just underneath the surface of all that was material—holding up the stretcher she was laid out on even as she was loaded into the ambulance. Alison entered the hospital vaguely aware of a sense of embarrassment at potentially bleeding all over the carpet.

Dr. Margaret Christensen was the consulting ob-gyn physician for the birth center and was on call for emergencies. When Alison arrived, she had already lost around 5 units of blood but was conscious and verbal. Dr. Christensen tried to do everything she knew to stop the hemorrhage, but nothing was working and she could see blood pouring through all the packing. By that point Alison's heart rate was close to 150 and her blood pressure was down to 85/60.

"It looks like your uterus will not clamp down or stop bleeding, so we're going to have to take you back and see if you have a piece of stuck placenta. If we can't stop the bleeding, then there is the likelihood we may need to perform a hysterectomy," she said to Alison and her husband.

Alison noticed that the "other presence" started to take over for her to help her communicate with those around her. She could no longer speak, but she felt the presence push words out of a very deep well from a distant place inside to guide her surgeon.

"Intubate me quickly, or I could die," Alison heard herself saying, as she was rushed into the OR.

As the medical team placed her on to the table, they were still trying to hold compression and keep her sufficiently loaded with IV fluids until blood and platelets arrived, before opening her up. But then, she started to crash—her blood pressure suddenly dropped to 40/0, she was unconscious, she was still bleeding profusely, and her heart rate slowed down until her EKG flatlined.

"Oh, my God, she's dying," Dr. Christensen realized.

There were a lot of people in the OR, including several residents, the anesthesiologist, and the doctor's new partner, a former Navy trauma surgeon whom she had called in to assist in the resuscitation.

"Alison, you cannot leave. You have two babies you have to take care of," Dr. Christensen said to an unconscious Alison while holding her face in her hands. As Alison lay dying on the operating table, Dr. Christensen estimated her odds for survival at around 10 percent.

The blood finally arrived and they pushed whole blood, plasma, fluids, and platelets into their patient in order to try to resurrect a pulse. It was not possible to make a surgical incision until Alison had enough blood in her system to keep her heart beating. That's when the surgeon took a pause.

Dr. Christensen had grown up Catholic but had completely rejected all religion by her teenage years after being disgusted with the fact that wars seemed to have started over whose God was better. At Rice University in Houston, she was very scientific and analytical, with a driven type A personality. She ranked in the top 10 of her class. She became fascinated with quantum physics and read *The Tao of Physics* by Fritjof Capra, followed by an interest in philosophy, ancient mystics, and the connection between Buddhism and quantum physics. She'd had several childhood mystical experiences but had dismissed them since she had no frame of reference for understanding them. During her third year of medical school, she had a powerful experience of enlightenment while in the deep pain of labor as she gave birth to her first child, an event that influenced her entire career. She felt connected to all the women through time who'd ever given birth and all the women around the world who were laboring along with her at that time.

The movie *Star Wars* was released around this time, and its concept of the "force," the idea that there was something larger than herself, this God thing that she could not wrap her brain around, deeply resonated with her. After medical school, she started her own practice and was highly influenced by the work of Christiane Northrup, author of *Women's Bodies, Women's Wisdom,* and Jean Shinoda Bolen, author of *Goddesses in Everywoman.*

Dr. Christensen was drawn to the concept of the divine feminine and eventually explored a return to church. She sometimes listened to the Unity Church broadcast on Sunday mornings as she drove to the hospital for rounds. She identified with these teachings because there was no strict dogma or guilt involved. God was considered a loving presence, and they used the term "mother-father God," which rang true to her. Caring for women's bodies was a sacred activity and prayer became a part of her medical practice. She prayed with her patients when they came in— whatever they wanted to pray and to whomever they wanted to pray; it made no difference.

"We need to stop, just for two minutes, and we are all going to do a prayer and we are going to call Alison back," Dr. Christensen said to the medical team. She began to pray, "Please guide us to heal Alison's body," she said, asking everyone in the OR to participate. "Please guide her spirit to come back into her body."

Meanwhile, Alison had become aware of her vital energy leaving her body through two areas simultaneously: her nose/mouth/throat and between her eyebrows, meeting somewhere ahead of or above her body. She looked down at her body, feeling something like indifference and something like compassion, but spent very little time dwelling on this. She recognized familiar energies as they began to swirl around her, pulsing their energy in a spiral of light as it propelled her up and up and up. She was so caught up in this joy and then they basically fell away and Alison drifted into the pitch-perfect, inky blackness that holds every other color and climbed to a leveling-off place. Then a wondrous being of light and sound appeared in front of her, emanating the purest, most profound, sacred and loving presence she had ever encountered. This was the unnamable, yet definitely knowable. More like feelable. She had no language, no words, nowhere else in the cosmos to be.

Then the profoundly sacred and magnificent presence gave to Alison a "thought," a communication straight to her beingness.

"You have a choice."

She was confused, then devastated, as she realized the inference. If she had a choice, that meant that there was somewhere else that wasn't here. She was deeply saddened by the knowledge that she would have to leave this serene place. As she began to try to comprehend what that "somewhere else" could mean, she became aware of prayers floating around her and behind her. These were the prayers that were coming from the people in that operating room in Dallas in a space-time day called April 25, 1999; these prayers were about Alison. She could not "listen" to the actual formed words (spoken in their minds) of these kind people in that trauma surgical room, but she could sense the heart-feelings and conscious intent of their expectation that she would live— live to know her baby girl, live to care for her son and return to her family. It was as though their conscious focus on her and her children, sent with love through space and time, created an awareness within her that reminded her that she was living a lifetime in a body on planet earth and spoke a linear language. She paid attention. It was heart-wrenching to detach from this magnificent unnamable being.

Alison thudded hard back into the room. She hovered around the right ears of the people who were praying. These people were praying in their minds, but she could hear them in her mind/spirit, outside her body. She began to remember that she had a body, that she had language, that she had children, a baby, and she knew what she had to do. So with excruciating pain, she contracted back into the darkness downward, into nothingness.

After Alison had been unresponsive for about 11 minutes, her heart rate started coming back and her blood pressure came up a little bit. Dr. Christensen was then able to start and successfully complete the hysterectomy. Alison ended up receiving 9 units of blood and many units of platelets to treat her thrombocytopenia, and she remained comatose in the ICU on a ventilator for five days. Part of her pituitary gland had died from lack of blood flow during her prolonged cardiac arrest (Sheehan's syndrome), so she was never able to breastfeed. Postpartum, she was not able to make cortisol, so she ended up having to take steroids for a time. She left the hospital with a hemoglobin of 6 (the normal range in women is 12 gm/dl to 16 gm/dl) and kept fainting and passing out. But eventually, she and her baby recovered. Alison speaks of this experience frequently to help others overcome their fear of death. She is intensely focused on exploring the healing powers of spiritual transformation.

This NDE account rang very true to me, resonating with some of the same key features as my own deep coma journey. It serves to support my own version of the perception of prayer energy, how it aligns beautifully with the healing energy of love so often described in such encounters, and how, seen from the other side of the filter, such trust and love serve so well in manifesting the reality that "all is well."

Alison's memory of how difficult it was to leave that realm reawakened in me the stunningly powerful feelings I remembered from the very end of my own NDE. My exit from that spiritual realm was one of the most emotionally wrenching and difficult aspects of the entire journey. Because I had been amnesic for my prior life experience during the entirety of my NDE, I did not remember any attachments or responsibilities to other souls.

But on that seventh day of coma, after hearing my doctors declare that it was time to let me go, my then 10-year-old son, Bond, ran into my room, pulled open my eyelids, and started pleading with me, "Daddy, you're gonna be okay," over and over again. Across the vast reaches of the spiritual realm, I sensed his presence very clearly, even though I had no clue who this being was and certainly did not understand his words. His imploring tone demanded my full attention, and sensing that strong bond between us, I knew I somehow had to start understanding the rules of this realm (including the earthly realm), for I had to do everything in my power to somehow go to him. And that meant returning to a realm that at that time was still completely mysterious to me. In the end, I survived and thrived, but sadly, that is not always the case.

As a neurosurgeon, I was no stranger to death. My forte had involved treating malignant brain tumors, often for patients who had been told there was "nothing that could be done," and that they had only a few weeks or months to live. While I had many successes, it's extremely rare in that world to have long-term cures—failure and death always lurk just around the corner. Death is the rule, but, of course, one tries to help the patients and families as much as possible through all phases of illness. After losing a patient to their disease and through ongoing connections following death, I would offer whatever comfort I could to a patient's family.

"We've done everything we can. I know you put your faith and prayer into seeing a more favorable outcome. I am so sorry we couldn't do more to help. At least we made her more comfortable in her final hours."

This was the best I could do. It appeased families to know that their beloved suffered the least amount possible. If a family member came to me with questions about their loved one's potential existence following death, about the possibility of a soul, I would say, "Yes, that could be"— maintaining my distance from the idea without squashing their beliefs. The truth was that back then, I didn't realize how much evidence supported the afterlife.

In 1980, just after I had been accepted into the neurosurgical residency training program at Duke University Medical Center, I had a memorable conversation with my father. I asked him what he thought his own biggest professional contribution was, expecting a description of some extremely difficult surgery to secure an aneurysm or remove a tumor. What I didn't expect was this: "That I am there for my patients and their families when there is nothing more I can do for them as a neurosurgeon."

His answer caught me totally off guard. It seemed to be a ready admission of steady defeat in the face of neurosurgical challenges. But he was right to be proud of supporting his patients when they really needed him most—when they were staring death and their own mortality straight in the face. He considered it a supreme gift that he was there to offer comfort and reassurance in the face of the greatest challenge of their lives. It took me years to finally appreciate at a deep level why he found this to be such an attractive aspect of his work.

Those familiar with my coma ordeal often write to me to ask what they can do for someone close to them who is presently in coma due to accident, illness, or other reasons. They are distraught at the thought of losing their loved one and wish to prevent it at all costs. Often they ask if prayers will make a difference. They are usually inspired by my inexplicable recovery and desperately wish to know if prayer will help their loved one survive and recover. The key thing to remember is that our existence does not end with the death of the physical body. Prayer can have tremendous power—remember that your prayers will get through to your loved one's soul on this journey, providing him or her with comfort and love. Whether or not the physical body recovers is not the end goal. If such recovery allows for growth in understanding our relationship with the universe in pursuit of our intended life lessons, then it becomes possible.

No matter how deep in coma a loved one might be, assume that the loving energy of your prayers will help you connect with their soul. Use the energy of that loving connection to manifest the highest and best good for all involved. This does entail detaching from the outcome, and asking that "thy will be done." The goal should be to connect to your loved one and let them know that they are loved and cherished; whether they return to their bodies or pass on is not an indictment of your prayers, or their choice, but simply different outcomes. It is crucial to realize that death is not the end of our soul connections with loved ones. Prayer often opens the door to show us that connection, as we sense that the soul of our departing loved one is not actually departed at all, even after they have left their physical body once and for all.

Typically, I encourage people concerned for their loved ones who are potentially close to death to trust their physician, who should be able to advise them on their loved one's prospects. Their health-care team can help with the decision as to termination of care, should that be recommended.

Such decisions in the sickest patients often rely on an assessment of brain death criteria. These criteria were first developed in 1968 in order to better define the point at which brain damage due to illness or injury has passed a point beyond which meaningful recovery is extremely unlikely. Brain death criteria can be a valid means of assessing one's prospects and, properly applied, they guide decision-making in such cases, especially as it pertains to making a choice about terminating care and life support.

The meningoencephalitis that afflicted me was of a severity that is almost always fatal. If I had not started to awaken, the next step in my care might well have been a formal assessment of brain-death criteria. If the patient's condition is one consistent with brain death, my advice would be to follow their doctor's advice, which might include withdrawing life support and letting him or her go. Personally, I am an organ donor and support the use of properly applied brain-death criteria in making such decisions. Even absent fully documented brain death, in certain situations, termination of care is sometimes the best course of action. When the prospects for functional recovery are nil, tremendous damage is done in such efforts that do nothing more than maintain a beating heart.

Generally speaking, some doctors view the death of their patient as a personal failure. But many people have shared stories of how the greatest gift they received from their loved one is some indication at the time of death, or thereafter, that their mutual soul connection outlived the death of the body.

Patricia (not her real name) reported that her father was in an ICU dying of gangrene and sepsis after an unfortunate surgery. After three weeks, he gradually lost all function and moved in and out of being aware of his surroundings. At one point he had not opened his eyes for three days and had not squeezed the hands of his loved ones when they spoke to him. After holding his hand for hours, to Patricia's complete surprise, he suddenly opened his eyes and raised himself up a bit on his elbows. He smiled and focused on her, making intense, loving eye contact that she felt in her soul.

"Look at you, you're back!" she exclaimed.

His countenance and energy were profound, not of this world. She then received what she called a clear telepathic communication: "It's all okay."

He then laid down against the pillow, his eyes rolled back, and returned to being unresponsive. He died the next day. She knew of no mechanism to explain how he telepathically transmitted a thought to her, but he did. She received it in an instant, an enormous amount of information, more like a *knowing*. The nurse entered and said she saw such warm bright light coming from the tiny room they were in, she came in to see what it was. Patricia was also aware of the glow of this light and, strange as it seems, in those moments it made sense. It changed her—from that moment on she has had no doubt of life after physical death and that love is all there is. Her dad wanted her to know that and she will never forget the seemingly simple and brief personal experience of receiving that message.

I've heard variations of this story hundreds of times. Hospice nurses and other health-care workers who have frequent experience with the dying usually realize this deep truth because they have seen examples of it time and time again. Recall that healing is to hallow or to make holy, essentially to "make whole." The reuniting with the infinitely loving creative force at the death of the body is a most beautiful lesson of the true oneness underlying our existence, the eternity of spirit and interconnectedness of all souls.

Our job, as caregivers and as loved ones of the dying person, is to share gifts—of recognition, of acceptance, and of forgiveness (of the departing soul, of siblings, and other family, but most especially of ourselves) to comfort and console the dying. Dying is a natural aspect of the cycle of life. Telling a dying person that it is okay, that you are also at one with it, offers powerful healing for all parties. Interpret what you witness with your heart, not your head. Stay alert throughout the dying process.

In *Glimpses of Eternity*, Raymond Moody explains shared-death experiences, which occur when the soul of a completely healthy bystander, either at the bedside or some distance away from a dying friend or family member, is whisked off to accompany the departing soul of the dying patient, even to the point of witnessing a full life review. Such experiences are often indistinguishable from the rich ultrareality of NDEs, except that they happen in people who are typically healthy. Such an experience often assists with managing one's grief, reducing fear of death and providing certainty that loved ones continue their journey beyond death still richly entangled with our common soul journey.

While most such reports involve spontaneous experiences, the Shared

Crossing Project, founded by William Peters in Santa Barbara, California, takes it a step further. As a hospice volunteer, William had shared in numerous mystical experiences with those making their final passage. In 2010 he was inspired by Moody's book, and developed ways to actively teach people how to intentionally create such an event for the benefit of both the dying and their surviving loved ones. He created protocols via the Shared Crossing Project's Pathway program, designed to assist others in accepting death as a natural process and specific exercises in how to establish "links" between the dying and their loved ones.

One such introductory exercise to facilitate this bond goes like this: "Take a moment to deepen into a relaxed and contemplative state, and focus on one particular close relationship. Reflect on a specific event or memory that evokes feelings of gratitude for this loved one. Perhaps this occurred at a time of great joy in your life, or when you most needed comfort. Allow these feelings of appreciation to form a bond across time and space, between you and this special loved one. Allow yourself to sense and feel the presence of this being, with you, now."

When practiced with some frequency over time, this visualization creates a link that stretches between this life and what lies ahead. Through a series of increasingly elaborate exercises, participants learn the landscape that leads from this human life into the afterlife and choreograph their transitions with loved ones. Participants who followed such protocols have attained a more meaningful relationship with death and numerous long-term benefits. These include increased appreciation for life, decreased fear of death, more manageable grief, and a deeper understanding of their own purpose in life.

Research reveals that these practices enable a variety of profound and healing end-of-life phenomena that Peters has identified and documented as "shared crossings." These refer to a kind of communication across the veil that yields a transformative gift, including predeath dreams/visions (where the dying express that they have been visited by a deceased loved one who provides them guidance and comfort); the shared death experience (where loved ones report that they went into the initial stages of the afterlife with the dying individual and experienced phenomena such as a shared out-of-body event, witnessing benevolent beings of light, encountering heavenly realms, and ultimately realizing that their departing loved one is safe, well-cared-for, and happy); postdeath coincidences (where an individual experiences a profound energetic event in which they know that a loved one has died, yet are alive and well); and many more.

As a physician who has come to realize the magnitude and scope of end-of-life phenomena, I believe a shift in the predominant hospice practices in our modern world is in order. Accepting death as a natural transition—similar to birth in the vast cycle of life, and *not* as an end to conscious awareness—helps foster an ambience of sacred celebration and gratitude for life. Children, family, and friends can participate lovingly in the transition of a soul from this world to the next—all in a fashion that fully honors the reality of ongoing connections between loved ones.

We are spiritual beings living in a spiritual universe. Fundamentally, this spirituality means we are all interconnected through the Collective Mind, and that the emotional power behind our hopes and dreams has a basis in reality that guides the unfolding of events in our lives. The very fuel of that spirituality is love, and the more we can express unconditional love for self and others, the more healing or "becoming whole" we will see. The best way to discover this is through cultivating a means of going within, often described as a practice of meditation or prayer. Any physical, mental, or emotional health must be firmly rooted in spiritual health, and prayer is a most natural means of invoking such overall wellness. As hundreds have shared with me, that sense of eternal connection is truly a life changer. We just need to be open to the possibility.

CHAPTER 8

THE PRACTICE OF GOING WITHIN

It is not the possession of truth, but the success
which attends the seeking after it, that enriches the
seeker and brings happiness to him.

—MAX PLANCK (1858–1947),
NOBEL PRIZE IN PHYSICS, 1918

Due to his lifelong appreciation of modern science, His Holiness the fourteenth Dalai Lama initiated a dialogue between Buddhists and Western scientists in the 1980s. This commenced an ongoing series of formal meetings and discussions at academic institutions throughout the Western world. His Holiness began to invite various scientists to study the brains of highly trained Buddhist meditators through his organization, Mind and Life Institute, eventually establishing the discipline known as "contemplative neuroscience." Science had been actively studying the brain to discover correlations with pathological conditions, such as depression and anxiety, but he suggested a novel approach. He was especially interested in learning what goes on in the brain of someone who is happy.

Inherent in Buddhism is the idea that happiness can be pursued through knowledge and personal practice to achieve mental peace of mind as a relief from suffering. Such practices go back thousands of years—Buddhists have passed down specialized knowledge of various techniques for hundreds of generations. One such technique is mindfulness, a form of meditation that can be accomplished in any moment simply by placing all attention on whatever activity is taking place, whether it's drinking a cup of coffee, sitting quietly, or walking through the woods. It involves a practice of constant awareness of the breath, the body, an object, or activity with the objective of moving the mind's attention away from negative or distracting thoughts. As our attention remains focused only on the present moment, the mind eventually becomes free of all other distractions. Once relieved of mental chatter, the practitioner achieves happiness or bliss, and freedom from suffering.

While this concept is simple to explain, it is not necessarily easy to accomplish. Buddhist monks are considered experts at meditation after 10,000 hours of practice. Thus, they are excellent candidates for measuring how the brain might be affected by such mental activity. Results indicate that in the brains of longtime meditators as compared with novices, there is increased activity in regions associated with states of attentive focus. There is an area in the forehead (Brodmann areas 9 and 10 in the prefrontal cortex) that contains a larger volume of brain tissue in experienced practitioners than in nonmeditating control subjects. Mindfulness training is correlated with a decreased volume in the amygdala, a brain structure associated with fear responses. Buddhist practitioners are able to hold a sustained EEG pattern of high-amplitude gamma brain-wave synchrony, denoting greater coordination of neuronal networks. The practice of long-term meditation seems to influence the physical structures in the brain through a process known as neuroplasticity.

As late as the 1970s, a basic principle taught in neuroscience stated that the human brain after childhood was relatively fixed in its structure, and that no new neurons could be created. The ability to recover proper function after any form of brain damage was thus postulated to be minimal. However, clinical experience in the late 20th century seemed to defy this hypothetical limitation and, in recent decades, remarkable evidence for the recovery of damaged human brains has been discovered in a wide variety of settings.

Neuroplasticity is the general term for this ability of the brain to recover from injury and to adapt in more normal circumstances ("activity-dependent plasticity"), including the ability to generate new neurons and interconnect them with the rest of the brain in a functionally effective manner. Further investigation of such cases of unexpected recovery have revealed a remarkable ability of the brain to rewire and rebuild itself in the normal setting of living and learning, outside of the challenges of recovering from significant physical damage. Such robust neuroplasticity seems to indicate the role of mind, or consciousness, in providing the template on which our physical brain changes to reflect our intentions and perceptions.

Research into the neuroscience of meditation reveals a wide range of emotional and behavioral benefits, including stress relief, reduced anxiety and depression, improved immunity, enhanced creativity, increased intuition, and lower blood pressure, among others. Meditative techniques provide a means to intentionally quiet the mind and discover a stillness inside. This allows the person meditating to reach profound states of focused relaxation, and presumably facilitates various recognized benefits through neuroplasticity. Meditators report a broad range of experiences, and some are able to regularly connect with the realm of loving oneness, either on purpose or quite unexpectedly, that I encountered during my coma. It should come as no surprise that those who regularly meditate are found to have increased ability to maintain focused attention.

I participated in formal efforts to improve the focus of my attention during my collegiate skydiving career in the 1970s at the University of North Carolina at Chapel Hill. During my time at UNC (1972 to 1976), our sport parachuting club trained more than 400 students who made at least one parachute jump. As a member of the UNC Sport Parachuting team, I made 365 parachute jumps, the vast majority of which were attempts to build group free-fall formations. This involved groups of two to twenty or more jumpers, a practice known as relative work, or RW.

Several members of the team interested in improving our skills, including myself, took a course entitled Silva Mind Control, a carefully proscribed method of applying mental focus to the improvement of challenging motor skills, such as those involved in flying one's body in free fall to safely and efficiently build formations with other jumpers. Our standard practice was to go through the intended formation build by marching through it on the ground before a jump. But with the added benefit of José Silva's techniques, we would also invoke our meditative state through his mind-control program and practice the various free-fall maneuvers necessary in our minds just prior to boarding the jump plane.

Our jumping proficiency improved after such mental rehearsals, but we never performed a controlled scientific assessment to compare our performance before and after using such techniques. I know that our sport parachuting environment was superior to that of any other college of which I was aware—the UNC parachute team at that time could build an eight-man star, whereas the US national collegiate competition involved teams of three, given that most colleges were lucky to have, at most, three sport parachutists accomplished enough to safely perform RW formations. Whether any of that apparent success was due to our practice of Silva mind control before jumps is an open question. Although I believe the Silva method helped me to become a better RW participant, I did not attempt to apply the practice to supplement other life activities. When I left UNC for the Duke University School of Medicine in 1976, I left behind my practice of focused visualization, not appreciating how it might assist me in so many other areas of my life. However, its principles are far more relevant to my life now.

During almost thirty years spent in academic neurosurgery, I frequently summoned up some of the most intense focus of my life while performing surgical procedures. I came to see the operating room as a sanctuary, a sacred space where I could focus completely on the matter at hand (whether it be resecting a challenging skull base tumor, or securing a difficult aneurysm), sinking into a sublime state that allowed me to achieve my loftiest goals in the OR. Time dilation was a common experience, where a particularly arduous dissection lasting hours might seem to last only minutes. My gratitude abounds to the nurses, residents, and staff who helped by insulating me from the calls and pages that threatened my cocoon—that is, trying to draw me out of my intense operative focus to attend to myriad patient issues outside of the OR. Calm, and intensely focused—truly a sublime form of mindfulness.

This attentive state of mind is sometimes referred to as a "flow state" or "being in the zone" and is often reported by athletes, creative artists, and musicians when they focus intently on a specific task to great satisfaction. Hungarian psychologist Mihaly Csikszentmihalyi first coined the phrase "flow" for this state of mind, claiming that happiness can be cultivated intentionally from within. In our everyday life, the flow state is not necessarily achieved at will but comes during intense immersion in an activity when all distractions (including a sense of objective time) fade from notice. We are not consciously thinking when we enter the zone—in fact, it feels as though the thinking mind is taking a break.

Brain-wave studies reveal some amazing things about this phenomenon. When in the flow state, activity is reduced in the prefrontal cortex, a region associated with analysis and monitoring our behavior. Typically, decisions must be reviewed by this part of the brain (as the center of what is called "executive function"), which often slows us down as we "overthink" what we are doing. Likewise, research reveals that expert Buddhist meditators with the highest level of training show *decreased* levels of brain activity in these same regions.

In related studies, scientific investigations assessing the action of various psychedelic drugs on the brain (specifically those that influence serotinergic receptors) reveal similar findings. One example involves a 2012 report from Imperial College London, in which functional MRI (fMRI) was used to evaluate various brain regions in subjects under the influence of psilocybin, the active ingredient in psychedelic mushrooms (the genus *Psilocybe* consists of more than 100 species).[1] The content of the subjects' mental experiences was assessed through a visual analog scale reporting on such features as blissful state, experience of unity, meaning, insightfulness, and disembodiment, with the most profound effects involving elementary and complex imagery, as well as audiovisual synesthesia (overlap of normally separate sensory modalities, such as "smelling colors" or "seeing sound").

The most remarkable finding of that study was that the activity of major connection regions of the brain was greatly diminished in those who were having the most profound psychedelic experiences, as opposed to the increase in brain activity originally anticipated by the investigators. In a very real sense, we seem to experience a greater sense of consciousness the less certain parts of our brain are actively functioning.

This result was so surprising to those who believed the brain creates consciousness that it prompted Christof Koch, chief scientist at the Allen Institute for Brain Science in Seattle, to write a column in *Scientific*

American entitled "This Is Your Brain on Drugs: To the Great Surprise of Many, Psilocybin, a Potent Psychedelic, Reduces Brain Activity." His column portrayed the extraordinary nature of the findings, especially because of the dramatic reduction in activity of the most complex junctional regions in the brain and the fact that *no* regions of the brain showed any increase in activity—widespread suppression was seen, and its degree correlated with the power of the psychedelic experience itself!

These results were confirmed by a Brazilian study published in February 2015 assessing brain activity through fMRI, this time in subjects under the influence of ayahuasca (which contains the active psychedelic compound N,N-dimethyltryptamine, or DMT, normally present in our brains, but in minuscule amounts).[2] Ayahuasca caused a significant decrease in activity throughout the main junctional network in the brain, known as the default-mode network.

The Imperial College group revealed similar results when examining the effects on the brain of the most powerful such drug, LSD (lysergic acid diethylamide-25). Again, the most extraordinary experiences were reported by those subjects who had the greatest inactivation of their brain's junctional center network activity, as measured through fMRI and magnetoencephalography. As the brain becomes less active, internal mental experience actually becomes more active.

This shocking revelation is completely consistent with my own experience in deep coma. While my neocortex was being dismantled by the invading bacteria, my conscious awareness greatly expanded to levels unprecedented in normal waking experiences, allowing me to connect with that profound presence of unconditional love at the core of all existence. Since my brain was unable to produce a hallucination due to its overall neocortical incapacity, it became apparent that that ultrareality occurred because the experience was real, although it did not occur anywhere in our four-dimensional space-time of the observable physical universe.

Although such psychedelic research is crucial in our evolving notions of consciousness and a better understanding of the nature of reality, I do not recommend the casual use of such substances in a nonsacred, recreational setting. In experimental studies, the quality and quantity of drug administered can be strictly controlled and monitored as the subject is

continuously supervised, which is not the case in most recreational settings, where such psychedelics can be dangerous to one's health, both
physical and mental.

Other means of connecting with the finer aspects of consciousness are
techniques that reduce, as much as possible, the steady stream of sensory
information that ties us down to the Supreme Illusion. Various forms of
sensory deprivation result in fascinating alterations in perceptual awareness.
By reducing the visual, auditory, and tactile stimuli that bombard us every
waking minute, we are able to connect more with that Collective Mind.
What remains of our conscious awareness when we shut down sensory
inputs? What is left? When we eliminate the "noise" (that is, the sensory
flood processed through our body's nervous system to perpetuate the
Supreme Illusion), we isolate a core aspect of conscious awareness itself.

Regular meditation trains the practitioner to be less bothered by
external stimuli, but for beginners, eye masks, light-blocking window
shades, noise-canceling headphones, and white-noise devices are common ways to reduce distractions. Note that a convenient form of sensory
deprivation has gained popularity in recent years through the expansion
of public facilities offering sessions in float tanks. While these efforts
help, special methods and devices have been developed for laboratory
studies.

German psychologist Wolfgang Metzger described in the 1930s his
discovery that gazing into a featureless field over many minutes could
produce altered levels of awareness, including what he labeled hallucinations, as well as corresponding alterations in the subject's EEG. Reports
from miners trapped in pitch-black conditions, as well as those from arc-
tic explorers exposed to a sea of white, also indicated that prolonged
exposure to a bland and featureless field of view provided a powerful
trigger for alterations in consciousness. These included occasional rich
visual experiences that seemed chaotic, and clearly unrelated to any local
stimulus in the subject's environment—a phenomenon referred to as the
ganzfeld effect (from the German for "total field").

The *ganzfeld* effect was utilized in experiments assessing psi effects
during dreams (notably, telepathy between a sender and a dreaming
receiver) at Maimonides Medical Center in Brooklyn in the late 1960s
and early 1970s.[3] These studies were later expanded to assess telepathy
in awake subjects, under the assumption that the *ganzfeld* effect reduced

the amount of neuronal activity in the brain's networks by greatly eliminating the river of sensory input we normally encounter in the world. By providing a bland, unchanging visual field, combined with white noise to the ears and a comfortable posture, they sought to reduce brain activity related to all sensory perception in the hopes of facilitating the telepathic transfer of information.

The general *ganzfeld* experimental setup included a sender who focused on the target (a randomly selected video short or picture) for 30 minutes or so, actively thinking out loud in a continuous stream of all that was passing through his mind concerning the target. Meanwhile, the recipient lay quietly in the *ganzfeld* state in another room, isolated from any excess sensory input. After the 30 minutes, the recipient was offered four separate stimuli, only one of which actually corresponded to the sender's target.

Two issues of the *Journal of Parapsychology* in the mid-1980s were devoted entirely to an analysis of the *ganzfeld* effect. They included commentary from both Ray Hyman, a skeptical but knowledgeable cognitive psychologist, and Charles Honorton, one of the most experienced investigators of the *ganzfeld* technique. This extensive review of the subject included forty-two separate studies conducted in ten separate laboratories around the world. Analysis of those combined studies revealed an overall hit rate of 35 percent, compared with the 25 percent that would be expected merely by chance. The probability of such a hit rate arising randomly is less than one in a billion, so they obviously indicated a real and profound effect. Even skeptical materialist scientist Carl Sagan noted that such phenomena are worthy of further study based on preliminary evidence.

In 1986, Hyman and Honorton agreed on more stringent methodology to improve the power of *ganzfeld* experiments, resulting in a procedure labeled *autoganzfeld*. Computers were used to run the experiments in a carefully scripted fashion by selecting images or video sequences and recording receiver's ratings. Honorton went on to conduct 354 experimental sessions over 11 separate experiments with 240 subjects. Even with the more stringent criteria, the hit rate remained an amazing 35 percent. Of note, they found that, compared with still images, dynamic targets (such as video, which contains more information) offered a substantially higher success rate.

Honorton also reported interesting qualities that improved the success of the receiver, including an active meditative practice, or being creative or artistically gifted. In particular, twenty music and dance students from the Juilliard School in New York achieved a hit rate of 50 percent, which rose to a record 75 percent for musicians alone. This incredible success rate was hypothesized to reveal an ability in these students related to their active creative nature. Their very creativity indicates a more natural and facile relationship with universal consciousness. They have a "thinner veil" than most, and thus their enhanced ability to receive telepathic information from others is simply another aspect of their broader channel of connection with that realm.

Many people who have contributed tremendous artistic works, scientific breakthroughs, and other insights concerning the interrelationships and structure of our world have admitted that their greatest creative visions seemed to come from outside of themselves. German-born physicist Albert Einstein, American inventor Thomas Edison, German composer Ludwig van Beethoven, Spanish surrealist painter Salvador Dalí, Scottish novelist Robert Louis Stevenson—all of these creative geniuses discussed how their greatest inspirations were not the result of prolonged intellectual inquiry or "thinking about" something. Rather, such creative revelations seemed to flash into their minds, willed by "the universe" or some force outside of themselves.

Einstein might drift in a small sailboat, staring into the sky for hours as his imagination wandered, during which time new possibilities for explaining reality appeared, that he would then work into his revolutionary ideas in physics. Edison learned to work for days on little sleep, gaining creative insights during the periods he continuously evoked by having weights in his hands that would awaken him by falling just as he was drifting off to sleep (very similar to a technique utilized by Stevenson to create the ideas behind his novels, poetry, and music). Each of these creative geniuses was thus able to harvest some of the more extraordinary insights they would gain during those cultivated intervals of transcendental states of consciousness.

They were aware of being active participants in the process, often by just opening their minds and following some process of mental liberation, which appears to set the stage for a form of free-flow daydreaming. This level of awareness is known as hypnagogia, the borderline between awake and asleep. All of us experience this hypnagogic state as we fall asleep, and again when we awaken. Pay attention during these moments each day and note how your sensory awareness is altered from the state you experience when fully awake. Often, we recall dream fragments and receive fresh insight or creative solutions to problems at these intervals. Such thoughts can be fleeting so it is helpful to keep a notebook and pen nearby to take notes for later reference.

Ultimately, by getting the brain out of the way, whether through meditation, achieving a flow state, or sensory deprivation, we are able to rise above the Supreme Illusion of our earthly space-time. The only way to truly grok the nature of underlying reality is to become more fully aware of it, from the outside, in order to take the broadest viewpoint possible. By intentionally going within to explore that infinite world of universal consciousness, we can access that grander viewpoint from a more expanded state of awareness. This is what advanced meditators and spiritual journeyers, including the great prophets and mystics who delivered the foundation of all of our religious beliefs, have done since time immemorial. All it takes is to establish a regular practice. In our busy modern world, this can be challenging to achieve but is well worth the effort.

As noted in Chapter 3, Karen Newell had embarked on a personal exploration to generate spiritual experience. She had learned that meditation was a valuable means for accessing greater knowledge outside of herself—but at first, it did not come easy. She was reluctant to join a meditation class since many seemed to require some sort of dogmatic belief system or acceptance of specific understandings, such as the worship of a particular deity. So she chose to try on her own by sitting quietly in a chair and willing her mind to empty. She had read that focusing on her breath or a simple phrase might help to distract her from her thoughts, but the thoughts were relentlessly persistent. As an accomplished information technology director and project manager, her mind was constantly planning and reorganizing ideas; it seemed impossible to stop that otherwise useful productive activity. Ten minutes seemed like a reasonable amount of time to close her eyes and sit still, but even that would seem like an eternity. She convinced herself that she simply wasn't capable of meditating.

Karen was not alone. A common challenge reported by those attempting to quiet the mind is the constant presence of mind chatter, the ongoing thoughts that never seem to stop. That inner voice is the linguistic brain, tightly tied to the ego and to the sense of self. The linguistic brain is the base of rational thought, logical inference, and human communications— but during meditation, it simply gets in the way.

Karen searched for tools and various guided meditation approaches to help quiet the mind. Eventually she attended a workshop led by Puran and Susanna Bair, who teach a form of heart-rhythm meditation with roots in Sufism. Karen was drawn to this approach because it was open to people from all walks of life, no matter what their underlying belief system. Heart-rhythm meditation involves coordinating the breath with the heartbeat in various repetitive patterns. For example, breathing out while counting eight heartbeats, then breathing in while counting eight heartbeats. The meditation techniques were demonstrated in the context of scientific research conducted by HeartMath Institute, an organization that studies the heart-brain connection and its relationship to stress and mood in humans.

Among other things, HeartMath research tests theories about the electromagnetic field of the human heart using machines that measure faint magnetic fields, such as those that are often used in MRIs and cardiologic tests. Remarkably, the heart's toroidally shaped electrical field is sixty times greater than that of the brain, and its magnetic field is 5,000 times greater than that of the brain. The heart generates the strongest electromagnetic field in the body, and its pumping action transmits powerful rhythmic information patterns containing neurological, hormonal, and electromagnetic data to the brain and throughout the rest of the body. The heart actually sends more information to the brain than the brain sends to the heart. In other words, the heart has a mind of its own. Studies reveal this electromagnetic field seems to pick up information in the surrounding environment and also broadcasts one's emotional state out from the body. Their measurements reveal that the field is large enough to extend several feet (or more) outside our bodies. Positive moods such as gratitude, joy, and happiness correlate to a larger, more expanded heart field, while emotions such as greed, anger, or sadness correlate to a constricted heart field.

At the seminar where Karen and I first met, we were paired up for an experiential exercise in which we practiced sensing or "feeling" each other's energy. We were instructed to take turns standing still while the other would approach and move back repeatedly from distances of 2 to 20 feet, noticing if we sensed anything along the way. As I walked toward Karen, holding up my hands, I became aware of a subtle but noticeable borderline of energy around her. This was a novel sensation for me, resembling a mild perception of change in temperature or air density. As I stood still while Karen approached me, I felt my heart respond with a warm connectedness, as if it was originating in her, but it felt internal to me, an entirely new phenomenon. At the time, I described it to her as the intermingling of our heart's energy into one—perhaps this research explains part of what I was sensing.

Fascinating research results point to the realization that our hearts interconnect and exchange information with others. In studies, subjects are trained to enact specific heart coherence techniques such as focusing awareness in the area surrounding the heart and generating a feeling of appreciation. Coherence reflects a higher state of balance and synchronization in the body's cognitive, emotional, and physiological processes, leading to lowering of stress reactions and more efficient function. Positive emotions are correlated with higher degrees of coherence, thus generating appreciation in the heart alone can beneficially affect the person's physiological functions, including the autonomic and parasympathetic nervous systems.

Subjects who performed such techniques even showed a measurable influence on the person sitting across from them, who was not practicing any technique. A related result was found when two subjects were holding hands. Likewise, when someone is in a coherent state, they are more receptive to information generated by other nearby heart fields. Maintaining awareness of the heart and an appreciative state of mind while listening to another person often results in improved clarity and increased awareness of more nonverbal aspects of what is being communicated, described as a higher sensitivity to the other person. Couples sleeping in the same bed have shown remarkable coherence between their two hearts throughout the night. It seems we communicate with more than our language, gestures, and other nonverbal cues through the energy of our hearts.

Karen was impressed by the research results demonstrating the value of coherent states and learned the technique at the workshop on heart-rhythm meditation. To monitor results directly, Puran and Susanna demonstrated a useful biofeedback tool (especially for beginners) called an emWave device, created by HeartMath. A clip is attached to the finger or ear and the other end is connected to a computer, which then displays information based on the person's measured heart-rate variability. Practitioners measure their success by viewing graphic displays, such as a nature scene being filled in with flowers and trees, or a special tone is heard as higher rates of coherence are achieved. This direct feedback was helpful to Karen in order to indicate when she had reached the desired state, often a very subtle but noticeable difference.

While these results were encouraging, the persistent mind chatter continued to distract her from reaching deeper meditative states. Inspired by the workshop and personal experiments with the emWave device, Karen enrolled in a five-week online beginner course facilitated by a mentor who had been trained by Puran and Susanna through their Institute of Applied Meditation on the Heart. Karen could practice meditation from the comfort of her home and report back to the facilitator and other enrolled students by posting on a private online forum. Students were given fresh instructions for each week of the course, starting with the task of maintaining a strict posture, sitting upright in a chair for 20 minutes, twice a day. At first, the task was simply to pay attention to the pattern of breathing. In this fashion, the observing mind begins to play an important role.

"Shortly after beginning to sit still and watch my breath, I developed pain in my middle back which eventually settled on the left side and radiated to the left shoulder. This was very distracting to the sitting-still process and in the past has been an easy excuse to stop, change position, or stretch. I sat through it and felt relief when I could move at the end of 20 minutes," Karen posted on the student forum.

"The left-sided pain you experienced today in meditation and that you have experienced before may be more than simply posture-related. The left side of the body is typically related to receptivity rather than expressiveness, and sometimes pain in one or the other side of the body reflects an imbalance that is asking for correction," the mentor suggested.

Karen was instructed to imagine her breath was moving in and out of the site of the pain. She tried this and found that the pain would subside a bit, or sometimes move to a different location. Whatever the cause, it was useful to have a method of relieving the pain, and it gave her something to do to distract herself from it.

To her dismay, the practice of focusing on her breath did not immediately diminish the constant mind chatter and the pain continued to come and go.

"I spend time thinking about how I'm going to later express my experience in these forum messages. I try to remember different sensations so I can report them accurately and have something to say. My thoughts are also busy planning future activities as opposed to reviewing past events. I do manage to multitask while that's going on, staying focused on breathing and looking for the heartbeat, whose sensation comes and goes," Karen reported.

"Sometimes we need to let the mind continue its background chatter while we find other ways to help energy move! We may never know the 'why,' but we know we feel better!" the mentor replied.

This is an incredibly common experience among meditation practitioners, especially when first starting out. Every person will have different obstacles and experiences, and it's critical not to give up if desired results aren't immediate. Karen had expected that her thoughts would completely dissipate but she began to see that it was okay for thoughts to continue while she focused her attention on another mental activity, whether noticing her breath, her heartbeat, or the shoulder and back pain. This allowed her to develop the vital and ever-present inner observer—the part of her that willed her mind's attention to tend to different tasks. One important step was to gain awareness of her physical heartbeat. Sometimes she could feel it, but when she couldn't, she was advised to place her hand on her heart to feel its beating as she sat in meditative posture. After a few weeks, she noticed herself regulating her breathing in relation to her heart without thinking about it as she went about her daily routine.

As she proceeded through the course, Karen quickly noted that each student had completely unique ways of experiencing the same activity. Some of the students expressed profound emotional connections, but this did not happen for Karen. She wondered if there was something wrong with her.

"You are certainly not the only person for whom this is true. There are people who do not have emotion as a predominant response to meditation, but who instead have more physical sensation, or energetic sensation, or imagery," the mentor advised.

It seems we are unique and react in different ways. It was interesting to compare experiences with the other students, but reading about how the others achieved deep insights and detailed visualizations caused a measure of distress. Karen's reports seemed rather dull by comparison.

"Sometimes as I sit, it feels like a chore to get through. I wish for it to feel like a pleasure to take these moments to myself. I long for a profound spiritual moment; I seem to have 'profound-moment envy,'" Karen shared with her group.

"It is easy to become impatient or disheartened when something we wish to attain doesn't come as quickly as we'd like or in the way we imagine it should. And then we sometimes miss the jewel we are really after, the one hidden within that requires the self-cultivation developed when we move one grain of soil, one tiny pebble at a time. And we may also miss the jewel that is lying in plain view, in front of our own eyes, but in a form other than what we expect," the mentor suggested.

Karen realized that attaining a certain level of spiritual awareness was an ongoing process, not one to be achieved with little effort. She continued to learn from dozens of teachers many different methods of achieving a quiet, still mind and other ways to explore within and expand her conscious awareness. Meditation was just the beginning. Sitting still in a chair focused on the breath and heartbeat was not the only way to experience expanded states of awareness, but learning to quiet the mind was a good basis for further practices.

Over several years, she embarked upon what she described as "spiritual boot camp." She applied herself to learn how to sense energy and expand her consciousness through practices such as lucid dreaming and self-hypnosis. She took courses in energy healing methods such as reiki, explored the spiritual properties of crystals, and learned how to communicate with animals and plants. She studied astrology and feng shui, and practiced interpreting Tarot card spreads. Some things made more sense than others, but by creating her own doorway to "extremely hidden phenomena," Karen no longer had to rely on other testimonies as proof of an unseen realm; her personal results and observations offered plenty of evidence. In a sense, her explorations became a modern passage to initiation in the spiritual arts, echoing the ancient mystery schools that she had longed to attend.

While awareness of the heart continued to be an essential tool, she found sounds produced by tuning forks, gongs, crystal bowls, didgeridoo, and Tibetan brass bowls all had a particular drone quality that would help to calm the incessant chatter in her head. Audio frequencies (known as binaural beats) embedded in specialized recordings used for brain-wave entrainment were especially helpful at supporting this goal, and my initial encounter with Karen found her already well along the path of this endeavor. As I was just beginning to learn the value of going within, I admired her perseverance and willingness to try numerous techniques. I identified with her open-mind and curious approach—an attitude I had acquired through the process of dismantling my previous belief that the material world is all that exists. Putting aside former opinions and maintaining an inquisitive mind-set is a valuable place from which to explore within consciousness. It was from this perspective that the next phase of my journey began.

CHAPTER 9

RIDING THE WAVE OF CONSCIOUSNESS

If you want to find the secrets of the universe, think in terms of energy, frequency, and vibration.

—Nikola Tesla (1856–1943), inventor

As an academic neurosurgeon, I was accustomed to *thinking* my way to answers. As much as that dogged pursuit of understanding through the linear rational and logical process so common in academics and much of daily human reasoning is ingrained into our culture, I came to realize how much the actual experience of my coma journey provided a more fundamental mode of *knowing*. I longed to reaccess that state of being in hopes that I could cultivate an ongoing connection to that realm.

In this context, two years after my coma, I became aware of audio recordings that contain binaural beats, used to alter conscious awareness. At first, I didn't view this as a form of meditation. My original attraction to binaural beat technology was related to my search for some means of duplicating the progressive dismantling of the neocortex that occurred during my coma journey but without, well, nearly dying. Binaural beats offered the potential to neutralize the information processing activity of the neocortex, the analytical part of the brain. I theorized that this might provide a robust enhancement of awareness similar to the transcendental state I experienced during coma. Like the flow state, lessening the information processing of the brain might allow the filtering function to diminish, allowing me more complete contact with the Collective Mind across the veil and setting my awareness free.

It seemed natural that sound might allow me to transcend our material world. As told in *Proof of Heaven,* music, sound, and vibration were essential to accessing the full spectrum of spiritual realms during my NDE. The spinning melody of pure white light that rescued me from the Earthworm's Eye View served as a portal leading up into the ultrareal Gateway Valley. The angelic choirs there emanated chants and hymns that empowered my ascendance beyond that idyllic valley through higher dimensions. My final destination was the Core, far beyond all space and time, the very boundary between the infinite eternal oneness I sensed and all of the emergent universe. It was in that Core realm that I felt the thunderous awe of om, the sound so intimately associated with that infinitely powerful, knowing, and loving being, that Deity beyond naming or description—whom some might label God.

Recordings containing binaural beats are designed to support the listener into achieving states of awareness correlated to brain-wave states as measured by an EEG. Brain-wave states are divided into five categories of progressively higher frequencies (expressed in hertz [Hz], or cycles per second): delta (0–4 Hz), theta (4–8 Hz), alpha (8–12 Hz), beta (12–25 Hz), and gamma (25–100+ Hz).

At any one time, any or all of these frequency ranges might be present across the surface of the entire brain. But consistent patterns of such frequency sets in specific brain regions, especially those dominant during any activity, correlate with various mental activities. Generally speaking, beta is associated with activities such as conversation, analysis, and processing of information, while the lowest delta waves are present during deep dreamless sleep and coma. Frequencies in the highest gamma level are found in individuals at moments of profound insight and peak physical performance. Alpha reflects a relaxed, calm, and focused mind, often prominent during dream sleep (REM, or rapid eye movement, sleep). Brain waves in the theta range correspond to meditation, enhanced intuition, and creativity. This is the state in which young children exist naturally during their normal, waking life and reflects a prime state in which to learn and absorb most readily from the surrounding environment.

In binaural-beat brain-entrainment audio recordings, each ear receives a slightly different frequency. The arithmetic difference between the two frequencies defines the resultant brain-wave state. For example, presenting 100 Hz in the left ear and 104 Hz in the right ear would deliver a 4 Hz signal to the brain stem. Our ears cannot hear frequencies below 20 Hz, but a timing circuit in the lower brain stem (the superior olivary complex) generates a strong signal equal to the arithmetic difference between the two (left and right) input signals. Through interaction with a region in the brain stem that serves as a major ignition or binding system for consciousness (the reticular activating system), this then seems to modulate the dominant brain waves of the neocortex.

Recall that the hypnagogic state is that sweet spot, in which our awareness hovers between awake and asleep, that many scientists and artists have utilized as a source of creativity and insight. Brain waves in this condition would likely be measured near the theta range of 4–8 Hz, a prime target for achieving a quiet but focused mind. Producers of brain-wave entrainment recordings utilize different combinations of binaural beats. Some also include isochronic tones, which are regular beats of the same frequency, like a drumbeat, but much faster. Different formulas, combinations that might include all of the brain-wave states, seem to offer support for various states of awareness.

I first listened to such recordings through headphones, lying quietly in a dark room, wearing an eye mask to eliminate any ambient light. This was an entirely new activity for me. The sounds I heard were remarkably different from regular music—similar to the vibration of an engine, but with a steady throbbing waver. The first few times I listened, I thought I might have fallen asleep. Unlike a typical nap, however, I felt as though I'd been quite active, not sleeping. I was curious as to why I didn't remember more of it. After a few listening sessions, as I lay there wondering what might come next, I suddenly became aware of a dreamlike floating sensation. I knew I was lying in my bed, but my awareness seemed to be separate from my physical body.

The etheric strangeness of the hypnagogic state was part of it, but I had a simultaneous sensation of drifting outside of the illusion of the material world. At first it was subtle, but the thing that really shocked me was a detachment from time flow. I became aware of a realm that was quite literally outside of the bubble of apparent here and now that is such a staple of our human existence. I had the sense of a grander aspect of my awareness from a perspective superior to anything I had witnessed, other than my coma journey. There was a powerful peace and acceptance to the experience, but also a sense of accessing much more complete and higher levels of comprehension and understanding.

Crucial to the process was the notion of letting go of any attachment to results and outcome. Through repeated practice, I have trained myself to resist the temptation to fill in the void with the chatter of my egoic linguistic brain. The binaural beats seemed to assist me in quieting my thoughts, but in that sensory-deprived setting, various images and complex visions would appear, initially seeming completely unbidden. By relaxing into a state of calm, expanded awareness, I found that the universe seemed to offer information to help me come to a richer understanding of some facet of my life.

I learned that I could stimulate a more engaged experience by expressing gratitude (for each little blessing in life) and trust (that higher consciousness would offer richer understanding), and then just letting go to see what the universe (and my higher soul?) might offer up in the way of knowledge. I learned to ask a question, and sometimes answers were revealed in this more expanded state of awareness. All of these steps allowed me to have a more rewarding experience. I later came to realize that this form of entering the realm of consciousness itself was a type of meditation, allowing me to connect more fully with my inner world (and the outer universe).

As I was just beginning to explore such methods of exploring within consciousness, Karen had been utilizing brain-wave entrainment audio recordings for several years. Along with her many other practices, she had discovered that recordings containing binaural beats were especially powerful and came to be a most useful tool in her personal explorations. Initially, Karen often fell asleep when listening to binaural beats, but persistence paid off. After acclimating her brain through regular listening sessions, she cultivated the ability to sustain her awareness for longer periods of time. She was quite dedicated to her personal exploration routines, and I was especially intrigued when she shared with me her

habit of listening to custom audio recordings with her friend and colleague Kevin Kossi.

They were attending a sound-related workshop when they first
became acquainted and, after listening to a guided recording, had gathered with the group to share their experiences. Several people took turns
relating what they felt or saw, sometimes colors, personal messages, or
bodily sensations, and then it was Kevin's turn. Karen had previously
heard Kevin describe his remarkable ability to describe things he encountered during out-of-body experiences (OBE).

An OBE occurs when someone might see a view of their body from
above during sleep or under anesthesia, and then realize their awareness
is floating up near the ceiling. Those having an OBE might find themselves in a familiar location in their home; others sense that their astral
body can travel through walls, and they can explore at a distance.
Attempts to duplicate such phenomena in a laboratory setting have been
elusive, but this does not make them any less real for those who experience them. Kevin had been traveling outside of his body since he was a
young child.

"As I separated from my body and started to rise above it, I felt something intriguing draw me toward Karen's room. I noticed there were several rows of images on the wall with colorful geometric shapes that
looked like portals. Using my etheric body, I began to dive into the portals to see what was there," Kevin stated.

As he told this story to the group, Karen had no recollection of sensing Kevin during her experience, which had been completely different,
from her perspective. However, she did recall the postcards she had
brought with her from home. They had arrived in the mail a few days
earlier and they were still in the unopened box, which contained dozens
of cards. Each displayed a different image on them, related to various
symbols found in crop circles. An artist had rendered these shapes into
colorful geometric patterns, each on a separate card. Karen offered to
show them to Kevin.

"Yup, that was them," he declared matter-of-factly later that day.

Had Kevin actually been aware of the same postcards? Now, this was
not a scientific study and there are all kinds of explanations that could be
invented to explain the situation, but it was not Karen's habit to casually
explain things away as mere coincidences. She paid close attention to her

personal experiences, practiced careful discernment, and remained open to all possibilities. Needless to say, she was intrigued.

Kevin revealed to Karen that he was interested in creating his own binaural-beat sound recordings. As a mechanical engineer, he excels at taking things apart and fashioning new inventions and shares Karen's highly innovative aptitude. When his dog was diagnosed with cancer, she was given just two months to live, and Kevin was inspired to seek alternative ways to cure her. This set him on a path to learn energy healing, and he succeeded in extending her life by two years. He had also practiced transcendental meditation and remote viewing. A near-death experience in 2006 sent him on a path, like me, to discover ways to revisit those realms. Here again was someone highly technical with a science-related career who also explored spiritual matters in his spare time.

Karen began to collaborate with Kevin, sharing a goal to enhance their respective personal explorations. For about a year prior to my meeting them, they had been creating experimental sound files that incorporated binaural beats and other forms of brain-wave entrainment techniques. Through analyzing Karen's vast library of sound recordings, they had deconstructed and reconstructed various sets of frequencies in all kinds of ways. Through trial and error, they found novel techniques that worked most effectively to achieve their particular goals. Most intriguing was that this process included frequently sharing simultaneous journeys into expanded states of consciousness. After listening to a recording at the same time, they would speak on the phone from their respective locations in New York City and Baltimore to describe their experiences. Karen found comparison of her perceptions with Kevin's to be especially useful and validating.

In early 2012, Karen and Kevin invited me to try out their sound recordings. They had not yet shared these recordings with another soul, so I considered this opportunity a rare treat. Kevin arrived at my New York City hotel room with a portable EEG device in his backpack.

"I'll attach the three electrical activity probes to your forehead to measure both the right and left frontal lobes," Kevin explained. "We can see in real time which brain waves are generally prominent and exactly when shifts occur as the recording is played."

The Interactive Brainwave Visual Analyzer (IBVA) was quite rudimentary compared to the EEG equipment I knew from clinical practice, but it had a robust graphic display that enabled us to analyze in real time the degree of synchrony and dominant frequency in the frontal lobes. Its simple design limited us to examining activity in the prefrontal regions (those in charge of executive function and decision-making), but those regions were among the most important to observe, as the flow state and meditation studies demonstrate. The IBVA system proved to be well suited for fieldwork such as this. Much of our more recent work involves a 20-lead EEG system, providing a more global look at the brain's neocortex, as opposed to the limited view measured through the IBVA.

As was their habit, Karen would listen to the same recording from her location, timing the push of the play button by texting her readiness to us. The particular recording we selected was their latest creation.

"Let's just notice what happens and tell each other afterward," Karen suggested, as we coordinated a plan.

"Sounds good," Kevin and I agreed.

As I adjusted my headphones and got comfortable on the hotel's couch, Kevin prepared to listen as well, with his own set of headphones. The recording began, and I settled into the sound journey. At first, I was taken by the power of the sound. It was richer than anything I had heard to date. I was careful not to have undue expectations, and I quickly found myself moving into the familiar state of being I had become accustomed to in recent months. I settled into the soundscape and allowed my experience to unfold. The powerful tones quickly supported an expansion of my awareness beyond the illusion of here and now.

As I removed my headphones after the recording ended, Kevin answered Karen's call and put her on speakerphone. As familiar as they were with trading their own experiences, they were especially curious to hear about mine.

"Wow," was about all I could muster, still reeling from the transcendental awareness of the tone-inspired inner exploration.

I was astonished by their power. Clearly, Kevin and Karen were onto something big, and I felt an immediate camaraderie. Although I had earlier sensed a powerful creative synergy between Kevin and Karen, I was now seeing it at a whole new level. They shared a chemistry that was well suited to this highly technical and elaborate effort to develop cutting-edge brain-wave entrainment recordings capable of invoking profound transcendental explorations into alternate realms of consciousness. I was just beginning to glimpse how my involvement might enhance their ongoing collaboration.

Kevin was especially adept at describing his journeys from a visual perspective. He meticulously reported detailed scenes and intricate interactions with energetic presences. In contrast, Karen experienced things more from a conceptual state. Through a sense of knowing, she described the same type of things Kevin could see, even as she claimed not to be as visual as Kevin. She sensed objects and events and would often have unexpected insights and emotional responses. This reminded me of how NDEs can be described in different ways, yet the lessons learned are so similar in nature.

I was invited by these two intrepid psychonauts to join them in their regular practice of listening to experimental audio recordings and trading reports of our experiences. Thus, a series of shared sound journeys began—from wherever I was located. I was delighted to be involved in this effort and found it an excellent opportunity to regularly practice expanded states of awareness. Several times a week, the three of us would coordinate our schedules and listen to the same recording followed by a three-way phone conversation.

In those early weeks of our shared journeys, I would drift in and out of awareness, perhaps notice imagery and sensations of connecting to something, but it wasn't always simple to articulate. We often listened late at night to accommodate our different schedules and I would sometimes have trouble staying awake. I was accustomed to floating in and out of my own awareness, letting go of all distractions and experiencing myself energetically. I found that engaging the linguistic part of my brain to form language immediately after returning from such meditations often proved challenging. At first, I didn't have much to add to our discussions, but as I practiced more frequently, I maintained more alertness throughout and found I could more readily describe my experience.

I paid attention to my breathing, with intense focus on its rhythm, and envisioned it as a natural oscillation that resonates with the harmonics of whatever aspect of my life I might choose to investigate (through a stated question or intention). With practice over years, this has become a very efficient process of detaching from the "here and now" existence. Beyond this point, I am only rarely aware of any thoughts in the form of words entering my awareness—I have entered a nonlinguistic realm, which is more consistent with the grand regions of expanded conscious awareness that I sense as realigning with my higher soul.

Just existing in the richness of the audible tones, floating in their rhythmic oscillations, allows me to sink into a soothing ocean of awareness, but one that is not tightly corralled within the confines of sensory input from the normal, waking world. This ocean is made from the comforting love that I have come to identify so perfectly with the spiritual realm of conscious influence and infinite potential—the realm of the higher soul. In that state, I leave my linguistic (and egoic) brain far behind, and thus find the interplay of concept and emotion to provide a fertile substrate for my meditative experience. This is the realm in which I began to sense the Collective Mind, of which all sentient beings are but a part.

While I enjoyed these shared journeys, I had a particular interest of my own. I wanted to return to my NDE—that is, to the state I had been in during coma. It seemed Kevin could create any frequency sets imaginable and I took advantage of that opportunity by requesting a recording that would return me to a coma state. We spent about two weeks experimenting with the "coma series" set of recordings that consisted of strong delta signals, the brain-wave state associated with coma. This particular attempt mostly succeeded in putting us to sleep! We managed to get into some deep states, but fortunately, did not induce an actual coma. In general, these recordings are quite safe. The tones provide an impetus for achieving deep relaxation, but the listener maintains the ability to manage the situation and can stop at any time, should that be desired, or simply fall asleep and awaken naturally.

As they had already discovered, a mix of tones that contained various combinations of delta, theta, and alpha were the most effective in supporting our goals. As it turns out, this is not a straightforward process at all—it required significant trial and error to achieve the desired results. Even then, the three of us responded in different ways—a one-size-fits-all approach, where each listener would have predictable results, was not readily apparent. For example, Karen generally preferred lower frequencies and had less preference for higher frequencies than I did, so it was not always simple to find the ideal combinations.

Kevin and Karen routinely collected original recordings of various sounds such as ocean surf, waterfalls, and birds to add to their repertoire of audio effects. They attended a conference in Sedona focused on topics related to ancient pre-history, such as astronomical alignments of mega-lithic structures, archaeological remains of ancient technologies and vast cycles of time related to the movement of constellations and planets. The presentations were fascinating, but they had another goal of exploring the adjacent area as part of their research.

While in a nearby but secluded location, they recorded a long stretch of dramatic rolling thunder from a brewing desert storm. This had provided the finishing touch to a favorite collection of recordings we came to call Portal to Unknown. Included was a spiraling sound effect that launched us into a variety of experimental frequency sets that occupied us for months in our shared journeys. The low and rumbling thunder slowly built to a crescendo; the tinkle of a Tibetan bell and other sound effects created an intense ramp-up, culminating in a spiraling sensation that propelled our awareness to deeper realms.

From there, we entered into a wide variety of experimental frequency sets. Kevin provided fresh recordings on a regular basis, with meticulous ongoing revisions based on our feedback. We defined the most successful frequency sets as those in which we sensed similar scenes or patterns, and these became foundations for future recordings. We typically attempted to find each other in our shared sound journeys in order to compare our own experiences with how the other two might have sensed us. The more alike these descriptions were, the more successful we felt we had been. In the Portal to Unknown series, the spiral effect was the constant, and each of us developed a unique, but similar, way of recounting it.

As the spiral sound began, I would sense the three of us standing on a raised metallic platform in the midst of a roiling, stormy sea, dressed in identical reflective, silvery suits. Dark gray luminous clouds swirled above the platform while giant waves pounded the pylons, showering us with salty spray as the spiral sound began to build. The clouds above whirled with increasing speed. Deep violet lightning bolts carved through the clouds above, splitting the sky with cracks of rolling thunder. Standing on the platform in a triangle, we floated up in defiance of local gravity. The swirling clouds assembled into a highly energized vortex, the complete sensory experience driven by the exponentially expanding spiral. We whisked up into a wormhole of infinite space-time confluence, as we zipped off to higher dimensional existence.

Kevin generally described the three of us using extensive details, as we gathered together on an island and then vertically rotated up into the air. Karen was less visual, but still, she sensed the three of us energetically joining and then flying through a vortex. We described this activity slightly differently, yet we all sensed our coming together, and it provided a consistent grounding point. Achieving this level of connection required extensive practice as a group. Even though part of it seemed to be coming from our imaginations, nonetheless, what caught our attention were the shared aspects of these experiences. We should not dismiss these encounters as merely the chaotic products of an overactive fantasy. As Einstein said, "Knowledge is nothing, imagination is everything."

Once through the spiral effect, different scenes or sensations followed. During one session in which we succeeded in finding the others, we each also identified three other beings who acted as our guides. We described them in similar ways, with two being taller than the third. Each guide paired up with one of us and provided a customized tour based on our respective interests. Remarkably, each of our descriptions during this journey was quite similar until we split up with our respective guides. Other times, we each described shifting through time to view flashes of scenes on earth taking place in the past or found ourselves traveling through a jungle scene together. The spiral effect became a useful sound cue that was our mechanism for launching into expanded states of awareness.

Karen's fascination with spirals stemmed from a lifelong curiosity about certain sacred sites that began when she was taught in school that the three pyramids located on the Giza plateau in Egypt were built by tens of thousands of laborers over two decades in order to serve as tombs for pharaohs. At the same time, historians were mystified as to how the incredible engineering feats of the Great Pyramid were achieved, such as the extremely precise alignments to the four cardinal directions and perfect 90-degree corners on a structure of such massive size, as well as how the enormous stones were shaped and lifted to be placed into position. There are many other such examples related to ancient ruins and archaeological anomalies. Evidence found at sacred sites throughout the world point to a lost awareness of humanity's true history and often contain repeated but mysterious symbols. One such symbol is the spiral, such as the triple spiral symbol found at Newgrange, a prehistoric structure in Ireland.

While intriguing, there is no consensus as to what the spiral meant to those who carved it into stone. Some believe it represents a portal to altered states of awareness. Karen had participated in a ceremony performed by Sufi mystics, known as whirling dervishes, in which they continuously spin their bodies with arms outstretched, the right hand pointed up and the left hand pointed down. As the dancers twirl, they move about the floor in a spiral motion, representing our solar system and the planets that revolve around the sun. In a sense, they join with the movement of the cosmos in order to more directly experience it, allowing for a transcendental shift in consciousness. Kevin agreed the spiral was interesting to explore as a potential impetus to achieving expanded awareness.

A particular kind of spiral is reflected through the Fibonacci series, a sequence of numbers related to the golden ratio. The golden ratio (or phi, the golden mean), was defined by the famed Greek geometer and mathematician Euclid in his *Elements* (ca. 300 BCE) as the "extreme and mean ratio." It was further elucidated by the renowned Italian mathematician Fibonacci (nickname for Leonardo of Pisa, 1175–1250 CE) in his *Liber Abaci*, published in 1202. Note that his book provided the first introduction of the Hindu-Arabic number system (originating in India prior to the 4th century CE) to the Western world, liberating it from the shackles of the cumbersome Roman numerals system. Fibonacci's contributions included several key concepts from the Hindu-Arabic system (including not only the nine digits, but also the concept of zero and the decimal place system) that allowed for the robust expansion of mathematics in Europe that continues globally today.

Fibonacci numbers and the golden ratio show up widely in nature, such as in the spiral structure of galaxies and orbits of planets; the structure of crystals, pinecones, and pineapples; the beautiful curve of the nautilus's shell; the design of the bee's hive; and myriad other instances, including the human body itself. The human mouth and nose are each positioned at the golden mean ratio of the distance between the eyes and the bottom of the chin. In measuring the length of the joints of our fingers, each section (from the tip of the finger moving toward the wrist) is larger than the preceding one by roughly the golden ratio. The golden ratio also appears in the helical structure of DNA, precisely followed in the dimensions of its molecular spiral. Even the cochlea of the inner ear is in the shape of a spiral, and while each human's anatomy is slightly different, the proportions are very close to that of the Fibonacci spiral. Our human way of receiving sound depends on this spiral shape as each point of the cochlea is related to a different frequency.

"It is probably fair to say that the Golden Ratio has inspired thinkers of all disciplines like no other number in the history of mathematics," the Israeli astrophysicist Mario Livio stated. "Some of the greatest mathematical minds of all ages, from Pythagoras and Euclid in ancient Greece, through the medieval Italian mathematician Leonardo of Pisa and the Renaissance astronomer Johannes Kepler, to present-day scientific figures such as Oxford physicist Roger Penrose, have spent endless hours over this simple ratio and its properties. But the fascination with the Golden Ratio is not confined just to mathematicians. Biologists, artists, musicians, historians, architects, psychologists, and even mystics have pondered and debated the basis of its ubiquity and appeal."

Likewise, Karen and Kevin have investigated ways to harness the golden ratio into their recordings along with other harmonics found in nature. As an engineer, Kevin is very adept with math. They found that tones incorporating various harmonic principles were more pleasing and/or effective than others. I was intrigued by this approach since sound was such a fundamental component of my traversing in the spiritual realm. Music is actually sound expressed in a mathematical form. Mathematical precision is found throughout nature and can define our physical world in ways that are anything but random. If our world is structured through mathematical relationships, it makes sense that creating sound reflecting those relationships might serve as an engine to explore consciousness itself.

I cannot imagine trying to negotiate life without a regular practice of spiritual exploration and love to share these tools with every soul I encounter. Thus, I encouraged Karen and Kevin to make these recordings available to others, leading them to create their company Sacred Acoustics. Listening to these audio recordings helps me to focus before a presentation, enables a respite from stressful situations, and provides an opportunity to tap into creative inspiration or guidance for a particular problem. I continue to assist in the development of tones with Kevin and Karen and try to spend at least an hour or so daily listening to them (sometimes as much as two or three hours per day, if possible). This regular practice has become my preferred form of meditation with a focus on exploring vast unknown regions of conscious awareness and to return to the realms, beings, and divinity that I first encountered during my meningitis-induced coma.

While I have succeeded in reconnecting to the spiritual realm, it must be stated that I have not achieved the full hyperreality that I experienced during coma. Nor have we been able to precisely duplicate the sounds I heard during that 7-day spiritual journey, despite many attempts to do so. For that, I expect I will need to wait until my physical body is no longer available to house my consciousness. The veil separating us from the spiritual world is powerful and is there for a purpose, to keep us focused on our lives here on earth.

These "sound journeys" far exceed simply recalling memories from my NDE. They involve a robust and expanding interaction with all aspects of those realms and lead to broad enhancement of my insight, comprehension, creativity, relationships, etc. By opening this door to the cosmos on a daily basis over years, I have come into a much richer alignment with my higher soul and with the universe at large. "I" am no longer simply a "part" of the universe, but in many ways my mental/spiritual being overlaps perfectly with the cosmos in a holographic fashion. This is another way of expressing the oneness that is the holy grail of so many seekers throughout human history.

CHAPTER 10

BE THE LOVE
THAT YOU ARE

Someday, after mastering the winds, the waves, the tides, and gravity, we shall harness for God the energies of love, and then, for a second time in the history of the world, man will have discovered fire.

—PIERRE TEILHARD DE CHARDIN (1881–1955),
FRENCH PHILOSOPHER AND PALEONTOLOGIST

One of the most profound realizations over the course of my spiritual awakening has been that emotions are what give us "skin in the game," that apply value and meaning to the lessons we learn in living our human lives, whether of love or of loss. This has been a paradigm-shifting realization. Like many, I was raised with the understanding that expressing one's emotions was not necessarily an admirable quality. In other words, I was taught to "stuff it," and not to bother others with my emotional reactions to the challenges of life. Keeping a stiff upper lip and soldiering on, no matter what, were qualities that I learned from my mother and father, two hardworking and lovable souls. They had grown up during the Great Depression and spent their early adult years dealing with the horrific existential crisis offered up by the Second World War.

Born from good intentions in a struggle to endure, many in our Western culture share this quality of emotional restraint, but it doesn't necessarily serve us well.

At a conference in Chicago, I met spiritual teacher Gary Zukav and his wife, Linda Francis. Gary is a graduate of Harvard University and had been a Green Beret in the US Army Special Forces during the Vietnam War. He became captivated with the fascinating revelations of quantum mechanics and in 1979 wrote *The Dancing Wu Li Masters: An Overview of the New Physics,* a helpful resource for the layperson on this dense topic. Ten years later, Gary wrote *The Seat of the Soul,* which addresses human consciousness from a spiritual perspective. After teaching a workshop in Seattle, Karen and I were traveling through Oregon with my son Bond and were pleased to accept Gary and Linda's invitation to visit them at their home in Ashland for a few days.

Gary and I enjoyed a lively discussion about some of the grand revelations that Einstein had drawn from musing over the equivalence of gravitational and inertial mass. This was a fact known by physicists for three centuries, but had been simply dismissed as a curious correlation. Einstein's brilliance was that he knew to pursue such observations much more deeply than had other physicists. I had a deep appreciation for Einstein's thought experiments, and how he had used his own consciousness as the tool from which tremendous insights about the universe would spring forth. Engaging in these practices demonstrated the fundamental power of the observer and its connection to the Collective Mind.

I enjoyed these scientific discussions, but Gary was most interested in hearing from me about any significant changes I might have had in my personal life since my NDE. My complete flip away from scientific materialism seemed to permeate every aspect of my life, but Gary meant something deeper and more intimate.

"We have talked a great deal about how this experience has altered your understandings, your thoughts, the way you look at the world now. What I'm interested in now is how have these experiences changed you. If you can feel such a change, how have they affected you in the way you relate to the people around you?" Gary asked.

I had to give his question some thought.

"It's very apparent in all relationships. I now see us all as eternal souls and have come to see much more deeply how those boundaries of self that

I often was so restricted by before my coma really are artificial in so many ways," I answered.

"Can you give me an example of 'boundaries of self'? What would that look like if I were a spectator at the time, if I had walked by and noticed you interacting with someone? How would that be different from how you would behave or speak or engage someone now?"

"It's really my perception of self as part of this grander self that would to the outside observer appear as a much smoother, more mature, authentic acknowledgment of that oneness, of the love, that we are all part of something that is moving in that direction of understanding. It's very difficult to . . ." I attempted to explain.

"I can see, because what we're talking about now is emotions. Can you think of emotions that you had before the coma? Especially painful emotions like impatience or jealousy or anger or resentment or humiliation or powerlessness? Do some interactions still bring up those painful emotions? And, if so, what's the difference between how you engage now when those painful emotions are roaring through you (if they do), and how you would have reacted in the past?"

I struggled to find a specific example. I was not accustomed to acknowledging my personal emotions—before *or* after coma.

Gary refers to "authentic power" as a process of aligning our thoughts, emotions, and actions (personality) with our higher nature (soul) and realizing our strength truly lies within. The logic and understanding of the personality lies in the mind, but in order to meaningfully engage the soul, we must turn to our heart. And this requires careful attention to our feelings. Gary maintains that in our efforts to survive, we seek to control our surrounding environment. Acquisition of money or knowledge, wars fought over valuable resources, seeking status, loving relationships, or an attractive body, are representations of "external power." Attempting to change these outward circumstances is a common approach to solving problems. "If only my boss were kinder to me, my life would be so much better," we might tell ourselves. As we pursue external power, we look outside ourselves to resolve issues rather than looking inward at the source of our emotional pain. To move past striving to control the external world, it helps to have a deeper understanding of our inner spiritual nature, beyond the five physical senses, in order to create authentic power—our emotions are essential to this.

As we talked about this emotional awareness, Gary gave an example of being in conflict with a difficult person. Maybe he's doing something that you think is going to affect your future in a negative way, maybe he's continually critical. Instead of pursuing external power to change him, you might find what you need to change is something in yourself, perhaps by reacting with less anger and more compassion. This allows you to move into your full potential and not to be bound by experiences of fear and resentment and negativity.

"Do you ever have to use your will to keep yourself from acting the way you would have before the coma?" Gary asked me.

"I'm still in the process of growing from this, so yes, I do have to be conscious and make a willful decision to be consistent with my evolving worldview of today because some of those automatic responses are still wired into my system. But I don't have to be controlled by them, and it's very liberating to come to see it that way. I realize now it's about how I can modify my own behavior, that changing myself actually has ramifications to all of those around me."

"That's what we call a responsible choice. Experiences come about from an aspect of either love or fear. If it comes from fear it's painful—anger, jealousy, or resentment. If it comes from love, it's patience, caring, contentment, and appreciation of all of life. A responsible choice is one that creates consequences for which I'm willing to assume responsibility rather than letting the conflict escalate. Deciding not to act as a frightened part of my personality is the moment of growing spiritually," Gary explained.

Despite not being able to outwardly express emotional awareness, I realized I had absolutely begun to make significant changes in my life. I now view all souls as eternal beings with unique qualities and purposes. Their actions result from issues in their own lives, and there are likely perfectly good explanations for behavior I might have previously taken more personally. Acting with compassion is far easier from this wider perspective.

Those who study near-death experiences remark that approximately 80 percent of marriages dissolve after one partner has had an NDE. The shift in one's worldview, interests, and perceptions about life engendered by such a life-changing experience can deviate so radically as to undermine even a previously stable relationship. My former wife, Holley, and I had had many happy times in our early lives together, including being blessed with two sons who mean more than life to both of us. However, our marriage had been difficult in the years before my coma, and my significant change afterward seemed to bring us to a choice point. I am forever grateful to Holley for the support she offered throughout our decades together, during my coma, and especially during my recovery from it. But it became clear that our lives together were not meant to last forever. Making a choice based in love, we separated amicably in 2012 and remain cordial and mutually supportive.

Every interaction in life is an opportunity to grow spiritually. Every interaction is perfect, in fact, for the spiritual growth of one's self and everyone involved, given the choices that each party has made. In a universe that is alive and wise and compassionate, we can use these opportunities to create authentic power and align the personality with the soul.

"Your emotions are messages from your soul that bring you priceless information. If you do not receive the information, it is delivered again and again. Once you move from being unconsciously controlled by fearful emotions to consciously choosing to act on loved-based emotions, you are in a position to change your life, your future, and your world," Gary shared.

Applying these concepts in his own life, Gary himself had transformed from an angry addicted man. He now actively lives the teachings he generously shares with others. I understood these concepts intellectually and had begun to apply them in my life, but I realized some patterns ingrained in my earlier days were still in effect.

As a neurosurgeon, I occasionally had to break the news to a family that a loved one had died. Such unremitting loss presented a challenge—I tended to bond with my patients and their families, and such losses could never simply become routine. However, I constructed a certain degree of protective buffering to shield me from the full onslaught of emotions accompanying daily exposure to death and its aftermath. I had come to believe that showing emotions was a sign of weakness. In essence, training from my youth to deny my feelings in an effort to stay strong in the face of such daunting hardship as regular participation in death and dying provided some respite. Such measures sometimes seemed like a small bandage trying to staunch the hemorrhaging from a mortal wound.

My neuroscientific training had implied that emotions were nothing more than the subjective expression of the interaction of various hormones and chemical neurotransmitters (the molecules nerve cells use to communicate with each other) with receptors on the cells of the nervous system. In discussions with my father around the topic of my adoption, he would always assure me that there was absolutely no way I could remember any of the events in the first weeks and months of my life, and thus I should have no emotional baggage around my adoption. He believed, like many, that infants were simply incapable of forming memories. Research maintains that memory formation, at least that to which we routinely have access later in life, begins around age 3. As the chairman of a top neurosurgical training program, I assumed that his words were true—after all, he should know the truth about the subject of memory. And so, I proceeded simply to ignore any feelings I had around the adoption issue, at least consciously.

I've since come to realize that he was wrong. In expanded states of awareness, I have recovered memories going back very early in life, and these have included the realization that the perceived abandonment by my birth mother, initially on day eleven of my life when I was hospitalized for "failing to thrive," was an event that was so dramatic and shocking that it left scars that are still apparent in my psyche. That abandonment event hit with such an impact that it left an afterimage with the smoking crater of my birth mother's absence planted squarely in the middle. Such abandonment often manifests as a feeling of low self-worth, i.e., that I was unworthy of my mother's love and was thus left behind.

There is no way to deny the power and effect of that deep emotional trauma, even though the specific details of such episodic memories can be difficult to recover. This is especially true when compared to the way we remember other events occurring after achieving the "age of reason" (around age 6 or 7). In theory, those earliest memories form before our linguistic brain has significantly constructed its library of objects and relationships, and are thus more difficult to retrieve once our dominant form of experience has become based in language. It is that difficulty in remembering the details of such an early trauma that contribute to making it so resilient and difficult to assuage or treat.

A story told to me about events in my young life helped to clarify some of the power of such an abandonment memory, applied in that same epoch. My parents married in 1942 and decided to adopt in the early

1950s when they did not seem able to conceive on their own. As often happens, they discovered soon after my adoption in April 1954 that they had indeed conceived a child, and so we were blessed with the birth of Betsy when I was 18 months of age. I did not fully appreciate the blessing as much as they did, for I reportedly stopped walking soon after Betsy arrived in our home in June 1955. Based on descriptions of my behavior (especially during the days Mom was in the hospital delivering Betsy), I was inconsolable and took weeks to get over this new challenge to my sense of importance in the world. I suspect my exuberant recoil at the arrival of a perceived competitor was rooted in my deep desire to avoid the pain of being given away again. After a few weeks of being carried around, I finally manned up to the situation and began walking again.

Of course, childhood abandonment and other types of emotional wounds are far more common than just those encountered in the world of adoption, and they often provide a source of perceived difficulty. Karen felt another brand of abandonment as an infant when her younger brother was born just 11 months after her. He suffered from hyaline membrane disease, a respiratory-distress syndrome found in newborns. Following a ten-day hospitalization, he naturally required extra attention. Karen cried incessantly and would be silenced only if her mother picked her up or if her mother was in direct line of sight.

Identifying such a wound—even those that are inflicted without intention—is absolutely necessary in gaining proper perspective of it. For especially deep issues, any truly effective therapy involves engaging the obscure emotional power of the original event, which is more difficult than dealing with other life traumas occurring after age 7. For example, one might have inexplicable anger issues related to an early trauma, yet be unable to make the connection that the angry behavior originates in that ancient abandonment wound. In my case, the *intellectual* knowledge that the perceived abandonment was actually a responsible choice by two teenagers trying to do the best, hardest, and most loving thing possible by giving their beloved baby up for adoption was not enough. It does not help in my dealing with the *emotional* side that only acknowledges the perceived abandonment and the life-altering impact it had at the time it occurred.

Gary's focus on developing emotional awareness seemed critically important. But some emotions are so deep that to fully address them is challenging. While my own experience is limited, hypnosis is a form of therapy used by psychiatrists and other therapists to help release emotional trauma. Using guided imagery and suggestion, the subject is induced into a trancelike, or hypnagogic, state, where the body is extremely relaxed, but the mind is attentively aware. Unlike stage hypnotists who command subjects to behave in strange ways, the subject maintains complete free will. In theory, the subconscious part of the mind is accessed as the conscious analytical mind takes a back seat. This allows for the therapist to make helpful suggestions for behavioral change—for example, to quit smoking. To address trauma, suppressed memories more easily come to the surface, allowing their examination from a fresh perspective.

Sometimes, traumas that are caused by severe physical shocks to the body can be addressed in a similar fashion. During a swim-meet delay due to thunder, New York hypnotherapist Paul Aurand was struck by lightning. His first stunned realization was that his feet and legs began to vibrate. His whole body then went rigid as a roaring buzz climbed up into his chest and arms. Every muscle in his body tensed and cramped as he felt the most excruciating pain of his life. His hat popped off as car keys flew out of his hands and glasses were torn from his face.

"Will it ever stop?" he raged against the relentless charge of energy. "Get out of my body!"

Like a missile, stiff like a statue, he was thrown backward 6 feet into the air and then fell to the street, his head bouncing on the hard pavement. His body jerked uncontrollably, but he couldn't will his legs to move; the parts of him that were not numb were in intense pain.

Forty-five minutes passed before Paul was rushed to a small country hospital in Warwick, New York. In the ambulance, Paul gradually began to regain the ability to move his body and the numbness lessened. He was relieved to realize he would likely walk again.

As he waited to be examined, Paul remained in shock, moving from sobbing and laughing to cracking morbid jokes and feeling grateful to be alive. Other times, he had the feeling of being superhuman and walked around the hospital with a blanket around his shoulders confident that he was the Savior, which wasn't even part of his belief system. He knew at the time it was strange behavior, yet he felt contained within him an invincible force of power beyond himself.

Days after being discharged, Paul's upper back was in constant pain and he had substantial short-term memory loss. For example, he stopped to put gas in the car and wondered why the tank was already full; his 3-year-old son reminded him he had filled it just a few minutes earlier. Hours before a thunderstorm, he could feel the same pain in his legs that he had suffered during the lightning strike and he would be frightened of a return strike. Conventional medicine failed to bring relief. After weeks of continued symptoms, Paul's energy level was still frustratingly low, his memory loss was frightening, and he continued to carry pain and fear from the experience. Knowing of the power of hypnotherapy from his own practice, he organized and participated in a workshop offered by David Quigley, founder of Alchemical Hypnosis, a therapeutic technique designed to release trauma. During this intensive weekend, David facilitated an individual session for Paul while the rest of the group supported the process. After assuming a comfortable position on a pad on the floor, David guided him to recall the memories of the day he was struck by lightning.

Paul began to relive the entire event in slow motion, at first in his mind's eye, right up to the moment the lightning entered his body. Then, his feet began to tingle and shake, slowly at first, then more violently. The shaking slowly rose up his legs following the same course the lightning had traveled, lasting much longer than his original experience. Ten or fifteen minutes into it, his legs shook harder and faster as the group looked on, quite alarmed. The shaking rose up into his hips and back as his whole body began to convulse in wave after wave as his body undulated on the floor. Each wave brought more memories of the terrible pain he had experienced, but each wave also released more and more of the trauma held in his muscles and nerves.

With David's encouragement, he stopped fighting and welcomed the lightning into his body. The violent shaking and convulsing gradually subsided and he relived the moment his heart stopped for a few seconds. Everything grew dark and he entered a great void of nothingness.

"Why did this happen? What are you to learn from it?" David gently guided Paul to ask.

In that moment, Paul felt bathed in that indescribable, limitless unconditional love, reminiscent of what he had felt while walking around in the emergency room.

"Listen with your heart," a message came to him. "Listen to spirit, meditate, turn inward, and listen. Spirit speaks to you constantly; all you need to do is listen. Use your wonderful mind, but listen to spirit."

Almost three hours had passed and Paul felt completely transformed, like a baby starting over. Remarkably, he realized the invincible superhuman power he felt within him directly after the lightning strike was actually the indescribable love he had touched. Years later, Paul is completely free of the chronic back pain caused by the lightning strike and is far less fearful of electric storms and electricity in general. The regression process through which David had ushered him allowed him to release the physical and emotional trauma he suffered by reliving the experience and letting it go.

I had experienced the full healing power of unconditional love when my brain inexplicably healed following my coma, but bringing the full power of that love into daily existence proved challenging. Many assume it is reserved for when we are in nonphysical form and, for a few years after my coma, I tended to agree. My focus had been on the mind, after all, and consciousness seemed very much related to the brain—I felt the answers would ultimately lie there. Belief systems can have quite a strong hold, and my pre-coma materialist mind-set was not so simple to relinquish when attempting to explain matters here on earth.

What helped me to move past this was Karen's elucidation of heart consciousness. Through her various experiences and practices, she had become quite adept at feeling and managing the energy surrounding her heart and could feel it expand and contract as it responded to different moods and environments, or how it shifted when altering her emotional state. When I described the incredible force of love I experienced during my coma journey, she seemed familiar with such energy.

"I have encountered that myself while in altered states of awareness, when being attentive to my heart or being out in nature. I can't say for sure it's the same thing you felt, but it is an amazing, expansive energy that I have been enveloped within and merged with on many occasions, often moving me to tears. We all have the potential to become containers of that love and radiate it to others here on earth. You don't have to wait for it to happen unexpectedly, like during your coma," she explained.

Karen had made her initial breakthrough in directly feeling her heart's energy after reading *The Biology of Transcendence* by Joseph

Chilton Pearce. He suggested that if you can't feel your heart, try conjuring a feeling of gratitude and then notice how the heart feels. That made sense, given HeartMath's data about the effect of emotional response on the heart's magnetic field. But actually doing it took practice. At first, there was nothing at all, but eventually she noticed a dull ache or heavy sensation in her heart. Still, it was better than nothing; she thought she was on the right track.

She considered what thoughts and feelings made her feel the most "warm and fuzzy." At age 6, Karen's family dog, Puff, had given birth to puppies under her bed—a magical childhood occasion that stayed with her. She discovered that when she imagined again being with Puff and her sweet, innocent, playful puppies, she felt (or created) a warm, soothing feeling in her heart area. She began to practice invoking this feeling in quiet moments. Later, when she described this to me, it reminded me of my postcoma experience with prayer, when I felt nothing but gratitude. Up until then, I had not considered the direct involvement of the heart.

"As I became more adept at feeling and managing the energy surrounding my heart," Karen recounted, "I began to feel it expand and contract as it responded to different moods and environments, or how it shifted along with my emotional state. At first it was sometimes painful, but I learned to release the pain through various methods, and eventually it became possible to feel wonderfully expansive heart energy that can best be described as love. The love I had felt previously came from my mind or thoughts, perhaps directed toward a person. But this love was different—it resided within me, and I recognized it as the source of my nonphysical self."

Some people seem to radiate heart energy naturally. If you think about the most generous, welcoming people in your life, you can probably call up an example. In my own life, my first time meeting His Holiness the fourteenth Dalai Lama during his visit to Charlottesville, Virginia, especially stands out. As His Holiness approached our position in the receiving line, I remember feeling a powerful wave of warmth as he came within 20 feet of us. As he drew nearer, he seemed to share a connection with each soul as he greeted them with a handshake and glance in the eyes. When he reached me, he held my hands in his as he peered deeply into my eyes with a warm smile and a twinkle in his eye. Time seemed to stand still. I'll never forget the way he made me feel seen and loved with his very presence.

I was intrigued about the love Karen experienced in the here and now and wanted to learn more, so she and I discussed these concepts at length. I often attempted to describe that love using the limited vocabulary of our language, but Karen encouraged me to actively *feel* it.

"Do you love yourself?" Karen asked during one of our early conversations.

"No," I stated frankly, after a few moments of earnest reflection.

I realized that, to some degree, feelings of unworthiness related to being abandoned by my birth mother were still in effect. Deeply ingrained beliefs, especially emotional wounds, are not so simple to completely release. Prior to this, I had found it easier to direct loving thoughts toward others rather than direct that love inwardly and really feel it. While much healing had taken place following the reconnection with my birth family that began in October 2007, it was not a matter of simply letting go of the emotional impact of perceived abandonment.

When this came up in a conversation with Karen, she was deeply sympathetic.

"We all have blockages like that, although some are more extreme than others. It's a universal wound that we feel inadequate or unworthy of being loved, so how could we possibly find it easy to love ourselves? Some feel so devalued, they even struggle to *like* themselves," she explained with familiar assurance.

I understood intellectually that loving oneself is a critical step to fully being able to love others, but I didn't know how to get past my blocks. One thing was clear: I would not be able to analyze or think my way into loving myself. It seemed a simple enough concept, but it was absolutely impossible to achieve through thinking alone.

With Karen's help, I began the work of releasing my blocks. This is a process of letting myself feel the original emotion and not avoiding its impact only to end up repressing it again. There is no way out but through. I tried to let go of any reservations that I was not worthy. Karen encouraged me to imagine that love already exists inside my heart. Over many sessions, I used the reference point of the love I felt during my deep coma journey and felt it grow within me. We have the potential to act as conduits for the healing power of that unconditional love at the core of all existence, and this seemed like a way to consciously achieve it.

You are deeply loved and cherished, forever, I recalled from my coma journey, and internalized that powerful message, along with the associated emotional state.

"Actively conjure up that feeling of being loved," Karen continued to remind me. "Eventually, it will become automatic, like breathing."

As I recognized the love coming from the divinity at the core of all existence as an internal part of me, here in my physical body, I began to create the earthly experience of feeling that love from within. I eventually became able to connect with this feeling of oneness and love quite readily during expanded states of awareness, and this has become a useful reference point when stressful events take place. I remain a work in progress as far as fully "becoming" love in my everyday interactions and relationships. I strive to recognize and constructively express my emotions rather than keep them stuffed inside. Life continues to present challenges that help me to grow. As I do this, I become more aligned with my higher self and more authentic to my true nature, as can we all.

CHAPTER 11

RESOLVING A KEY QUESTION

I shall not commit the fashionable stupidity of
regarding everything I cannot explain as a fraud.

—Carl G. Jung (1875–1961),
Swiss psychoanalyst

Near-death experiences and related lines of evidence suggest that our awareness does not end following death and, very possibly, that our souls are eternal. The ultimate evidence for such survival would be a demonstration that the distinctive personality or memories of a given soul remain intact after departing the physical body when the brain is no longer available to support ongoing consciousness. There are multiple lines of evidence to validate this concept, including not only near-death and shared-death experiences, but also after-death communications, deathbed visions, and dream apparitions. These sorts of phenomena typically occur spontaneously, making them challenging to study scientifically. But there is an enormous amount of evidence to suggest that they do occur, frequently, and that some people are able to tune in to departed souls intentionally, and quite fluently.

The ability to communicate with the dead and pick up on their signs are skills held by psychic mediums. Movies and television shows often characterize mediums as complete frauds, with elaborate demonstrations revealing how information is gathered ahead of time that is delivered at the right moment through a hidden transmitter near the alleged medium's ear. There are courses that teach one how to perform "cold readings," which entails making general statements and then reading subtle body language and reactions in people to determine what next to say, often fooling desperate people who wish to make contact that their loved one is present and speaking through them. It's saddening that there are instances of deception, but it is crucial to point out that this by no means indicates that *all* mediums are frauds. Many seem to have natural skills, while others open up to the spiritual realm after establishing a regular routine of meditation.

Many modern scientists remain skeptical (especially those ignorant of the research), but those who seek comfort following the death of a loved one often turn to mediums in their state of grief. Many are amazed at the information that is provided, often details that no one else could have known. These experiences defy scientific explanation, but seem quite real to the person who receives the remarkable information. Some psychic mediums are aware that their extraordinary abilities are potentially latent in us all, but people tend to distrust their own intuition, conceding that any personal communications with the souls of departed loved ones might be just wishful thinking or the result of an overactive imagination. Hence, to garner such information from another person, notably one who should have no way of acquiring such information though standard channels, serves to validate its authenticity.

That's precisely how it worked for me after I met with a medium for the first time. Up until then, my only personal experience had been about a decade prior to my coma, when my sisters had consulted a medium named Blanche in California and talked about our family. Blanche seemed to be tuned in to future events concerning our parents and my sisters, but she had not mentioned me.

"What about our brother?" Betsy had asked toward the end of their reading, curious as to any information the psychic might be picking up about my energy.

"Oh . . . oh . . . he is not long for this world," had been Blanche's ominous reply. My sisters were so upset by this dark premonition that they never told me about it—at least, not until after my coma.

Of course, they could have shared their concerns with me back then, and the materialist scientist in me would have scoffed at the idea that a psychic medium could know anything worthy of actual concern. I would have paid it no mind.

I've learned a lot since then.

Just as people are comforted by my message that our souls are eternal and survive beyond their physical death, mediums bring comfort by connecting with the deceased and delivering messages to those still alive here on earth. Distraught people often find comfort from such communications, relieving them from sometimes devastating and crippling grief. But are these messages authentic? Or are people simply gullible and more susceptible to deception in their distressed state?

I was fortunate to have the opportunity to learn for myself. A few weeks after meeting John Audette at the first IANDS meeting where I presented, he offered to arrange a psychic reading. He and Edgar Mitchell had been greatly impressed by recent readings from a medium named Laura Lynne Jackson, author of *The Light Between Us*.

"She is quite good. Amazing, in fact," John shared with me over the phone.

"I'm game. It might help me understand more about my experience," I admitted.

The only information Laura had received was my full name and the fact that I had experienced an NDE. My story had not yet been made public through the publication of *Proof of Heaven* and therefore, aside from John telling her about it (which he and she denied), I could not think of a way she might have learned any details about my experience.

"I have a male stepping in. This is a father figure for me. Your dad has crossed, yes?" Laura Lynne began.

"Yes," I replied.

"Okay, because it's a father figure for me. I'm supposed to acknowledge, you have a son here, yes?"

"Yes."

"Okay, he wants me to acknowledge a son here and being very proud, so that's his grandson. And I know you share your father's name, obviously, because you're the 'third' correct?"

"Right, yes."

"All right, then you have a son who is the 'fourth,' yes?"

"I do."

"Okay, on the other side, the name goes back generations, but then there's a generation that it skips. So it's almost like if your father's named after his father, who's named after his father, there was a generation without the name, but then a generation prior to that the name repeats. Do you understand this?"

I was careful to keep my responses short. I didn't want to reveal anything that might give her additional information to read from. But inside, I was struck by Laura Lynne's remark. It was a complete mystery to me how she could have picked up on the fact that the "Eben Alexander" naming tradition had shifted several generations back. My sisters did not even know the details of that altered lineage! In fact, my grandfather Eben Alexander Sr. was originally Eben Alexander III. Since his own father, Eben Alexander Jr., had already passed, rather than name his son (my father) Eben Alexander IV, he decided to begin the naming tradition again. From that point forward, he referred to himself as Eben Alexander and his son as Eben Alexander Jr. Thus, I became Eben Alexander III rather than Eben Alexander V. It was remarkable that Laura Lynne had picked up on this change in naming. This was an incredibly obscure fact that I had become aware of in discussions with Dad early in my life. It had never occurred to me to discuss it with anyone else because it seemed so trivial.

Up until then, I had the mind-set of conventional scientists who simply dismiss all mediums as frauds. But Laura Lynne was a Windbridge-certified research medium who is actively involved in scientific experimental assessment of this phenomenon. I was shocked to learn there were research protocols for studying mediums.

Windbridge Institute is an organization that has gone to great lengths to create strict scientific protocols in order to investigate the abilities and methods of mediums. Through a rigorous eight-step screening process, they have identified pool of talented and reliable mediums with whom to perform regular research. Following rigorous training and a series of demanding quintuple-blind exercises to test their abilities, certain mediums become certified to be Windbridge-certified research mediums. Windbridge follows a unique and stringent protocol to determine mediumship skills and maintains a strict code of ethics that the mediums must agree to follow in order to participate in ongoing scientific research.

The strictest part of their evaluation protocol occurs with two blinded phone readings. They anticipate all potential influences on the outcome by eliminating any possibility for cold readings, fraud, experimenter cues, general statements, and evaluation bias from the sitter (the one receiving the reading).

Windbridge has collected the first names of more than 1,000 discarnates (departed loved ones) from volunteers who desire to make contact. From that list of discarnate names, two are chosen by Experimenter 1 (E1) that are judged to be distinctly different from each another. E1 works with the sitters to explain their role in the process. They are coached by E1 ahead of time to request in their mind that the desired discarnate actually shows up to provide the specific data needed for verification. E1 then hands off the two first names of the discarnates to Experimenter 2 (E2) who is completely isolated from the sitters and descriptions of the discarnates. E2 then schedules two separate phone readings (about a week apart) with the medium to be tested and in each reading asks a standard list of questions about the discarnates, including a physical description, hobbies, personality, cause of death, and any messages for the sitter.

The recorded conversation is simplified into definitive statements, such as "curly red hair" or "worked with trains." A third experimenter (E3) then emails the statements to the sitters (whose emails are provided by E1), who then score the statements for accuracy. Each sitter evaluates both readings with an attempt to select which qualities best match the discarnate known to them. This is why two very different discarnates are selected by E1 in the first stage, so that the descriptions are easily distinguishable. This process ensures five levels of blinding in order to prevent any undue subjective influences.

Study results using these parameters demonstrate that this phenomenon is quite real. In one study, the results indicated a statistically significant 76 percent accuracy rate.[1] It is impressive that, given these strict parameters, there is *any* accuracy at all! During a typical reading outside of research studies, most mediums speak directly to their sitters, yet these mediums were given just a first name with no other information and were able to provide enough details for 76 percent of the sitters to accurately identify them. This protocol is designed to ensure mediums aren't poten-tially picking up information telepathically from the sitter. While the results do not unequivocally point toward survival of the soul after death, a curious part of the experimental protocol involves the sitter requesting active participation from their discarnate loved one prior to the reading. It seems our intentional interaction with the deceased is part of the process, as we seem to be forever connected to others through our love for them.

"I have to tell you," Laura Lynne said to me, "your father comes in very formally and very nobly to me and I feel like he's a great man and he did a lot of great deeds when he was here as well. Does it make sense to you, that he was a hero when he was here?"

"Oh, yeah," I replied.

"That's how I get it. I feel he's a teacher. I have a sense that he was renowned in his field and yet there's no ego on his part. I'm reading all this through his energy, but it's not like he's telling me, 'I was renowned' or anything like that."

Laura Lynne was right. Dad was the consummate hero of my life. He was eminently respected by his colleagues as a highly intelligent, compas-sionate, and capable neurosurgeon. He had been the president of several national and international neurosurgical organizations, head of the Harvard Medical Alumni Association, and was chief of staff at the then-named Baptist Hospital and Wake Forest University Medical Center for more than twenty years. My encounters with hundreds of colleagues, staff, patients, and patient families over the years drilled into me their great admiration of his exceptional qualities as a physician and human being. He treated everyone equally and with respect and, in spite of his extreme self-confidence and competence, always presented a warm and humble presence.

"Okay, I feel like when you were on the other side, you met him there and there was knowledge that was shared; that's how he's giving it to me. But I feel like you've been allowed to remember most of it; that's how I'm getting it."

"Uh-huh, yeah, I do remember most of it and, in fact, he was *not* there. That was one of the interesting things, although I did . . ."

"Yes, he was. Maybe you will remember this later."

Behind my blasé responses, my heart was pounding. I was absolutely shocked at Laura Lynne's revelations. Laura Lynne knew I had had an NDE, but she knew none of the details and nothing else about my life. My father had passed over just four years before my coma. If my NDE had followed the general layout of those reported over the last few thousand years, he would have been there front and center as an important part of my journey—yet in my coma memories he was nowhere to be found. That absence made me feel confused, but also cheated—why hadn't I seen him? Was he prevented from visiting in some way? Had he chosen to withhold contact? Had I misunderstood the nature of my experience? It seemed a cruel trick indeed to have undergone such a profound spiritual journey, but never to have encountered my father, whom I dearly missed.

Some mediums report that we all have these same abilities to communicate with the souls of departed loved ones, but that we have not developed these skills like they have. Many people who do have such communications with their loved ones who have passed naturally wonder if it is just wishful thinking, perhaps due to their overactive imagination. That is why many prefer to have a third party (i.e., the medium) serve as the messenger—their lack of personal knowledge about the departed soul allows for validation if they provide sufficiently detailed information that they should have no other way of knowing.

Sometimes such a personal communication from the beyond requires no validation whatsoever. Shirley (not her real name) lingered after a luncheon talk I gave at an IANDS meeting to share this story.

Shirley's dad had died three years earlier, and she had asked and prayed for him to give her some sign he was still present for her, yet such a message never seemed to come. One day, she was driving 70 mph on an interstate highway during a rainstorm when, suddenly and unbidden, she heard her father's voice for the first time since his death.

"Shirley, you should pull over into the left lane. That tractor-trailer truck coming up behind you is going to blow a tire, and I don't want you to be hurt," he said calmly.

She reacted quickly and carefully steered over into the left lane just as the truck sped past and, as it passed, there was a loud bang as strips of rubber flew everywhere in the predicted tire explosion. She had never witnessed a tire blow with such a ruckus, but by being an extra lane over, her car was undamaged and she continued on. She was absolutely stupe-fied by her father's voice and warning, yet she felt calm and serene. Since then, he has appeared to her in dreams, and occasionally he coaches her in major life decisions. But she'll never forget that first contact!

I had not communicated with my father in any such fashion and hoped that using binaural-beat brain-wave entrainment to return to the realms I had encountered during my coma journey could help me solve the mystery of my father's absence during my NDE. The critical develop-ment came quite unexpectedly one Thursday morning in February, eight months prior to my conversation with Laura Lynne. In the early stages of using sound to access expanded states of consciousness, I was learning about the work of Robert Monroe, whose institute was quite near my home. Monroe was an early pioneer in researching binaural beats to achieve out-of-body states. I started listening to a 45-minute sound jour-ney to address the question that nagged at me: "Am I on the right path?"

Ten minutes into the recording, I had returned to the scene familiar from recent listening sessions—a magnificent white marble bridge reach-ing out across a deep gorge filled with roiling mists and clouds (in my mind's eye view). Illuminated mainly by a soft glow from the bridge itself, I saw numerous dark silhouettes of the denizens of this realm, progres-sively obscured by the distant fog. I sensed them to be souls of the departed, here to interact with visitors from the incarnate physical realms, like me, as well as with guides and angels.

The richness of the scene increased as I allowed the tones on the recording to take me deeper and deeper. My awareness broadened as unbridled consciousness enveloped me. My perspective shifted slowly as my awareness rose up and over the side of the glowing marble bridge, lighter than a feather, and then slowly descended into the clouds churning over the gorge that dropped steeply out of sight beneath me. I felt deep reverence and blissful joy, and surrendered to the full force of my higher soul taking over.

A black-and-white checkerboard pattern began forming up out of the mists—a smooth floor hewn into the very walls of the gorge. Figures emerged into view—a café with scattered patrons, some pairs absorbed in deep conversation. My awareness floated toward one small, round table near the edge. Two young men were there, deep in discussion and occasionally laughing. I was shocked to recognize the man facing away from me at an angle—my father!

Thinking of that moment of recognition still sends chills up my spine.

Although my mother and sisters had shared occasional stories of sensing my father's soul in dreams, I had not been similarly blessed. I'd sought him intentionally in other meditations to no avail, but now, deep in this brain-wave entrained journey I was taking to explore the question of whether or not I was on the right path, he suddenly appeared.

The man sitting across from my father was Agnew Bahnson, whom I recognized immediately to be my father's college roommate at the University of North Carolina at Chapel Hill in the early 1930s, although at the time I had no idea why he was his companion in this particular scene. Both men were in their early twenties, glowing, at the absolute peak of health. They both appeared so young and vital! That was no surprise, given what I had been learning about the myriad after-death communications that pepper humanity with the evidence that our souls do not end with bodily death, that our relationships with other members of our soul group continue on. All physical impairments present at the time of physical death have often vanished when one encounters lost loved ones in that spiritual realm—they appear as their perfect form at an ideal age, often late teens to early twenties, not as the age at which they passed over (whether it be older, or younger).

As I recognized my father, he turned to look directly at me. With a broad and knowing smile, absolutely filled with love and truth, he winked at me, then turned back to rejoin the animated discussion he was having with the other handsome young man at the table.

It was the same wink he used to give me to punctuate a story or lesson he might have shared in life when I was but a young lad. It triggered a tsunami of understanding in answer to my stated inquiry for this particular listening session: "Am I on the right path?" Typical of the unfiltered flow of information I received during my coma and often encountered on such meditative journeys, his answer came as a rich, multifaceted network of communication—what I sometimes call a "thought ball." It was an affirmation, but it also included all of the relevant nuances and variations necessary for more complete comprehension: Yes, my journey would bring deeper understanding of the nature of consciousness, and greater knowledge about the nature of reality. Yes, through differential sound-frequency enhancement of transcendental conscious states I could access those realms; and, yes, I would be equipped to participate in the expansion and sharing of that technology.

Though it went beyond mere words, that wink somehow communicated so much. Dad was letting me know that his soul was deeply involved in my NDE (as Laura Lynne had picked up), but that it was crucial that he not be "apparent" to me during the NDE (I attribute the double entendre nature of the word *apparent* to him, and his smiling wink). If I had recognized his presence as my guide during my NDE, if my NDE had followed a common pattern others have been through, I might have been more willing to assume my experience was simply "a trick of the dying brain," as my doctors had initially assured me.

That was why my guardian angel had been the lovely girl companion, my birth sister whom I had never known, and not my beloved father. I had described her appearance and my knowing of her in detail to family and friends soon after awakening from my coma, and had been struck by how clearly I remembered so much about her, yet also had sufficient clarity in those memories to know I had never met her in my life before coma. Those issues had haunted me in my efforts to comprehend my experience, yet they had driven me to seek better answers. Now it all started to make more sense.

The beta audio tones signaled the termination of the sound-journey exercise, as my expanded awareness felt the constriction of returning to my physical human form. My mind was still reeling from the experience and struggling to make sense of it. But I was giddy nonetheless.

This beautiful experience helped me to further open my mind to the grand possibilities and connections that we all share, and to trust that the universe will provide us with the evidence we need to demonstrate our shared purpose and connection, and that death is not so final. We simply need to open our minds and hearts to receive the message.

Typically such communications come as a surprise, like this encounter with my father. Those in grief who receive such contact often feel great comfort and relief from their sadness, but how can all of us get reassuring messages from deceased loved ones? According to many mediums, those on the other side often try hard to get our attention, but we simply don't notice. After-death communication (ADC) is not uncommon, as illustrated in hundreds of stories recounted in *Hello From Heaven,* by Bill and Judy Guggenheim, who collected more than 3,000 examples. Messages come in a wide variety of forms, including during dreams or meditation, through signs and symbols, electronic anomalies, inexplicable synchronicities, or, more directly, through visions, smells, sounds, or touch.

The first step to manifesting an ADC is to be open to its possibility. Often, all it takes is to mentally ask to be shown a sign that a loved one is still present. After asking, it's critical to stay patient and alert to anything significant that might appear in your path, often in repetitious or unexpected fashion. While some ADCs are obvious and profound, many are subtler and require us to pay extra attention. Those that come in continuous patterns are especially powerful. A sign may come in the form of a butterfly or other type of imagery, but whatever it is, it will be something obviously related to the deceased person and often quite personal and unique. While falling asleep at night, imagine you are with the person who passed, really feel what it was like to be with them, and request that they show up in a dream. It may not happen right away, but keep trying, as it can take weeks or even months to develop sufficient sensitivity.

ADCs cannot be willed into existence, but becoming more receptive to inner promptings can help. Along with its many other benefits, a regular meditation practice will improve intuitive skills and create a peaceful stillness within. This state of being connects us to the spiritual realm and is a wonderful space from which to invite an encounter. Learning to trust that connection brings countless benefits.

CHAPTER 12

THE ANSWERS LIE WITHIN US ALL

We cannot teach people anything; we can only help them discover it within themselves.

—GALILEO GALILEI (1564–1642),
ITALIAN ASTRONOMER

It is incumbent on each of us to pay attention to why we are here and what is our purpose. Focusing on our role in the larger scheme offers tremendous power over our lives. Consciousness is a continuum in which at every stage we have the opportunity for learning and growth. Many people, like myself, find such revelations through a near-death experience or other impromptu connection to the spiritual realm. But any of us can achieve the same goal by cultivating a connection to our own higher nature. One must intentionally "step outside" of mundane waking consciousness to perceive a grander view—it cannot be fully appreciated from within the Supreme Illusion. When one accepts that the physical brain does not create mind but serves to allow in universal consciousness, "going within" is actually the means of "going out" to know more of the universe.

It is the awareness, or the observer, within each of us that is at the heart of the deep mystery of the mind-body discussion and confounding experiments in quantum physics. Through regular practice, strengthening our connection with that inner observer allows us to apply profound understanding and influence in the course of our daily lives. Developing this awareness enhances our link with our "higher soul," which connects us to Collective Mind.

Karen and I regularly teach workshops in which we demonstrate techniques for exploring consciousness and exercising that inner observer. One of our main teachings is on how to engage the heart in these practices. I remind people of the powerful force of love I encountered in the deepest part of my coma journey and how we all can become conduits of that love. Karen then relates how to begin to do exactly that by increasing awareness of the heart. She describes how to imagine something for which you are grateful and then noticing how that feels in the area surrounding the heart. For her, that was her recollection of playing with puppies. But for someone else, it could be the memory of a beautiful sunset or a joy-filled occasion; each of us will select something different.

As we inhabit the thought and feeling of that memory, the energetic heart will begin to respond. The feeling may be subtle at first, but after a time, a lighter or more expansive sensation in the heart becomes more obvious. You can do this in quiet moments while lying in bed or daydreaming during a break from work. It might start as a warm or tingling sensation, perhaps a fluttering or quivering feeling. Once you increase awareness of this, you can begin to manage it. Practice this repeatedly throughout the day; there is no limit to how frequently, but just a few minutes each time is enough to start.

That feeling that you have is being generated and felt within your heart. Realize what that means: You *are* the love; it is generated from inside of you. Rather than directing loving thoughts *toward* yourself, simply *be* the love that you are. As this becomes more comfortable, begin to practice expanding your heart field to positive effect on those around you. Knowing that our heart fields expand around the body, as you consciously become more of this love, it begins to radiate out to others and starts to affect them in remarkable ways. Try expanding like this when you're in a meeting or stuck in a long line and notice how others respond—you don't have to say a word to begin noticing a difference. For example, during a tension-filled business meeting, Karen quietly focused on radiating love with her energetic heart and watched as the stress dissipated. If each of us takes personal responsibility for managing our heart's energy (not someone else's), imagine how the world might change.

I now consciously incorporate this heart awareness regularly into presentations. As I prepare during the moments just prior to speaking, I check into my heart space, I feel more deeply into it, and then I let it expand to encompass the entire group. The actual words conveyed in my talks are always somewhat different, as those who have heard me speak repeated times know. For example, sometimes I focus on more scientific concepts related to quantum mechanics and the measurement paradox. Other times, anecdotes I've not previously shared with an audience unexpectedly come to mind. I visualize that I am resonating with the collective heart fields of the entire group in order to tailor my delivery to the needs of the specific audience. This seems to help guide the particular direction of my message and connects me to the group in ways my medical presentations before coma never achieved.

A highlight of our workshops is offering the opportunity to generate firsthand experience. For this, we employ brain-wave entrainment audio recordings produced by Sacred Acoustics (the company Karen and Kevin formed to make their recordings available to others). We recommend listening with headphones to receive the full power of the binaural beats embedded in the sound, but at workshops we make an exception and play the sound over speakers. Having a large group of people focused on the same process seems to enhance the power of the experience. Imagine all of the individual heart fields interacting with all the other heart fields in the room: Together, we form a resonant harmonic convergence toward a mutual objective.

Karen instructs the group not to have any overriding expectations of what might occur, but simply to allow the experience to unfold in a natural way. Whether one is a beginner or experienced meditator, these recordings can have a wide range of effects, from powerful and immediate to none at all, depending on the makeup of the individual listening and their mind-set at the time. A state of gratitude for whatever might occur is a useful starting point.

Typically, we play a recording for the group focused on the heart. As the powerful tones emanate from the speakers, filling the room, Karen uses her voice to guide our audience through a relaxation process.

"Relax your body, quiet the mind," Karen says.

"As you breathe in, silently say, 'Let.'"

"As you breathe out, silently say, 'Go.'"

"Let—Go."

I'll join in the meditation with the others. As I relax, I usually offer a brief prayer of gratitude, then mentally state my intention for that meditation. It might concern growing love awareness or broaching crucial boundaries that have recently hindered soul growth. Or it might be so wide open as asking the universe what I most need to know now. Then I "let go"—that is, I allow my conscious awareness to coast comfortably on the waves of sound coming through the speakers, letting my linguistic brain, or my egoic identity, take a break. For me, such sound meditations are a form of centering prayer in which my awareness merges with the oneness of all creation and the divine love there available for "becoming whole," or healing. Worldly concerns dissipate like a puff of smoke in a strong gale.

"Now, move your awareness to your heart center.

"Imagine your breath is moving in and out of your heart."

Karen continues to guide the group through the act of visualizing the breath filling up a bubble surrounding the entire body—the electromagnetic torus field encircling each of us that interacts with those around us.

I follow along with everyone else and *feel into* my heart awareness, a palpable sphere of energy that expresses the love that I am, originating in my heart but expanding freely into the space around me. That "space" should not be viewed as a three-dimensional spatial construct because it is more a structure in the spiritual realm. This perceptual environment acknowledges that we can know and influence events and entities outside of the immediate physical environs in which our body might exist.

Our awareness and influence in that spiritual realm are not as restricted as our conscious awareness seems to be in the physical realm. It is thus not limited to the confines of the here and now of our normal waking consciousness. This empowers us to connect with a higher good that is most beneficial to all involved. It embraces the similar energies I detect in the individual heart fields of members of the audience.

Following the exercise, Karen will invite participants to share their experience. I typically do not share my own experience to avoid any influence on our audience's expectations. Each person reacts in a unique way, and Karen is especially adept at assisting participants in understanding their experiences.

"I felt a weird tingling in my hands and feet," audience members often say.

"This is rather common," Karen will reassure them. "The tones seem to activate the energetic part of us, our energy body, which we typically don't pay attention to. It can feel like buzzing or going from hot to cold very quickly; sometimes it's even painful. Remember that the tones are activating something already inside you, not *causing* whatever is happening. Simply take note or, if it bothers you, imagine that it is releasing, removing itself from your energy body. Or shift the focus of your attention to your breathing."

"I felt a pressure on my forehead, between my eyes."

"You may be activating the third eye, often described as a gateway to the inner world," Karen will offer.

"My hands seemed to be rising off my lap on their own, but I don't think they actually moved," another participant might report.

"Yes, that is sometimes a precursor to an out-of-body experience. Others might feel strong vibrations or shaking sensations. Some can feel their energy body activating before it leaves the body and sometimes that can feel like physical movement of different body parts, especially with closed eyes," Karen will explain.

A few participants have even reported full-blown OBEs during our workshops, although this is rare.

"I saw a lot of colors, especially blue and purple."

"Yes, that is common in deep states of awareness. Did others see colors?" Karen will ask, and typically many audience members raise their hands. "Any colors might show up, maybe bright, maybe blurred, but a shade of bluish purple might indicate being at a ready state, or a sign that you have made connection with your energetic self."

"I noticed a sense of spinning, like a whirlpool, and it made me feel dizzy."

"Think of this as a vortex, or portal, that opens up as you become more energetically aware. It can be a sign of a transition point, and you might choose to imagine your awareness actually entering the spinning energy and notice what happens next," Karen will recommend.

Brain-wave entrainment is often used to help quiet the constant chatter going on in the linguistic brain. This is one of the biggest challenges in establishing a regular practice, especially in our busy modern Western society. While some find that the specialized recordings quickly and efficiently quiet that monkey mind, others find the audio support only somewhat helpful and need to employ additional techniques.

"Developing an awareness of your inner observer can be most useful," Karen encourages. "Begin to consciously notice your thoughts and emotional responses from a different part of yourself—with no judgment. This part of you that notices the thoughts is objective and neutral. Once you start to notice them, realize there is a part of you that is separate from your thoughts—that is the key. It does not analyze, it simply observes. This is the first means to finding that larger part of you that exists beyond the physical world. As you create more conscious awareness of this observer, you then *witness* your thoughts, allowing them to exist, but separate from your observer."

This can sound rather strange if you're not used to this concept, but developing the inner observer we all have within allows you to move one step out of the Supreme Illusion. To become more aware of your observer, practice being in a completely neutral state, with no attachment to specific outcomes, and offer a wide-open acceptance to whatever shows up. If thoughts arise, simply note them in your mind with no judgment, and no analysis. Watching your thoughts like this on a regular basis brings you more in touch with the inner observer.

Distracting mind chatter might appear as "What will I have for dinner tonight?" When your observer is paying close attention, such thoughts are more detached and may simply fade away as another thought arises. However, if you become attached to a thought, your mind is preoccupied with perhaps a dinner menu or which restaurant you might choose, possibly leading you into a labyrinth of ongoing related thoughts. When you notice this has occurred, you have activated your inner observer and can begin watching again from that perspective. This process can be tedious, but its repeated practice brings beneficial results.

To honor and cultivate the *observer* within while exercising its ability to be neutral allows one to assume a much broader perspective. To feel and note thoughts and emotions that may occur, while maintaining the neutrality of the observer, is a fine balancing act that might come with certain experiences and knowings. By remaining open to all possibilities, we allow new insights and wisdom to emerge that have the potential to offer us strength and healing. This can be challenging at first, but with regular practice, it becomes a natural process. This can be useful to exercise while in a meditative state, but also during quiet moments throughout the day.

Eventually, it is possible to move into a neutral state more easily, even during the height of an emotional situation. The goal is to shift one's mind to that impartial observer and witness the emotional content from a more detached perspective, providing a broader context. This aids in more fully understanding it, noting one's thought process in the heat of the moment and realizing one's reaction is often pointing to a larger issue, sometimes completely unrelated to the event at hand. Such a process can bring surprising revelations as to the source of our seeming difficulties.

Once distinguishing a contrast between the inner observer and mind chatter, begin to note what goes on in your mind as you achieve more expanded states of awareness. You might notice colors or images, insights and inspirations, messages or symbols—even entire scenes. You might feel different sensations in the body or deep emotions. Allow your experience to unfold, trusting that whatever occurs will be useful in some fashion. Trust that the universe will provide the structure and information that best allows you to make the requisite choices in your life.

Sometimes, first entering these states can be confusing. Not every perceived experience is equivalent in its importance or in its linkage to our soul's journey, or even to ultimate truth. The importance is simply in discerning the difference. Most of us have a well-developed sense of intuition around such matters, but we are trained to ignore it in favor of more rational thought. Practicing states of expanded consciousness will bring intuitive senses more to the surface. Pay attention to how an experience feels. You will learn from whatever shows up if you allow yourself to remain open and curious.

The more important messages often come packaged with an imprimatur, or a mysterious feature that doesn't make sense in the moment, as in seeing my father's college roommate sitting with him in that deep meditation a little over two years after my coma. It would have been more than enough just to have the experience of seeing my father, his brief glance and wink at me, and the huge volume of "knowing" contained in the "thought ball" that came to me during that memorable exchange. Such tremendous bundles of knowledge might seemingly arrive in an instant.

These visions or "knowings" seem to pop up out of the blue, with no leading thought stream or apparent reason for their appearance. The presence of Dad's roommate was absolutely *not* expected, and presented a deep mystery to me. I had known immediately that the other man was Agnew Bahnson, Dad's close friend and college roommate. On his way to visit one of his sons in school in 1964, Agnew suffered a mishap when trying to land a small plane, his beloved Beechcraft, during a thunderstorm. Tragically, he struck power lines and immediately perished. Why was Agnew there in my vision? What did his presence add to the value and power of the message I had received?

To unravel this mystery, I started with my parents' social network in Winston-Salem, North Carolina. As fate would have it, around two months after my experience, Sophia Cody, a close family friend, offered a crucial clue: She told me that Agnew Bahnson had been close friends with Robert Monroe, whose work I had been exploring during my meditative encounter with Dad. I reached out to children of both Bahnson and Monroe, seeking to assemble their memories of the men's relationship.

Later, I received an email from Agnew's daughter, Karen Bahnson (now known as Osha Reader). She shared that she had worked for Robert Monroe in the 1960s, helping to transcribe his 1971 book *Journeys Out of the Body,* the first of three books he wrote on the subject of out-of-body experiences.

"My father, like Bob, was a man ahead of his time," Osha's email said. "He too was a creative, successful businessman, but having a keen interest in antigravity, philosophy, and the paranormal was very different from most of the people around him in the South of the '50s and early '60s, which is surely one reason why he and Bob became such good friends."

This naturally contributed to answering my original query, "Am I on the right path?" Agnew's forward-thinking scientific nature and his common interest with Monroe in the paranormal was plenty to make me realize I was onto something with using sound to induce altered states of consciousness and with becoming more open to the reality of the paranormal. The fact that my conservative father was college roommates with one of Bob Monroe's close friends was completely unexpected.

"The last time I saw Bob was sometime in the late '70s," Osha continued. "He did tell me, during the time I was working for him, that when Daddy crashed while landing his Beechcraft in Wooster, Ohio, June 3, 1964, he 'came through' to say goodbye to him on his way out."

I was especially amazed to note that on June 12, 2011, the day I received Karen Bahnson's email communication, I had just driven past the Wooster County airport in Ohio, the exact location where Agnew Bahnson's plane had crashed almost exactly 47 years earlier. I had never been within 200 miles of that site. I found it a striking synchronicity that she had sent the email at the moment I was driving by that airport a short while before. This sort of synchronicity offers further compelling data to ponder on the interconnections we all share.

Only by going through the process of unraveling this mystery was I able to come to fully realize my father's continued involvement in my soul journey in a way that fostered my soul's growth. Such an imprimatur then serves to authenticate the overall experience. These elaborate constructs often occur for a reason: to help us in our soul journey, even when they seem to appear quite randomly in that moment. Thus the overall information content—not just of the experience itself, but of the identifiable relationships with all else we know in our lives—can provide a crucial clue as to the reality of that particular perception. Such a stamp of approval helps in validating that our experience might be more than just fanciful imagination and in seeing its specific relevance to our soul's journey.

Surrendering to the process when going within is a useful approach, especially when just starting out or if you don't have a particular goal. However, adding *conscious intention* to your practice often yields significant benefit and direction. Performing the same act but with a different intention can bring about diverse results. You might wish to achieve a peaceful mind or contemplate a particular question. Perhaps you are curious about gaining more sensation of your energetic body or seek creative inspiration. Many are interested in connecting with their higher soul and the collective oneness of which we are all a part.

Intention is a tool of your inner observer's focused attention that can be employed to achieve these objectives and many others. Attention is fundamentally the linkage between consciousness and any aspect of the world around us. Attention is what sets the stage for the choices and observations we make that force the cloud of infinite possibilities to become an actuality (to "collapse the wave function," in the parlance of quantum physics). There are many ways to approach focused intent using various affirmations or visualizations, but Karen offers a simple technique to our audiences.

"Try setting an intention using just one word," she will suggest. "Select a word that represents the state of being you would like to have once your objective is achieved. Imagine what you would *feel* like in that state; really feel it, as if it has already happened."

Thus, if you are asking for an answer to a nagging question, imagine how you would feel when the question was finally answered—*clarity*. If you're seeking a solution to a problem, imagine what it would feel like when the solution was found—*success*. If you don't have a particular goal, simply open yourself to all possibilities—*trust*. Think of your question or problem first and associate it in your mind with the word—but while listening to the brain-wave entrainment recording, focus on just the one word. There are countless approaches, but the critical part is to use your *feeling* state and not just the literal definition of the word.

"Combining the emotion of a word with the thought of a word creates a powerful force," Karen will explain during a workshop. "Imagine that this blend of your thoughts and emotions then becomes part of your heart's electromagnetic field and emanates to the world around you."

Even back in the 3rd century, Egyptian philosopher Plotinus knew the power of resonance, and how "like attracts like." Resonance explains how patterns of any type can reinforce similar patterns, just as wave patterns demonstrate constructive and destructive interference. This can greatly amplify the power of the information that overlaps between such interacting forces.

"My intention was joy. I felt an amazing connection with everyone in the room and all of humanity. It brought tears to my eyes to feel the loving oneness we all share," someone might describe.

Intention is creating an imagined state of being for something you wish to achieve as if you had already attained it—truly feeling as if you have already gained what you desired. Expectation of exactly how that outcome will be accomplished is a detriment to success. Resolution to issues often comes in completely unexpected ways. Thus, it is vital to maintain an open mind to any path that might present itself.

Sometimes, despite their focused intent, an audience member is surprised to experience something unpleasant, seemingly unrelated to their goal.

"My intention was 'clarity' but I didn't get an answer to my question. I just felt a lot of anxiety and started to cry, but I don't know why."

"This is not unusual," Karen will calmly suggest. "Just as the tones can activate our energetic body, they can also trigger our emotions. Unresolved emotional trauma can get stuck when we don't properly process it. Having anxiety rise up in a state of expanded awareness is an excellent opportunity to release it."

The source of a particular emotion that arises may or may not be obvious. But in these moments, allow yourself to feel the particular emotion—don't try to make it go away and don't try to analyze it. The act of *feeling* the emotion often acts as a release in and of itself. It doesn't necessarily mean it's gone forever, and it might be activated again in the future. Each time an emotion arises, repeat the process of allowing yourself to actively feel it. Like peeling an onion, each layer of emotion will eventually be released. Later, that space of release is often filled with unexpected positive emotions.

Each of us is unique. It may take some trial and error to find what works best as an ongoing practice for any individual. But to find out, one must try. Many listeners find Sacred Acoustics brain-wave entrainment recordings useful in some fashion, and others do not. Everyone is unique and will find that different methods bring varied results, although consistent patterns do emerge, such as a quieting of distracting thoughts, increased intuition, greater relaxation, and deeper sleep. Some experience benefits right away, while others take more time. One Sacred Acoustics listener reported that after eighteen months of daily listening, she began to have spontaneous OBEs, which subsequently led to more profound spiritual growth and awakening. Others have shared profound life changes and realizations after using the tones for a much shorter time.

There are countless other methods for achieving expanded states of awareness, including qigong, yoga, trance dance, chanting, float tanks, countless meditation practices, and more. It may be that a practice *not* involving sound brings the best results. The key is to experiment and find what works best for you.

Naturally, I encouraged my two sons to listen to the same sound recordings I had found so helpful in hopes they would find similar benefits in their own lives. My younger son, Bond, was quite skeptical that there could be any effect at all, having been influenced throughout his life by my materialist scientific worldview. Despite my NDE, he remained dubious. I understood this; it had taken my firsthand experience to get my attention. His initial encounter occurred during our first visit to Gary Zukav and Linda Francis's home in Ashland, Oregon. Karen had brought along the Interactive Brainwave Visual Analyzer (IBVA) device that I had first tried when meeting Kevin in New York a couple of years earlier, and I was hoping to entice Bond by engaging him in research with sound recordings and brain-wave states.

While Gary and I enjoyed a lively discussion on matters of physics and consciousness, Karen showed Bond his brain-wave activity using the portable frontal-lobe EEG device. After getting settled in the sunroom, Karen attached the device to Bond's forehead.

"You can put your attention on different things and see what's occurring in your brain," Karen explained.

"Wow, that's so cool. Look how it changes when I move my arm like this," Bond said, experimenting.

He could see directly in real time how movement and different thought processes and states of mental focus would affect what displayed on the laptop screen and quickly discerned that he could modify the display by managing his thoughts along with his gestures.

"I'm going to play a recording for you, but since you haven't listened before, I don't want to influence your experience by telling you what to expect. Just pay attention to what you're feeling or sensing, and we'll talk afterward," Karen instructed.

Bond reclined on the couch and adjusted his headphones, being careful to avoid the sensitive EEG wires. He then listened to a nonguided 39-minute Sacred Acoustics recording.

Karen checked on Bond in the sunroom after the recording was complete and saw that he had fallen asleep. Maintaining an alert level of awareness in the hypnagogic state without dozing off can be challenging at first—*and* we had been driving a lot. She let him sleep.

"How was that?" Karen asked Bond, as he came out of his groggy state later.

"Not much happened. I think I just fell asleep, but I had this crazy dream," Bond replied.

"What do you remember from the dream?" Karen asked.

"It was strange—I was walking around Gary and Linda's house, even though I've never been here before. I remember seeing that picture in the living room, the furniture, and those plants," Bond explained.

As he recounted the different objects, it struck Karen that there might be more to his dream than it seemed.

"I think you might have had an out-of-body experience," she suggested.

Karen had taken courses a few years earlier on how to induce an OBE. A five-week online class included preparatory exercises for learning how to sense the body's energy, usually performed while lying in bed. For example, she would imagine the sensation of a soft brush or feather moving on her hands or feet, then her legs and arms. One exercise was to imagine her body's energy moving completely out the top of her head in an infinite direction, then back through her body, out the bottom of her feet, in the same fashion. Further mental techniques involved visualizing the sensation of moving down a never-ending staircase, pulling herself up with an imaginary rope, or rolling out of bed. This imagined movement was designed to activate awareness of the energy body with the goal of eventually managing it more consciously. One of Karen's first OBEs occurred during a dream. The instructor offered that we often interpret "real" OBEs as dreams until we fully realize we can actually achieve such states.

Bond was unconvinced by this explanation. To his mind, he could easily have been recalling what he had already seen when being shown around the home a few hours earlier. But later that evening, after dinner, Gary escorted Bond and me to a different building on their property, where Bond would be sleeping in a guest room. As we entered, Bond was surprised to recognize more furnishings and artwork from the "dream" he had had earlier.

"I saw this painting; I recognize this hallway. But this is the first time I've been here. How could that be?" Bond remarked, as he recalled his earlier "dream."

He felt as if he had actually been in this location previously, even though neither he, nor any of us, had entered the structure until that moment. This seemed like further validation that Bond's awareness did travel around the property while his physical body was lying still in Gary's sunroom. But as an "extremely hidden phenomenon," only Bond could verify whether it really happened. He could choose to trust his experience, or not.

He later recounted a dream from about two weeks earlier, where he recalled seeing the same complex of buildings on our host's property, but it was unfamiliar and thus did not make sense at the time. While he wasn't fully convinced of his own abilities in out-of-body perception, he felt more open to the possibility that it wasn't just his imagination.

Bond was intrigued by his experience at Gary and Linda's home. As Karen and I continued to listen to experimental audio files developed by Kevin, we invited Bond to listen as well. One particular recording included verbal guidance through stages of relaxation and letting go of mental chatter.

"Relax the tension in your body. Calm your mind. Allow any distracting thoughts to fade away and gently focus your attention on the breath."

Once Bond started experimenting with guided visualization, he realized he could manage his experience with his mind and intention rather than simply waiting to see what happened. Verbal guidance alone wasn't enough, and he continued to find that the audio tones greatly enhanced his process of complete relaxation. Bond had been experiencing some recent insomnia and we provided him with an experimental recording designed to support sleep. An interesting side effect is that on these nights, for at least two weeks straight, he recalled having an incredibly clear dream every single night.

Bond would often become aware that he was dreaming during these ultraclear dreams, yet instead of awakening, the reverie continued—a state known as lucid dreaming. Lucid dreaming is relatable to meditation in that we become aware of our inner observer from within the sleep state. Lucid dreams can be induced through various methods, such as specialized glasses that flash a light when REM sleep is detected in order to alert the person wearing them within their dream. After "awakening," the dreamer can actually manage the dream and perform feats like flying or time travel, face fears and anxieties, or even solve problems and tap into creative inspiration. Bond's lucid dreams continued for a few more weeks, although not on every night, and gradually became less frequent. He felt that his mind eventually adapted to the tones he was hearing and reverted back to regular sleep. More than three years later, he can recall a select few of the most vivid dreams as clearly as if they happened yesterday.

People have recounted ultraclear memories of their NDE more than half a century after the event, often claiming that they remember it as vividly now as when it first occurred. Bond recalled his most lucid dreams in much the same way. So, in interpreting our experiences, it is helpful to look to the degree of lucidity, ultrareality, and emotional power for clues as to the meaningfulness of a given experience.

One strong indicator to discern the difference between a less significant versus a deeper encounter involves the emotional power and lucidity of an experience, whether in meditation, a dream state, or another spiritually transformative experience. The most powerful experiences are notorious for seeming ultrareal, or "way too real to be real," as I, and others, often explain their experiences. Such memories are typically very persistent, far more so than most memories of our life events, and especially more so than our average dreams and imaginings.

In workshops, we often recommend keeping a journal, in part to record experiences and musings (including perceptions in meditation and dreams) as they occur, since the patterns may not be presented in the nice linear and logical manner to which we are accustomed in our daily waking consciousness. The answer often comes before the question. If Bond had recorded the dream he'd had two weeks prior to being in Gary's house, he would have had notes available to compare any pertinent details to his later experience. Anything we encounter along the way can help us to reach a deeper understanding of our existence by exploring the rich tapestry of our interconnections.

Generally speaking, our culture has been conditioned to dismiss impressions that come from within—fully trusting them can be a challenge. It is easy to discount a message or vision as simply a product of the imagination, especially when there is but one witness to it—the observer within. But there are ways to validate information received through psychic means, and scientific study of remote viewing, a method that allows such validation, has shown fruitful and encouraging results that suggest such effects are quite real.

By tapping into the Collective Mind, our conscious awareness can access many layers of the information substrate underlying physical reality. Some would call this substrate the quantum hologram, or Akashic field. We can access not only the information pertaining to our experience, but extended information across much broader swaths of space and time through methods such as remote viewing. Some readers are no doubt aware of the CIA's 23-year-long remote viewing or "psychic spy" program managed by nuclear physicist Ed May and laser physicists Hal Puthoff and Russell Targ, who were based at Stanford Research Institute. The intelligence arms of other governments (China, Russia, and Israel, among others) have hosted similar programs, especially given the fact that there does not seem to be any mode of defense against such mental probing techniques, necessitating active offensive programs.

Many of the more significant research findings of the American investigators have been published in such esteemed scientific journals as *Nature* and *Proceedings of the IEEE*. Widely known successes of remote viewing programs include the location of US hostages during the Iranian hostage crisis (and the prediction that one would be released because of poor health), discovery of crucial clues in solving the kidnapping of newspaper heiress Patty Hearst, identification of a top-secret Soviet weapons factory in Semipalatinsk, the location of a missing Soviet Tu-22 bomber in Zaire, and the viewing of the ring around the planet Jupiter prior to its official discovery by the *Voyager 1* spacecraft, among others.

The public perception of the program was besmirched by the 1995 American Institutes for Research report, which concluded that the information provided by remote viewing was "vague and ambiguous, making it difficult . . . for the technique to yield information of sufficient quality and accuracy for actionable intelligence." However, this assessment that the quality of information retrieved through remote viewing had no valid operational utility is quite different from realizing that the remote viewers *far exceeded chance* in their abilities to discern information.

Dr. Jessica Utts, the chief statistician for the study, stated, "Using the standards applied to any other area of science, it is concluded that psychic functioning has been well established. The statistical results of the studies examined are far beyond what is expected by chance." Overall review of the field of remote viewing supports this extraordinary modality as being a real effect. Although the specifics of technique are crucial to its success, it seems anyone can learn how to do it.

During remote-viewing courses, Karen was provided an eight-digit number and instructed to draw or write her impressions on a blank sheet of paper. The number was associated with the target in question, merely through its random assignment by the instructor. Somehow, that conscious act of assigning the number to a particular place, thing, person, or event creates an informational connection, an entanglement of sorts. No one knows *how* this works, but, remarkably, it does.

The task was to enter a neutral state, focus on the number, and then note whatever came to mind—shapes, colors, emotions, sensations, textures, or temperature—with no judgment or analysis. After a short period, the class was shown a photograph and other information associated with that number. Karen was amazed to see the shapes, colors, and images that came to mind often corresponded to elements of the photo they had been shown, sometimes rather accurately.

Occasionally, the target was an actual person at a location somewhere on earth, but the students tuned in the same way. Others in her classes had varied levels of success, but most found at least some encouraging results. She noted that her most successful attempts were accompanied by a distinct sensation in her abdomen, sort of like a nervous excitement, but not uncomfortable. She validated her abilities in the classroom and also practiced regularly at home, completing hundreds of sessions over several years. This helped her to understand the difference between random thoughts and accurate intuitive information. While she became more self-assured over time, initially she was stunned by her ability to access such information.

In *One Mind*, Larry Dossey suggests that such information is available through a shared intelligence reflected in the connectedness of all minds and cites remote viewing as a compelling source of evidence to support this concept. But he doesn't stop there. Along with many other related topics, he discusses countless stories of animals and their connections to both humans and each other. These stories include instances of dogs who found their way home from thousands of miles away; dolphins who rescued not only humans, but also dogs and whales; cats who knew when someone was near death; and other stories involving cows, gorillas, and bees. This amazing collection of stories supporting the interconnectedness of species simply cannot be explained with traditional scientific models. Such anecdotes are made more viable when viewed from a perspective of the oneness of universal consciousness.

Many animal lovers feel as though they are able to communicate with their pets, even beyond simple training commands. A special bond between animals and humans has seemingly always existed, but can we really know what animals think and feel? During one of Karen's animal communication courses, dog owners brought their pets to the class. The students had absolutely no prior knowledge of the owners and their beloved dogs. Karen followed the instructions to connect with one dog at a time by emptying her mind and imagining that her heart was making the connection. This made sense given the HeartMath research with which she was familiar. Then, she simply posed a question in her mind and allowed her impressions to come forth. Like remote viewing, the most important thing was to note her first inklings with no second-guessing. This is *not* a process of guessing one's way to the correct answer.

"Is there anything you would like to change about your living situation?" she tentatively asked a white poodle in her mind, selecting a question from a list provided by the instructor.

Karen noticed impressions enter her mind, and dutifully wrote them down as instructed. When her turn came, she read her notes out loud to the dog owner.

"This sounds so random, but I got that he would like to have his bed moved by the window," Karen reported.

"Our dog doesn't have a bed," the owner replied, "but just yesterday, we borrowed one from a friend to see if he might like to have one. We placed it by the window and he stayed in it all day long, napping or gazing out the window overlooking trees and a playground for kids."

"What is your favorite toy?" Karen silently asked a black Labrador retriever.

"A blue ball," the dog answered quite definitively.

"He doesn't really have a favorite toy," the owner later explained. "His attention to specific toys regularly changes, but a couple of days ago during a walk, he found a blue ball and has kept it near him ever since."

Dogs, especially, show a devotion to their caretakers generally unmatched in human-to-human relationships. Animals offer reliable emotional support, often assisting with conditions such as anxiety, depression, and suicidal thoughts. But are animals conscious in the same way humans are? I am often asked if animals have souls and if we will see our beloved pets in the afterlife. In the Gateway Valley of my coma journey, I witnessed children playing with dogs who were jumping with joy. For me, this allows for the possibility that yes, animals, along with humans, also are involved in the afterlife.

As children, we easily see the divinity in animals, but as we get older, conventional science teaches us that animals are instinctive creatures, acting from thousands of years of instinctual evolutionary behavior. Due to our linguistic and rational conceptualization, many scientists assume that humans are superior to animals. In fact, I've come to realize since my coma that the ability that truly sets humans apart from animals is not something as profound as language, it's simply that—we cook!

Given the realization that our language capabilities and constant internal chatter seem to limit deeper understanding, perhaps animals have an edge on humans after all, being much more in touch with that spiritual side, unencumbered by self-limiting thoughts. But if animals have no language, how do we understand what they are saying? The pure conceptual flow of information gleaned in altered states of consciousness reveals the limitations of linearly constricted verbal language, and much of our communication with animals occurs without a linguistic bottleneck. Perhaps there is something more profound going on and we truly are connected at a deeper level.

Outside the classroom, Karen often practiced her intuitive connection to animals when her dog Niko would get lost. He was an accomplished and agile escape artist with abilities to scale 5-foot chain-link fences, locate vulnerabilities along the perimeter of enclosed areas, or simply stay alert for that door occasionally left ajar. There was no predictable place he might wander throughout the surrounding neighborhood, and Karen was consistently challenged at following his trail. She strategically used intention by remaining calm and feeling as if she had already found Niko, while simultaneously broadcasting her intention to find him with her heart. Somehow, nearly always, she knew where he would be.

Once, afer escaping into the darkness of a cold winter evening, Niko had worked himself into the crawl space under a neighbor's home and become trapped there. Following an intuitive prompting without knowing exactly why, Karen went directly to this area, where she then heard his faint scratches. He had never been found here previously, and it was completely unexpected. He could not get out the same way he got in so she had to pry open the lattice panel to allow him out. Many of us have strong connections to our pets, and such uncanny encounters are not uncommon.

Such experiences speak to the Collective Mind of which we are all a part. The answers truly do lie within, and learning to trust our intuition is an important facet of spiritual discovery. But achieving such abilities is never the end goal. Of highest importance is to be more aligned with our higher self, resonating our oneness with the universe. As we become more familiar and comfortable with our inner essence, our unique qualities begin to shine. We more easily access guidance and creative inspiration, and gain a deeper understanding of personal events taking place in our lives. Meaning and purpose flourish in such an awakened environment.

CHAPTER 13

LEARNING OUR SOUL LESSONS

Live as if you were to die tomorrow. Learn as if you were to live forever.

—MAHATMA GANDHI (1869–1948),
INDIAN PACIFIST AND LEADER

We are much vaster than our physical bodies. We are greater than our thoughts and personalities, much more than the roles we play as doctor, teacher, engineer, mother, or father. We are spiritual beings, living in a spiritual universe. Truly, this way of perceiving the world affects our approach to daily life in remarkable ways, including how we view death, manage our health, and understand our relationships with others. Rather than being separate individuals competing for resources, driven by the concerns of the ego, we are part of a larger whole, connected to each other in ways that bring meaning and purpose to our lives. We are not dependent on a functioning physical brain—our awareness outlives our bodies. Our observed reality exists as the stage setting on which we learn and teach ongoing lessons.

A useful approach is to consider our collective earthly existence as time spent in "soul school"—and it seems we don't have only one chance to get it right. This grand evolution of consciousness was beautifully elucidated by the French Jesuit priest, paleontologist, and geologist Pierre Teilhard de Chardin in his 1955 masterpiece, *The Phenomenon of Man*. He expanded the concept of mere biological evolution in his attempt to combine modern science and philosophy with Christian thought. In essence, he envisioned a far grander purpose for consciousness in the universe, quite aligned with the views presented in this book.

This evolution is not chaotic and random (as in the popular form of Darwinian selection) but convergent toward what he called an Omega Point by a force of infinite love that guides our pathway through such learning and teaching of which we are all integral parts. To even use the words "part of" is misleading, though—our very language conspires to obscure the fact that our conscious awareness is one with the universe. Teilhard de Chardin theorized that the progressive growth of consciousness itself is ultimately the purpose of our existence, and each of us plays a crucial role in this process. We return repeatedly through multiple lifetimes over vast cycles of time to participate in this shared endeavor.

Reincarnation is a process of education for all beings in the grander evolution of consciousness. This apparently standard procedure was part of the lessons I learned in my coma journey. Reincarnation was presented in the Core realm as part of the very fabric of all existence—not as some blind mechanistic wheel (as in some interpretations), but a process that is more directly related to our soul's purpose of existence and transformation. Reincarnation was the best way to reconcile the omniscient, omnipotent, omnipresent, and infinitely loving deity I encountered with the suffering of innocent beings allowed in our world, especially children and animals.

Supporting evidence for reincarnation is found in the research of Dr. Ian Stevenson and Dr. Jim Tucker, from the Division of Perceptual Studies at the University of Virginia in Charlottesville, who have assembled more than 2,500 cases of past-life memories in children in which reincarnation is the most straightforward explanation. Their research focuses on young children who spontaneously report that they had another family or lived somewhere else, or describe details of events that have not taken place in their current lives. This typically begins at age 2 or 3, and usually these memories fade around 6 or 7 years of age. Scientists who delve into the fringes of acceptable research must be especially careful with their approach so as to maintain credibility. Such stories are easy to dismiss as fantasy or wishful thinking. Of course, some such claims are just that, but that doesn't mean they all are.

While it can be tempting to dismiss this sort of thing, for those children who provide enough details, researchers have sometimes been able to identify a specific "previous personality" that the child recalls having been before, at times within the same family and other times as strangers in another location. Some children display curious behaviors and habits or exceptional abilities, such as athletic or musical talent. Others relate specific names or places, and identify former family members.

Researchers are meticulous in their care to apply discernment as to how and from whom the data are collected. They search historical records and family connections to compare the reports to actual events. Fascinatingly, with sufficient details validated, it seems reincarnation turns out to be a viable explanation in more than 2,500 cases. All of these together form an impressive database, each case coded on 200 variables, allowing for useful analysis. The strongest instances contain elements that cannot simply be dismissed out of hand.

A rather striking example, reviewed in Tucker's book, *Return to Life,* is the case of James Leininger, whose nightmares of being in a plane crash indicated his connection with a World War II pilot shot down in the Battle of Iwo Jima. Starting around age 2, while dreaming, he would shout, "Airplane crash on fire! Little man can't get out," and thrash about, kicking his legs in the air. Upon awakening, he described being stuck, unable to get out of the sinking plane. Some nights at bedtime, James talked about memories of his plane catching fire after being shot by the Japanese. He identified the boat his plane flew off of as "Natoma," referred to himself as "James 3," and claimed he was with someone named Jack Larsen.

Later, James's parents learned about a Casablanca class escort carrier named the USS *Natoma Bay* that was stationed in the Pacific during WWII. Historical records revealed that a pilot from this ship named James Huston Jr. had perished after his plane was shot in the engine. Remarkably, three surviving eye witnesses confirmed it happened precisely the way young James described. Jack Larsen was eventually found to be still alive, a fellow pilot who had flown on the same day of the fatal crash.

James made many other explicit statements that were corroborated in similar fashion. For example, between the ages of 3 and 5, James acquired three G.I. Joe action figures that he played with constantly and even slept with at night. He named them Billy, Leon, and Walter and explained that these were the three friends who met him in heaven after dying. Later, his parents learned three of the ten men from James Huston Jr.'s squadron who had been killed before him were named Billie, Leon, and Walter. Incredibly, their respective hair color matched that of the action figures. Investigation indicated that he had no way of having acquired such knowledge through normal means. No evidence of fraud was found, and there was substantial documentation for verification.

Researchers have concluded that children who report past-life memories often recall having died suddenly and relatively young in their previous lifetime. The memories appear to pick up where they left off, much as James's nightmares seemed to reenact his death. Notably, reports indicate that 70 percent died of unnatural causes, such as accidents or murder, and where enough data exist, the median interval before rebirth is 16 months although the average interval is 4½ years. Perhaps the emotional power associated with such an untimely passing leads to more urgency in reincarnating.

In fact, the level of emotional intensity is directly related to the strength of a given case. In 35 percent of reports, children have phobias related to the previous death, such as a fear of water in those who remember drowning. More than 200 cases have been documented where children have birthmarks or abnormalities that match usually fatal wounds received in the previous lifetime, such as a discoloration where a bullet entered the body. Somehow, the memory of such a trauma seems to affect the physical body.

While most children's reported memories involve moving directly upon death from one body into the next, in 20 percent of cataloged cases, children recall events that take place before entering the current incarnation. Many of the elements are similar to NDE reports, such as encounters with deceased relatives or visiting another realm. Just as in NDEs, children's past-life memories do not describe the exact same elements, but remarkable patterns do emerge. This should come as no surprise. If we took a group of twenty people and dropped them all into Paris, France, and retrieved them twenty-four hours later, they would all have different things to report.

Some children reveal they chose their parents, sometimes witnessing events prior to entering their mother's womb. In discussions with Dr. Raymond Moody on this topic, he shared that his adopted son spontaneously began to talk about his family in China around age 2 or 3. While Raymond and his wife, Cheryl, did not attempt to validate his claims, they listened with rapt interest. During one of these times, he related that while perched in a tree, he witnessed Raymond and Cheryl lying on a blanket in the grass before he was born. As it happens, during a trip to Ephyra, Greece, at the Oracle of the Dead, Raymond and Cheryl stopped to rest and laid on a blanket in the grass, surrounded by trees. They remember it clearly because, as they rested, they began the first of many discussions about plans to adopt a child. Five years later, they adopted their newborn son, Carter. I encourage those with a child younger than 6 to ask them, "Where were you before you were here?" Have no expectations and ask no leading questions. Simply ask, apply no pressure and accept any answer you are given.

This phenomenon of reincarnation supports the observation that memories do not seem to be stored in the physical brain. Finding a location for memories within the brain has completely eluded neuroscientific efforts (see Chapter 5). Just as filter theory allows that the brain is not the producer of consciousness, likewise, we use the brain to access memory from an information field (e.g., the quantum hologram or Akashic record) that exists outside of it.

In our effort to explain the nature and workings of the world, we must explain these cases of well-documented past-life memories in children with no other way of having acquired the memories. It would be wise to accept the existing research findings and dive even deeper into its scientific study. This is not simply a discussion of what one wants to believe, but, as much as possible, we must address the world as it is. We must consider that reincarnation is apparently something that happens to us all (with or without our belief in it) and offers a richer view of our lives here on earth.

Part of our earthly existence seems to also include a programmed forgetting of our plans, but sometimes it seems we can retrieve some of these memories. Techniques for going within to retrieve such memories can be utilized on your own with skill and discipline, but the assistance of a practitioner might also prove beneficial, especially when first starting out. Similar to deep meditative states, guided hypnosis induces the subject into a hypnagogic state, allowing them to access heightened focus and insight, and to respond to suggestions to control pain or modify behavior, such as in addressing an addictive habit. These things can certainly be achieved in meditative states, but a trained professional can often get us past more stubborn issues.

Paul Aurand, who had suffered from and then released persistent pain due to a lightning strike (as described in Chapter 10), worked as a hypnotherapist in a medical center with doctors who specialized in helping patients manage chronic pain and illness. Paul's role was to perform traditional hypnoanesthesia in order to facilitate less sensitivity to pain in the mind of the subject—basically, numbing their symptoms with hypnotic suggestion. This is not a new concept; in fact, hypnosis was used as an anesthetic during major surgery starting in the 1800s, prior to the introduction of chemical anesthesia. Paul's pain-numbing procedure would sometimes be successful, but he wished the overall results were more satisfying.

Rather than trying to numb the pain, he noticed that he could guide the subject to become an objective observer and enter into a dialogue with the pain and its source. Evoking the observer while in a hypnotic state allowed the subject to bypass their conscious thoughts and analysis and tap directly into their inner wisdom. Paul then guided the subject to literally ask the pain for assistance within their mind, and they would get answers. Sometimes the source of pain would be a specific childhood trauma or perhaps a dysfunctional relationship. Other times, they would be told to eat differently or change a lifestyle behavior. The key seemed to be that they received advice from within, rather than from an outside source.

It was not unusual for the source of a pain to be related to an event from the past. A woman who had suffered chronic shoulder pain for seven years had received every possible diagnosis with no relief. She'd tried steroids, painkillers, immobilization, and physical therapy, and now her doctors had suggested exploratory surgery. She wished to avoid surgery and hoped that anesthetizing the pain through hypnosis might help. Paul induced the woman and gave the usual instruction to regress back in time to the source of the pain. Rather unexpectedly, she spontaneously regressed back to a time when she described herself as a slave having an experience of stealing food for her starving child. She recounted being caught and, in the process of beating her to death, the attackers broke her shoulder.

"Is she fantasizing? Did she have a psychotic break?" Paul asked himself as he listened to her relate the tale. He knew she had not been a slave at any point in her life, but she appeared to be living out a scene she had actually experienced in a previous lifetime. He guided her, as usual, to release the pain. He didn't know exactly what had happened, but she came out of the session with no remaining shoulder pain. Remarkably, over time it became clear she was permanently free of the pain.

This sort of thing happened several more times, and Paul realized he would be able to better benefit his subjects if he learned to guide people more intentionally. He began to learn specific techniques for guiding people into recalling past-life memories. He didn't always start by suggesting, "Let's go to a past life," because that wasn't necessarily the first place to look. But some issues clearly seemed to be a residue or carryover from a previous lifetime. This is not to say that information gained under hypnosis alone can be used to establish definitive proof for a past life, but it can sometimes prove useful for purposes of personal growth.

Paul studied another approach using hypnosis, designed for people to recall memories of what occurs *between* our lifetimes on earth. Dr. Michael Newton, counseling psychologist, describes this process in *Journey of Souls*, where he documented the patterns found in reports of thousands of hypnotically regressed patients, noting the most common consistencies among them. Similar to past-life regression, the subject is guided to return to a lifetime previous to the current one, then guided to the time of death. Remarkably similar to NDE descriptions, some feel an immediate sense of euphoric freedom as they observe their dying body and sense a bright light. Unlike an NDE, rather than return to their physical body, they then go on to recall what occurs next, as their awareness under hypnosis fully enters the spiritual realm. Many describe a familiar return to home as they encounter souls of departed loved ones and spiritual guides.

Compiling thirty years of data, Newton created a potential road map of what might happen, at least for some, during the time spent between death and rebirth. Among other things, this body of data suggests that we actively *plan* each of our lifetimes, including choosing our parents and physical bodies, and selecting the challenges (such as illness and injury) and gifts that will most effectively teach us that which we came here to learn. According to Newton's data, we ostensibly make agreements related to our plans with others in our soul groups, those other souls we encounter and interact with throughout our lives who play both good and bad roles, often trading off to help each other learn crucial lessons.

Paul was among the first hypnotherapists in 2001 whom Newton trained in his methods to conduct a "life between lives," or LBL, hypnotic regression. He was also later asked to gather a group of therapists Newton had trained to form the Michael Newton Institute in 2005. Paul served as president for four years and since then has continued as director of education.

Cynthia, a 42-year-old client of Paul's, wished to address her issues of low self-esteem and body image. She wondered if persistent teasing from childhood was related to her current poor self-image. Obligingly, Paul regressed her back to childhood, where she recalled being teased relentlessly for her big nose. She was mocked by other children, but also by one of her uncles, who was especially cruel. He then guided Cynthia to continue further back in time, seeking the original source of her issues.

"I seem to be in some kind of an open-air temple. I need to rest here for a while. I am in spirit. I have just died and returned home. I need some time to adjust. It's so bright here!"

After adjusting to her new surroundings, she found herself experiencing a time of contemplation that involved looking back at the life she had just completed.

"I was a very beautiful and tall woman. It was an elegant life, but I was actually rather vain. Oh, I was really awful. I felt I was so much better than everyone else. . . . This is very hard for me to see. How could I have been so arrogant? And not just arrogant; I was really conceited. I didn't treat people well at all. Oh, this is so difficult. I felt so superior just because of my beauty. I ridiculed and made fun of others who were not so beautiful. I was actually, well, really mean. I am not at all like that today. How could I have behaved in such a way? Now I understand why

I am so harsh with my two children if they ever tease or ridicule someone."

The insights gained from this life review were difficult for Cynthia to absorb. Paul sensed there was something more here to be explored.

"Looking back over that life, as a result of the experiences you have just reviewed, what thoughts and feelings are you left with?" Paul asked.

"I am horrified with my conceit and meanness. My beauty was so important to me. I find myself never wanting to be like that again," Cynthia replied.

"As a result of the experiences you had in that life, what do you decide to do or not do in your next life?" Paul probed further, anticipating that Cynthia's soul answer would give insight into the experiences that were troubling her in this life.

"I certainly don't want to be beautiful. I want to find out what it is like to be made fun of. I want to be teased and ridiculed. I think it would be better if I was small, short, and unassuming. Yes, that would be better. And, I should have an unattractive face. Maybe a big nose would be good? Yes, a big, ugly nose. That's it. I should have a big, ugly nose that everyone will notice and make fun of. I want to be teased so I really know how it feels and never act this way again."

This was not the kind of instant karma, "eye for an eye," or punishment from a judgmental God that had been imposed on Cynthia for improper behavior. This was a decision made by her soul in order to learn from direct experience in the life she was currently leading. Paul's clients have reported these kinds of decisions being made soon after leaving the physical body during the life review, but before fully entering the higher realms of unconditional love and more enlightened awareness.

Research indicates that the life review ("your life flashing before your eyes") has been commonly encountered in NDEs over the last few millennia (reported in 30 to 50 percent of NDEs, depending on the study), no matter what one's prior faith and belief system. Shortly after leaving the physical body, participants relive each situation in what seems like real time, sometimes noted as taking years to complete, even if just seconds or minutes had passed in earth time. A fundamental lesson of life reviews concerns their revelations around the ephemeral nature of time and the apparent boundaries of the "self"—we become those other souls impacted by our actions and thoughts, to experience the feelings our actions elicited in others as we relive key moments of our lives.

The life review ritual exists in order for us to feel the emotional impact of our behavior from another perspective, both good and bad, especially those situations that might still harbor residual lessons for us. This allows us to witness and assess the progress of our spiritual growth, ultimately across multiple lifetimes. Judgment is not cast upon us from some other "higher" being—we judge ourselves (not from an egoic perspective, but from that of our own higher soul), and we apparently do so more harshly than any third party might. Thus, one who has handed out much pain and suffering to others, who has been more ego-driven, selfish, and greedy, will face a relatively unpleasant life review that might even resemble a type of hell.

I suspect our very concepts of "hell" arose from the life reviews of those who had been particularly selfish, greedy, or prone to handing out pain and suffering to others. Through the mirroring process of the life review, feeling the sting of their thoughts and actions would be quite grim. Life reviews serve in our learning the lessons of life, providing balance and justice to our growth.

A particular ordeal in life might also be related to another soul's important lesson, as seen during a highly emotional exchange that took place as Cynthia continued to explore her time between lives with the very person she really did not want to meet, her deceased uncle.

"No, not him! Of all the people I could possibly meet here in spirit, why would he be here? This is the uncle that abused me for years. He constantly teased me. He was so cruel to me. I don't want anything to do with him. He's coming toward me, arms outstretched. He's crying. He's hugging me. I feel such love from him. He really loves me! I thought he hated me. Now I am crying, too. It's like a reunion. He has missed me so and, strangely, I too feel as though I have missed him. This is so confusing. We are hugging and crying."

"That was one of the most difficult things I have ever done for you," her uncle explained. "You made me promise to tease and hurt you to help you overcome your tendency to tease and hurt others. I didn't really want to do it, but because I love you and you insisted, I agreed. It was painful for me to hurt you like that."

It took time for Cynthia to absorb all of this. Imagine, after almost forty years of feeling victimized by her uncle—and many others, for that matter—what a different perspective she achieved! It seemed she had requested assistance from a soul she was very close to in order to overcome her tendency to be conceited and mean.

"I am happy about my choice of a smaller body and even my nose. They have helped me learn to be more loving and accepting. As for my uncle, I have a very different feeling about him and what he did to me. I don't feel like a victim anymore. Strangely enough, I appreciate what he has done for me."

Consider all the relationship issues many of us have endured, whether as parent-child, husband-wife, or boss-employee. This school of thought implies we make such plans together, knowingly and with love. To explore this concept, it is not necessary to fully accept it as truth. Simply ask yourself, "What if it *is* true?" Then look back on specific life events, especially those that were catalysts for change, and contemplate, "Why might I have planned that?" or "Did something useful result?" Pay attention to your answers, and trust your intuitions.

In some of my meditative explorations, I have sensed an awareness of the soul agreements of my adoptive parents, birth parents, and birth grandparents to set up their lives in the ways that resulted in my personal adoption drama, but of course validation of such sensations can be quite difficult. It seems the whole matter of the infertility of my adoptive parents and my birth parents giving me up were agreed on by them before birth, and ties together our soul journeys.

Even my great-grandfather, then known as Eben Alexander Jr., made himself known during a series of fund-raisers I spoke at for the Children's Home in North Carolina. Readers will recall this is the organization that cared for me as an infant and arranged my placement with my adoptive parents. Brian Maness, the president and CEO of the Children's Home Society of North Carolina, was delighted to share with me the book *Adoption Means Love,* a history of the Children's Home. The book includes a mention of a previous Eben Alexander, whom I confirmed to be my great-grandfather and namesake.

He was one of the original concerned citizens who in 1903 wished to create a home for babies and children in need of families and helped to start the organization that would one day become so crucial to my journey. Little did he know at the time the influence the CHS would have on the life of his unborn grandson, my father, Eben Alexander Jr., by providing him with an adopted son in 1954. We can all look back on our lives and open our minds to the synchronicities that occur, and this kind of connection can potentially reflect that we are part of a grander plan.

Recognition that the soul lessons resulting from the hardships, struggles, and conflicts in life might serve a purpose offers great insight in living our lives. And the more open you are to accepting the opportunities that these challenges present to become stronger, the more you are able to spare your future lives that continued suffering. If a particular lesson wasn't properly learned, you might plan an even more daunting situation in the next lifetime. Should you successfully learn the lesson, it would never have to be repeated again and you could move on to the next challenge.

This concept may seem counterintuitive, especially when it comes to extreme hardship and adversity. We might find it difficult to accept that we have intentionally planned less than ideal situations for ourselves. But when we make these plans, we have full knowing that the situation will be temporary and we will be generally unaware of the underlying arrangement during life. To add to the confusion of programmed forgetting, often we choose an experience opposite of something we wish to learn in order to understand from a different perspective. From the vantage point of here and now, some of our decisions seem to be illogical, but nonetheless a pragmatic choice at the time it was made.

Another of Paul's clients was a woman who experienced difficulty with becoming pregnant. In her regression session, she recalled being a Native American with two children when her village was raided. Nearly everyone in the village was killed, including her children, but she was wounded and survived. She lived out the remainder of her life in isolation in another village, and when she died she said to herself, "I couldn't protect my children. It's my fault they died. I don't deserve to be a mother; no children next time." And so, she carried that guilt into this life, but also had a physical problem in that she couldn't get pregnant, even with in vitro fertilization.

Paul has found three primary things that come up during hypnosis-regression sessions. One is stored emotions or feelings carried over from our previous experience—happy, sad, angry, afraid—that are triggered by experiences in our current life. Finding the source and releasing those stuck emotions can help us tremendously. The second is our beliefs. When we experience something, whether it's from a previous life or this life, we form certain beliefs. These beliefs are often related to problems and thus are typically self-sabotaging—"I'm not good enough," "The world's a cruel place," or "It's my fault." These beliefs are a vital aspect of why we make certain choices. The third thing is strategies for survival—what we learn to do in order to stay safe and be loved—"I'll choose others' needs over my own," "I won't have children," or "I'll be invisible." Those strategies comprise the program that is running beneath our superficial level of awareness—that is what truly rules our lives.

These programs occur not only in childhood, but also in the womb, where our soul joins with the body. We bring them in from previous lifetimes as well—that's the material on which the soul is working. There are life lessons and soul lessons. Life lessons are stepping-stones that can be accomplished in an individual life, leading toward grander lessons. For example, Cynthia chose an unattractive appearance to learn to accept all souls equally, regardless of their outward image. Those hardships that especially demand our attention are likely related to our chosen lessons and act as catalysts for changing perspective or making significant changes.

Some lessons aren't learned in just one lifetime and serve more as compass points guiding multiple incarnations toward a deeper lesson of understanding. Soul lessons continue from one life to the next and may comprise the most ambitious lessons, such as forgiveness or serving as a full embodiment of unconditional love at the source of all existence. There are not always enough opportunities for complete resolution within just a single lifetime. We make choices with the very best of intentions, although it may not always appear to serve us well, at least on the surface.

Aysu (not her real name) arrived at Paul's office in Istanbul having suffered a lifetime of chronic pain and fatigue that made it impossible to work, strained her family, and had ruined more than one relationship. She wanted relief and was desperate to understand why she experienced so much suffering in her life. Aysu had tried various medical treatments and numerous therapies, all to no avail.

Paul regressed her to a traumatic event early in childhood where she felt alone and very afraid. He guided Aysu, as the loving woman and mother that she is today, to hold her scared child self in her arms and to love and protect her. Next, Paul guided her back into the womb, where her physical body was developing.

"It hurts. I don't want to be here! It's so uncomfortable," Aysu reported.

Paul quickly recognized that Aysu had brought pain with her into this lifetime so he directed her back to the previous lifetime, where she recalled being beaten to death. Aysu experienced a sense of drifting, floating upward like a balloon, and eventually arrived in a place where she found herself surrounded by three guides.

"We want to work with you on your basic misunderstanding about pain. You believe pain teaches. You believe you have pain because you think you can receive love through pain. You believe that because you hurt others in the past, you deserve to have pain now," her primary guide said.

The guides were very clear and direct, but Aysu struggled to understand. Her beliefs had been carried with her through countless lifetimes.

"You are so focused on the pain, you cannot go beyond it. You are holding on to your pain because you fear that if you let it go, even worse things will happen to your children, your family, and your friends. It has gone on for lifetimes. Trust us and let it go. Let go of these beliefs and let go of this pain," they suggested.

The guides were loving and persistent and Aysu eventually opened herself to the love and healing energy being conveyed to her and burst into tears.

"They are comforting me and telling me to let everything go, not to hang on to anything."

"Now your soul is happy with a newly healed body. We thank you for working with us. There are some other things in your life that will now be resolved also," the guides said.

Paul was delighted a few months later when he followed up with Aysu. She was free of chronic pain and working again. She was full of smiles and reported that things were now so much better with her family at home.

Letting go of past trauma often leads to resolution of certain issues, but some challenges are more difficult to understand, especially when it involves the death of a loved one. Often, we cannot understand why someone in the prime of life might suddenly be taken away. Reasons for this are usually not readily apparent, but sometimes deeper understanding results from a change in perspective.

A woman from a country in eastern Europe whose fiancé had been killed in a car crash sought assistance from Paul. Her fiancé had been driving to her parents' house to announce their engagement when he skidded on black ice and was killed. They had been together for about a year and had fallen in love, just like a magical fantasy. Her question was why—why had he been taken away from her? They loved each other so much. How could God be so cruel? She made contact with her beloved fiancé and, much to her surprise, he told her, "No, I was not taken away. I was given a life extension so we could have that year together."

She went from being devastated about not having him with her anymore to being grateful that she had been with him at all. And it seemed their relationship was not over. She had received twenty to thirty text messages from him after he died. They were originally text messages he had sent to her when he was alive that would mysteriously cycle back to the top of her phone's message list. She would be listening to their favorite song on the radio, and then a text message he had written her many months before about that song would be viewed again as a new message. Perhaps they will plan to meet again in a future lifetime.

Time flow on earth does not operate in the same fashion as what I refer to as "deep time." Deep time takes precedence over earth time and is applicable to our higher souls and soul groups. Deep time is the higher ordering of all that unfolds for beings in their higher journey so that no soul reincarnates in any fashion that would remove them from the appropriate interactions with other members of their soul group at the right time. In other words, they would not reincarnate too early and thus be unavailable to, say, escort the soul of a loved one across when the second one to pass over does so.

A reincarnation could even happen *before* an incarnation (from the viewpoint of earth time), if that helps in optimal presentation of the life lessons being learned and taught within an evolving soul group. The ordering of events in deep time trumps any ordering within earth time. Deep time concerns more the plot and theme of a soul group's lessons, as opposed to earth time, which is more simply the stage on which events of the drama unfold.

As you begin to realize your role as a player in the arena of life, reasons for certain circumstances come more sharply into focus. Take a step back and view a situation in your life on a much larger scale. Reflect on the seeming hardships you have had and recall important lessons you have learned. For example, getting caught in a childhood theft could be quite humiliating at the time, but years later you might realize it was important to have that experience in order to learn the value of proper integrity. Reaching clear insight in the moment it occurs might seem impossible, but deeper understanding often comes following its resolution. Our own issues are often the hardest to see, though exercising our neutral inner observer certainly helps.

Rather than waiting for a life review at the end of life, what if we could enact a daily or weekly review, where notable events are assessed as potential lessons? Such reviews can bring significant life lessons to the surface while we still have time to make changes to our attitude and conduct. This takes place in one's mind, perhaps during meditation or a contemplative moment, and can lead to extraordinarily transformative effects. Pay attention to what triggered you emotionally—this is a clue that you are possibly dealing with an important lesson. Note any situations you may have encountered that perhaps could have been managed differently for a better outcome. Are you proud of your reactions? Might you have tried another approach?

A focus on modifying one's own perspective and behavior is vital, not dwelling on how the actions of others should change. Imagine how you might have behaved differently and plan to modify your actions the next time you are faced with a similar situation. You might even choose to apologize for a particular behavior. The point is not to dwell on and remain stuck in past incidents, but to review them in order to educate yourself about how you interact with the world. With practice, it's possible to make changes in the exact moment a stressful situation presents itself rather than reviewing it at a later time. This is best accomplished by developing the neutral inner observer in order to view emotional reactions from a broader perspective.

Ultimately, the plans we make seem to relate to the underlying theme of love and service to others. We can learn these concepts intellectually and understand their value in our minds, but the greatest learning comes from immersing oneself in actual situations of life here on earth. Even someone who seems to be struggling with every aspect of life is playing a significant role. Whether they are learning compassion or patience for their situation or providing an impetus for another person's growth, as we learn and grow as individuals, we contribute to the ongoing evolution of the entire universe by modeling our lessons to others through our actions and behavior.

When we fully accept that we are eternal souls and make plans to be faced with certain challenges, we are no longer victims of circumstance. Something that seems unfair can suddenly seem purposeful, and we come to respect even more those who gain acceptance or pull themselves out of undesirable circumstances. These people are learning their life's lessons. We each offer a unique aspect of the whole and, collectively, we are the self-awareness of the universe, and thus serve in cocreating its evolving destiny. We learn lessons of love and compassion by planning the events in our lives—both hardships and happy times. Ultimately, through learning the underlying truth of our soul lessons, we gain deep inner peace and understanding of such events from a higher vantage point.

CHAPTER 14

THE FREEDOM OF CHOICE

I believe that we are solely responsible for our choices, and we have to accept the consequences of every deed, word, and thought throughout our lifetime.

—ELISABETH KÜBLER-ROSS (1926–2004),
SWISS-AMERICAN PSYCHIATRIST

The choices we make are directly related to the experiences that take place in our lives—not only those plans that we have forgotten before coming into this lifetime, but the choices we make on a routine daily basis. Learning about our prelife goals is certainly helpful in some cases, but what if, instead of waiting until after departing the physical body, we gained understanding of our life lessons while we still had a chance to make different choices?

Our choices involve not only our specific behavior, but the intention or attitude that underlies them. As Gary Zukav points out in *The Seat of the Soul*, "What you choose, with each action and each thought, is an intention, a quality of consciousness that you bring to your action or your thought." We make countless choices each day—most of them are reactions to circumstances without conscious thought. Gary reminds us that each choice of intention creates a consequence and advises that we pay close attention to the ramifications of our choices. Becoming more conscious of our unconscious decision-making process allows for greater awareness of how our unfolding reality comes into being.

By realizing you actively create the events in your life with your free-will choices, you rise above merely reacting to situations as they occur. Gaining a bigger picture of this individual power provides a tremendous asset in managing difficulties that take place. One choice leads to another, and looking back at the series of events throughout your life might reveal repeated patterns of suffering. It is easy to feel like a victim of circumstances and stay stuck, but through recognizing the power of choice (whether conscious or not), it's possible to break these cycles and literally change the future.

Karen struggled with helping her daughter Jamie manage angry emotional outbursts and anxiety throughout her teenage years. Jamie often got in trouble at school for arguing with teachers, and sometimes was even suspended and not allowed to go to class. She skipped school a lot. Keeping Jamie engaged in learning became a vicious cycle. She began to use drugs and alcohol to distract her from her troubles—a form of self-medication. After Jamie reported suicidal thoughts and self-mutilation to her doctor, she spent a few days in a local mental-health facility, where several prescription drugs were recommended due to a bipolar diagnosis. Karen was concerned, but knew her daughter best and felt this was rather extreme. She refused the doctor's advice, worried that it would only enable Jamie to abuse drugs even more than she already was if she had her own prescriptions.

At age 19, Jamie learned about hypnotherapy and told her mother she'd like to find a hypnotherapist to help manage her emotional issues. She was drawn to it partly because she would be placed into a relaxed state and guided with suggestions, rather than being required to describe her problems as she had attempted (and avoided) in talk therapy. Karen knew her daughter might be difficult to guide since she was headstrong and resistant to authority. Frustratingly, the first therapist declined to treat Jamie because she felt Jamie was too stubborn and untreatable. Undeterred, Karen searched for a practitioner specializing in teenage issues and her efforts were rewarded. The appointment began with a review of Jamie's overriding issues.

"What is going on when you get in trouble?" the therapist asked.

"Usually, I'm bored," Jamie replied.

At Jamie's request, Karen remained in the room during the hypnosis session. She observed Jamie gradually relax as the therapist used a soothing voice to guide her. Soon, she entered a hypnagogic state. After a few minutes of questioning to establish an easy rapport, the therapist cut straight to the issue at hand.

"Go back to the time when you were first bored."

Jamie's voice sounded a little different from her normal voice, speaking a bit slower and more deliberately from her deep state of awareness. She described a scene from younger in life when she was bored in school.

"Was this the first time you were bored?"

"No," Jamie replied.

"Let's go back a bit further."

"Now I'm a baby in a baby swing," Jamie described.

The therapist proceeded to guide Jamie to identify the potential source of her boredom from her early days and how it got her into trouble. The next step was to provide a solution.

"Now I'm going to ask you to move forward into your future. If you make no changes in your life, what will it be like in ten years?"

Jamie described a scene where she was unmarried, had two children, and was living with her half brother. She didn't have a job and was struggling to make ends meet.

"Now let's assume you have made constructive changes in how you handle your life. Move forward ten years and describe what your life is like."

Jamie then related a completely different scene, where she was independent and had a fulfilling job. She was content and involved in a loving relationship. While in this hypnagogic state, the therapist asked her which future she would prefer to experience in real life and, not surprisingly, Jamie chose the latter. The therapist suggested she could ask this "future self" to help her anytime she wished since that self had created a happy and successful life and could be a useful advisor.

Following this therapy, Jamie began to turn around and gain more control over her life. She loved the idea that it was her future self, a part inside of her and not someone else, that could advise her, and this seemed to empower her as she moved forward. Nearly ten years later, she is generally well balanced, content with her job, and happily married to a loving, supportive husband—they are expecting a child of their own.

Shortly after graduation from high school, Jamie had divulged to Karen that she was grateful she had not been given her own prescription drugs during high school. She admitted to sometimes purposely acting in extreme ways so she could acquire prescription drugs of her own as some of her friends had done. Jamie had observed some of her peers' reactions to various substances over the previous years. She concluded that she would have been worse off had she taken even more drugs and was glad that she had found effective ways to manage her emotional reactions. She continues to have successful results using self-hypnosis to address other issues in her life. Hers has not been an easy path, but more of a gradual road to improvement through a conscious effort to make different choices through the guidance of her future self.

Having faced my own alcoholism in the early 1990s, I came to see the dark aspects of alcoholism and addiction in general as potentially representing a spiritual hole in the core of one's being that they are trying to fill with nonspiritual substance. That hole is unfillable, except with "spiritual matter." Think of spiritual matter as the connection of ourselves with others and the universe, a linkage that goes beyond the physical. Even in those pre-coma days, when I was struggling with faith in a higher power, the role of spiritual lack as a root cause seemed quite evident, within myself and in every other recovering soul I encountered. Spiritual emptiness stems from a sense of isolation and separation, which is false, but devastating to the human who suffers it. Filling a void of spiritual emptiness with something in the physical world, like drugs, alcohol, or sex, often seems to ease that pain, but only temporarily.

In the depths of despair, finding a permanent solution might not be so simple. Some even resort to taking their own lives in hopes of escaping extreme despair. Your progress in life is measured by the choices you make in every moment, but what choice to make is not always obvious. The straightest pathway to success is through perfect manifestation of unconditional love for all fellow beings, starting with oneself. However, this can be difficult to achieve—we have the free will to do otherwise.

Choosing otherwise, however, involves a more arduous pathway, often wrought with angst and increased challenges. Regardless, either path will eventually teach us the fundamental lessons of love, compassion, forgiveness, acceptance, and mercy, although not necessarily within a given lifetime.

Karen received a startling phone call from her mother in May 2006 with news that her stepfather had died. While this was upsetting, it wasn't completely shocking given his condition the last time she had seen him. She was better prepared than most to handle the news that someone close to her had died; due to her full understanding that death is a transition, and not the end of awareness, she knew that Randy was simply continuing his soul lessons in the spiritual realm. Along with the details of what had taken place, Diane shared something rather unusual.

"The ceiling fans in all the rooms came on in the middle of the night, all at once," she reported. "I got up to turn them off and I felt Randy's presence, like he was really there." She did not necessarily believe that dead people could communicate with us, but she knew her daughter was open to such things and Karen knew that electronics were one of the more common modes of communication from the other side.

"Yes, it very likely was he who set off the fans!" Karen agreed, knowing it would bring her comfort. "Maybe he'll be back. Pay attention to any signs. I will, too."

"Will you let me know if he contacts you?" Diane asked.

"Yes, of course," Karen replied.

Karen was somber but relieved that Randy's physical suffering was over. She lit a candle and sent thoughts and feelings of compassion, comfort, and love to his spirit in transition, wherever he was.

"Please know we love you, no matter what," she implored.

Randy had been a major influence in Karen's life from the time she was a child. One of her strong memories of him was when he had helped Karen to acquire a paper route at age 11. She began by delivering newspapers each afternoon by bicycle to thirty-five homes in her neighborhood in Salem, Oregon. Over time, she graduated to a route with hundreds of daily deliveries of the local *Statesman Journal* newspaper, necessitating the use of a car. Randy accompanied her each morning and it quickly became evident that Karen's ability to drive would make the job easier, so he taught her to drive before reaching the legal driving age.

That way, they could develop more efficient ways to deliver the papers in tandem. Throughout her high school years, they spent the wee hours of nearly every morning together, driving the route on deserted streets, bringing newspapers to people's homes. He was naturally witty and charming and would often good-naturedly tease Karen, but always with kindness.

The circumstances leading up to his death offer meaningful opportunity for reflection. When Karen's younger brother left home for college in 1983, Randy and Diane moved from Oregon to Arizona. Because of the larger market in the greater Phoenix area, Randy decided this would be a great opportunity to get back into the radio industry, where he had thrived in the '50s and '60s as a rock-and-roll DJ and, later, as a music director and sports director/announcer. He was offered a job as a weekend DJ, but he felt the position was beneath his level of experience, even though it had been ten years since he had worked in radio. He made the choice to wait for a higher-profile job—an offer that never came.

He found odd jobs here and there, but none of them met his dream of returning to radio. Increasingly, he began to suffer from anxiety and was prescribed Xanax. Eventually, he found steady work as a truck driver, from which he retired in 2000. Shortly thereafter, depression set in. He had nothing to do except take daily walks with his majestic gray and white Siberian husky, Leica, with one blue eye and one brown eye, who had often accompanied him on long road trips.

As time went on, Randy's depression worsened. While seeing a doctor, he admitted to having thoughts of suicide and was referred to a psychiatrist, who prescribed antidepressants along with the antianxiety drug Xanax, which he had continued to take. He had stopped drinking and smoking cigarettes years earlier, but regularly took medications to treat symptoms of high cholesterol, high blood pressure, and a hiatal hernia. Karen and Jamie paid a visit to Arizona in 2004 and found Randy to be an empty shell. Gone was the humorous teasing, which had extended to young Jamie, and they both missed his amusing, playful nature. They found it demanding to hold even a brief conversation with him. He seemed dull and uninterested in engaging in any way, as if nothing at all mattered.

To make matters worse, Randy had recently been diagnosed with shingles, an extremely painful viral infection of the peripheral nerves with no medical cure, but which added a pain-management prescription to his cocktail of medications. The next blow was on March 9, 2006, when their beloved dog Leica died after nearly twelve years of loyal companionship.

On the Monday before Memorial Day in 2006, Diane drove to work as usual. Randy had been in an extra-surly mood the night before and, while it wasn't her habit, she felt prompted to call him at home around noon. He answered the phone, but his words were slurred.

"What's wrong?" Diane asked.

"Nothing," he replied. Just then, she heard a crash in the background.

"What was that?" she asked.

"I fell, but I'm fine. Don't come home," Randy insisted, and hung up the phone.

Diane sensed something was desperately wrong and immediately requested permission to leave work. As she made the hour-long drive through Phoenix along the 10 freeway to the 202, she prepared herself for what she might find. Upon walking into the house, she first noticed a bottle of Jack Daniel's whiskey in the kitchen, and next to it an empty Xanax pill bottle and a note. She found him sitting in an armchair in the bedroom, holding photos of her in his lap. He was not responsive, but still breathing, and she called 911. The paramedics tried to revive him and transported him to Mesa General Hospital for further attempts, but it was too late.

Suicide is often debilitating for those left behind. Diane constantly reviewed what she might have done differently to prevent such a loss. She was wracked with guilt in the here and now, and Karen did what she could to alleviate her mother's self-reproach.

For months after his death, Karen attempted to reach out to Randy in expanded states of awareness. Such intentional attempts to communicate with loved ones can be elusive since we are often too emotionally charged to allow for the necessary clarity and neutrality. This could have been upsetting or discouraging, but she knew that the souls of departed loved ones might also appear in dreams. She was determined to remain patient.

On June 7, 2007, Karen was rewarded with such a dream, as recorded in her journal:

"I visited Randy. He was happy and conversational; he told me he was a spirit. We talked while he sat in his favorite chair. Later he was driving a bus in a tunnel and I was in the car next to him. He seemed to make sure I could see him on my left and waved, then pointed to his left, across the lanes, to a memorial of him—photos, flowers—in a niche in the tunnel. At one point in the earlier conversation, he expressed frustration or jealousy of a person Mom knew and spent time with. He referred to the man as being at their house three times. Also, Randy had a full, healthy head of hair."

The dream showed Karen that Randy seemed happy and had returned to his usual plucky self. His full, healthy head of hair had not been present since he had been much younger. Just as I had viewed my father and Agnew while listening to binaural beats, Karen viewed her stepfather in his ideal physical state, his light body. They were both driving in the dream, reminiscent of those many hours spent driving together to deliver newspapers. She noted that the dream was accompanied by atypical vibrations and the sense of falling.

Thus far, she wasn't ready to declare she had actually communicated with Randy. Well-practiced with applying discernment, she felt this all could be information that her subconscious mind made up to provide comfort, easily dismissed as a manufactured self-fulfilling vision. That is, until she talked to her mother. Diane and Karen did not speak on a regular basis—many months would pass between conversations and they did not routinely share details of their daily lives. But the encounter with Randy required a phone call.

"Mom, I had a dream about Randy," Karen began.

Diane kept an open mind and was relieved to hear that Randy appeared to be happy and had a full head of hair. But her comments regarding Randy's concern about a new man in her life were the most interesting.

"This is so strange. I've been seeing another man, an old friend from high school," Diane explained. "We have been out to dinner three times and he picked me up at home each time. I've recently decided not to see him again since I'm just not ready to start dating anyone seriously."

In the dream, Randy had expressed frustration or jealousy about a man her mother spent time with who had been to their home three times. Since Karen had absolutely no knowledge of her mother's recent activities, this provided meaningful validation that she had potentially inter-acted with an energy she identified as her stepfather, who apparently had communicated to her facts about what was going on here on earth.

Diane shared in this amazement and the news brought her solace as it seemed Randy really was okay and continued to watch over her. Karen's dream about Randy contributed greatly to Diane's ability to move past her guilt and grief. The idea that he was watching after her was comfort-ing. Following five years of self-imposed penance and keeping their cre-mated ashes at home, Diane arranged for Randy and Leica to be buried together in Cascade Locks, Oregon, under a Harry Lauder's walking stick plant on a bluff overlooking the Columbia River. Diane is now at peace with all that occurred and continues to maintain a positive outlook on life.

"Where is the soul of my departed loved one who successfully com-mitted suicide?" I am often asked, with great concern.

One of the most consistent observations of Dr. Raymond Moody, spanning more than four decades of study, is that attempted suicides who witness any of the features of an NDE, especially the life review or the feeling of overwhelming unconditional love, come back to this world and generally never attempt suicide again. That is very remarkable given that the more typical pattern for attempted but failed suicides is that they do try again, often repeatedly and, sadly enough, eventually with success.

The interjection of common NDE features—including the presence of love and the life review, where they realize the love others (and the divine Source) have for them, and the pain and suffering they've caused others through their act of suicide—reveals the extraordinary power of the NDE in correcting the entire path of the soul group. Some report going through an extraordinarily rich life review, a whole process that seems to be effective at preventing reattempts at suicide because what the person encounters in that life review is overwhelming evidence of the extraordi-nary love that was in their life, but unrecognized by them during such a "dark night of the soul" that allowed their suicide attempt in the first place.

The important thing to recognize is that those who take their own lives are choosing an especially arduous pathway and may very likely choose to essentially relive the same circumstances they are attempting to leave behind. We are all essential to this evolution of consciousness, and we cannot simply opt out. No one gets out of here dead—there is ultimately no escape from the continuum of conscious awareness. It is wise to embrace this glorious gift of physical life, and to rise to the challenges it presents to afford the possibility of true learning, growth, and transcendence. This is not to say such a thing is easy, especially in our modern culture.

The 2015 Nobel Memorial Prize in Economic Science was awarded to two Princeton economists, Dr. Angus Deaton and his wife, Dr. Anne Case, for their research that revealed a startling reality about our society: The death rate among middle-aged white Americans is rising steadily as compared with every other age, ethnic, and racial group in America, and compared with similar groups in other developed nations. This rise in death rates is not due to the usual suspects of cancer, diabetes, and heart disease, but rather to a steady growth in death by suicide and the consequences of alcohol and other substance abuse (particularly heroin and prescription opiate overdoses).

Other economists have been shocked by this alarming trend. Even the HIV/AIDS epidemic has not caused such a major dent in life expectancy in our country in recent decades. A major culprit in this pattern is likely related to the spiritual vacuum that has crept into our secular culture. Mainstream Western society takes its lead from conventional science, which denies the reality of soul and spirit in our lives. Our society simply doesn't support the value of a rich, internal spiritual connection.

Believe me, I do understand the desolation of spiritual emptiness; I have touched it myself. I often proclaim to be a grateful recovering alcoholic. Many might not understand that the gratitude is not simply for breaking free of alcohol—it is for being born alcoholic in the first place. Without this difficult challenge, I never would have received the "gift of desperation," of hitting a bottom that was not quite as low as death (though frighteningly close), and the start down a pathway that would lead, eventually, through my coma journey, toward truly knowing the love of a higher power (an intelligent, loving, and supportive force, which some call God and others call their higher self). Similar challenges might lead us into hopelessness, but it is our choice whether or not we go there. Gratitude is the most appropriate response to life and, with it, everything begins to shift from a position of hopelessness to one of hope, no matter what your life situation presents.

Twelve-step programs, like the archetype known to the world through the remarkably successful Alcoholics Anonymous, depend on the principle of turning one's life over to a higher power. It makes no religious demands on the identity of this higher power—one of my early friends in recovery said that the higher power could even be a lightbulb. The important step is not feeling responsible for overpowering and driving every event in one's life, but actually turning it over and trusting that the higher power will assume the navigation of our lives, that we are not ultimately responsible for forcing every outcome that our ego demands of us. In our proposed program of meditation, this "turning over" process is accomplished through invocation of our "higher soul," an aspect completely free of egoic concerns, as that higher power.

In the most acute setting of life's challenges, administration of certain medications can be quite valuable, but not necessarily for long-term use. When the fundamental problem is one that's more deeply spiritual, it needs spiritual addressing, not only biochemical. While medication might be necessary in some cases, exploring the benefits of some sort of spiritual practice is a must. For many, the adage "Let go, and let God," says it all. I submit that this process is greatly facilitated through any practice of "going within," of centering prayer or meditation, of getting in touch with that spiritual core that is within us all.

The "Serenity Prayer," at the heart of twelve-step programs, states in elegant simplicity the power of this turning-over process:

> God, grant me the serenity to accept the things I cannot change,
>
> The courage to change the things I can,
>
> And the wisdom to know the difference.

> —*Reinhold Niebuhr (1892–1971)*

This is a simple but powerful appeal to practice acceptance, to act with courage, and a request to be blessed with the insight to discriminate between that over which we have power, and that over which we do not.

Importantly, we can find through the associated spiritual growth that we have tremendous power over our lives, but it begins through the understanding that our wisdom of discrimination originates within—with our higher souls, not with our ego or some limited form of our being in the material realm. This is the same higher soul that I routinely access through daily meditation. Note that, for me, while in that expanded state, that higher soul has not a trace of ego still encumbering it—it is fully devoted to the higher good.

The ego is an important psychological structure that plays an important role in a human being's dealing with the world, but it is not ultimately who we are. In fact, the ego can create powerful blockades of pride, shame, and fear that prevent too many people from opening themselves up to love and healing. Ego is often to blame when someone refuses to ask for help, or won't commit to a treatment, or doesn't even want to admit that they have a problem. Some in addiction medicine have even developed a ritual that dramatizes the death of the ego to allow for its rebirth in a far more healthy and harmonious state.

Dr. Stanislav Grof and his wife, Christina, developed such a method using specific breathing techniques and other elements—a therapy they named "holotropic breathwork." Holotropic refers to the state of "moving toward wholeness," or "becoming whole." This method utilizes a precise way of breathing and other specific practices to achieve a hypnagogic state. The particular breath patterns seem to occupy the analytical part of the brain, similar to brain-wave entrainment recordings. This leads to expansion of consciousness and access to insights associated with an "inner healer" not typically possible using conventional psychotherapy. The subject performing the breathing technique is closely supervised, often in a group setting, and time for interpretation and integration is a critical part of the process.

During a session, it is necessary to surrender completely to the process and allow anything that arises to be expressed. Some experience profound states of love and connection to the cosmos, while others report feelings of fear or intense guilt. Memories from traumatic experiences are frequently evoked. Often, people are able to break well beyond typical defense mechanisms that occur during talk therapy. Sometimes, just the act of crying will trigger a release of past emotional trauma. Participants respond in unique ways specific to their personal makeup, but consistently report benefits such as relief from depression and chronic pain, release of emotional suffering, and a greater sense of contact with their spiritual self. They find meaning and purpose in life, intuitive insights and support for addiction recovery.

Another useful therapy for accessing and processing traumatic memories is eye-movement desensitization and reprocessing (EMDR), often used to address symptoms associated with post-traumatic stress disorder. After a thorough case history of issues to be addressed, this process involves inducing a pattern of rapid back-and-forth eye movements that seems to allow greater access to past memories.

Note that brain-wave entrainment audio recordings have similar profound effects on altering our state of consciousness, attributed mainly to the left-right oscillation in the lower brain stem, where these sounds are perceived (specifically in the superior olivary complex, near the reticular activating system, which is the ignition system for binding consciousness into an apparent whole). I surmise that the mechanism underlying EMDR, as well as hypnosis, similarly accesses expanded states of consciousness through a common influence of such low frequency left-right oscillations in the lower brain stem.

EMDR therapy consists of several phases of treatment over repeated sessions, including desensitization to the original trauma memory, resolution of disturbing emotions, and replacement of unfavorable memories with something more positive. Successful subjects report letting go of anger and depression, and replacing it with inner peace and acceptance.

Addressing emotional trauma is something we all struggle with at times, some more extremely than others, and feeling more whole often involves a lifelong journey. But the rewards are well worth the effort to make different choices that might bring an end to dismay and distress. At age 16, Caroline Cook (a reader who shared her story) was confused and intensely sad, feeling so much emotional pain that she hurt physically, with an unbearable intensity. Traumatic childhood events, her mother's mental illness, and her parents' divorce spiraled her into a life dominated by a need to be loved that could never be fulfilled. At some point, she became aware of a terrible, wrenching sadness that she felt in her solar-plexus region—a large, hard, tense ball that she came to call her "great ball of sadness." She reached a point where she couldn't stand another minute of it and wanted the peace she believed death would bring, so she swallowed an overdose of sleeping pills with the intent to end her life.

After being unconscious for a time, she was found and taken to a hospital, where she remained in a coma for three days. Upon awakening, she was shocked to recall a vivid memory, overshadowing everything else, of what seemed to be a real experience. Different from a dream, Caroline's recollections remain as clear today at age 63 as they were all those years ago (a hallmark of NDE memories).

"I suddenly found myself standing in a beautiful, lush, green forest, looking out over pastures filled with flowers with snow-capped mountains in the distance, all beneath a brilliant blue sky. The colors were vivid, yet everything was bathed in a white light, even the sky. I felt joyful and happy to be there."

Then, beside her appeared a very old man dressed all in white with white hair and beard; he, too, was bathed in white light. She felt no fear as he emanated deep caring and understanding.

"You cannot stay here. It is not your time yet and you must go back and finish living your life," he gently said to Caroline.

Even though she wanted to stay in the beautiful place where she felt that sense of peace and well-being for which she had longed, she accepted that coming back to earth was the right thing to do. She realized that suicide doesn't solve problems or take away pain—the problems go with you. You can't escape them this way; ending her life was more than wrong, it was futile. The only way to get off the merry-go-round of life is to ride it until it stops naturally, as it will. When we commit suicide, we don't get off the merry-go-round at all—we stay on it, and our pains and problems stay with us.

Before she left the hospital, and only a day or so after waking up, a nurse asked Caroline if she would like to visit sick children as she recuperated. It was terribly sad on one level, yet they modeled how to be brave through the simple acceptance of their own pains and struggles. Many of these children were dying, and she was uplifted and inspired by their stoic attitudes to live fully during each and every minute of their lives. They, too, taught her that suicide is not the right way to die, and that it is in the struggling with illness or hardships that we truly learn to live.

In the hundreds of presentations I've given since my coma, I often encounter parents who are grieving the loss of a child. Most often, no matter how far along they are in the grief process, these parents tell me their child seemed to have immense strength in the face of imminent death—in fact, they often report the child to be the greatest pillar of strength holding the family together around such a tragic loss. It became apparent that these children were advanced souls, indeed.

Following her release from the hospital, Caroline continued to feel sadness, depression, and anxiety, and suffered panic attacks. Thoughts of killing herself continued, but aside from a few minor attempts as a cry for help, she never seriously attempted suicide again. But her problems weren't over and the great ball of sadness was ever-present. She occasionally sought help from medical professionals and took antidepressant medications for a couple of years on two occasions. But nothing seemed to make a difference in the long run. In her early fifties, her latest relationship came to a crashing end and she felt the rug of her life had been pulled out from beneath her, sending her into yet another deeply distressed state. Caroline had a supportive friend with a simple, strong, and unwavering faith in God who one day said something meaningful to her.

"Remember that God is there for you and you can be healed through faith and prayer."

This did not have an immediate cure-all effect, but it did remind Caroline of her experience at age 16, when she encountered the loving man bathed in white light who brought her such a strong sense of peace. Thus began a journey of rejuvenation. She developed a habit of daily prayer, and one day she thought to ask in her prayers that the great ball of sadness be taken from her—and it was. In the days and weeks that followed, her awareness of this grew stronger and she soon realized she no longer carried that terrible burden. She felt lighter and filled with hope and, while she still battled depression and anxiety, from that moment forward she never had another suicidal thought. She stopped looking for love in all the wrong ways; the longing to be loved dissipated and was replaced by a knowing that it is enough to be loved by God.

She came to understand what "surrendering to God" really means. She once thought it meant relinquishing her independence and identity and to be ruled over in some way. Now she understands that in surrendering we are freeing ourselves and tapping into the tremendous power of love, with all its healing, comforting, and nurturing. She is grateful for the guidance, teaching, discipline, protection, and grace that she has experienced in her life (which she now knows were always there, even when she didn't realize it).

Caroline considers her instinct and intuition as God's voice in her heart and mind, and she now trusts that inner voice without a doubt. She is not conventionally religious—but through knowing God, she nurtures her deeply personal connection with that loving force. The impact and benefits in her life are amazing and miraculous. She has found a peace and contentment in herself she had never thought possible here on earth. She has learned to accept what is thrown at her, bearing all pains, hurts, sorrows, and difficulties. She is now fulfilled with love from her personal community that includes her son and his young family, her canine companion, her friends, and her students.

Like a caterpillar struggling out of its cocoon only to transform into a beautiful butterfly, the struggles in life are worth it because the joys really can outweigh the burdens. Through forgiveness, we release pain and prevent destructive bitterness. Practicing gratitude or praying every day reinforces a connection to a higher power. While life is not perfect and we wrestle with finances, health, and family issues, it is vital to focus on doing everything we can to nurture our souls and trust in our connection with a higher life force. By becoming more conscious of the choices we make in our lives, we learn to create more fulfilling experiences.

CHAPTER 15

MIND OVER MATTER

There are two kinds of people: Those who think they can, and those who think they can't, and they're both right.

—HENRY FORD (1863–1947),
FOUNDER OF THE FORD MOTOR COMPANY

No matter what our beliefs, they are highly influential in our lives. Many beliefs are so ingrained in our systems that they are recognized more as truths than as beliefs. Even recognition of truth is subject to our underlying assumptions. Our beliefs affect the analysis and understanding of any experience, whether it be the interpretation of a scientific experiment or the description of an NDE. In the end, each of us has a completely unique blend of beliefs and attitudes that affect every aspect of life, including our health.

While presenting a workshop in Aspen in July 2015, Karen and I noted the power of attitude when we had the pleasure of getting to know Laurie MacCaskill. She had been diagnosed with pancreatic cancer nine years earlier. Those familiar with cancer of the pancreas will know that the typical survival time following diagnosis is counted in months, not years. Remarkably, during a lunch we shared, she appeared completely healthy and fit.

"How is it that you've outlived all expectations?" Karen asked, with her usual frank curiosity.

"You know, I never believed I was sick," Laurie answered.

Laurie was an exercise enthusiast and quite active, routinely participating in 100-mile bike rides, skiing, and high-altitude hiking. She maintained a healthy diet and tended to her overall health with "well-check" medical screenings. Following a persistent pain in the lower right side of her back, Laurie's diagnosis at 55 years of age came as quite a shock.

Following a Whipple procedure (a complicated abdominal surgery for pancreatic cancer) soon after her diagnosis, Laurie began an aggressive three-year chemotherapy regimen, which had its ups and downs. Some days left her nauseous, weak, and exhausted, while other days her activities proceeded fairly normally. She viewed her treatments as "just another thing on my calendar," and never used language like "my cancer" or "my final days." She followed all her doctors' instructions and advice using Western medical techniques, but remained detached from "owning" the illness.

After three years, chemotherapy was no longer effective and she was told she had four to six months to live. Following twelve liver biopsies, she was diagnosed with a liver infection and, medically, it seemed that this was heralding the end. Laurie was prescribed a daily treatment that involved receiving medication via intravenous (IV) injection for two hours twice a day over the course of one month. Typically, this is carried out in a hospital or, alternatively, through regular at-home visits from a nurse. Given her travel schedule, Laurie asked if she could perform the treatment herself. While her doctor had never received such a request, he arranged for the proper instructions.

"One day, I wanted to go on an early bike ride, but my IV was still going," Laurie shared. "I simply packed everything up and put it in my fanny pack while my husband and I rode up a canyon. When the IV stopped, I found two bearproof containers on the side of the road, pulled out my small towel, syringes, and alcohol swabs, disconnected the tubes, flushed with the appropriate drugs, and off we went. I felt I was responsible, careful, and, most important, living my life!

"Attitude—it has an incredible impact on our lives. The remarkable thing is we have a choice every day regarding the attitude we will embrace that day. I am convinced that life is 10 percent of what happens to me and

90 percent how I react to it. Through my 'survivorship,' I have learned that contentment is not the fulfillment of what you want, but the realization of what you already have," Laurie added.

It is especially important to emphasize her statement that "we have a choice" regarding our attitude in life—with or without contending with a cancer-treatment regimen. Laurie chose to believe her illness did not own her. She continues to enjoy good health and now serves as a motivational speaker. Her inspirational outlook can be applied to any perceived hardship someone might face.

Anita Moorjani, who describes her experience in *Dying to Be Me,* was faced with a cancer diagnosis of her own. For decades, she had been afraid of not measuring up to other people's expectations and felt constant fear and anxiety about not fitting in. The choices she made throughout her life were usually based on her fear of disappointing someone. Following the news of her best friend's diagnosis of cancer, and subsequently the same in her brother-in-law, she learned more about cancer and its many causes and treatments. It seemed that nearly everything could cause cancer, and this knowledge evolved into an obsessive fear of contracting cancer.

She was wholly committed *not* to get it herself and thus developed a strict regimen to eliminate consumption of certain foods and substances reported to cause cancer. Pollution in the environment, microwaves, plastic containers, mobile phones—it seemed everything was a potential cause of cancer. Despite her avoidance, she was devastated when she later was diagnosed with cancer of the lymphatic system. Compounding her fear of contracting cancer was her fear of chemotherapy, a primary treatment for cancer. She had witnessed the damaging side effects suffered by her best friend and brother-in-law and refused all radiation treatments.

For several years she tried alternative therapies, but in February 2006 she was admitted to the hospital already in coma, as her organs were failing and she appeared to be losing the battle. While doctors informed her family that she was hours away from death, Anita's awareness left her body and became part of the spiritual realm, where she met with the souls of her departed father and best friend. Anita was awash in the force of unconditional love, free from earthly attachments, and viewed events throughout her life in a whole new light. She understood that her illness had started on an energetic level prior to any physical symptoms.

In the process of choosing whether or not to return to her physical body, she attained a knowing, without any doubt, that if she chose to complete the dying process, "everything was exactly as it should be in the grand tapestry of life." Likewise, if she returned to her body, she would experience a complete healing. Either choice was freely available with no judgment. Initially, she made the decision to let go and die, but at that point an important truth became clear.

"It was then that I understood that my body is only a reflection of my inner state," Anita explains. "If my inner self were aware of its greatness and connection with All-that-is, my body would soon reflect that and heal rapidly."

After thirty hours in coma, Anita awakened. Within days, the lemon-size tumors throughout her entire lymphatic system began to shrink. Much to her doctors' amazement, after two weeks there were no tumors at all. While they continued to run tests to find the cancer so that it could be properly treated, Anita insisted they would not find any sign of it. Over the weeks, months, and years since then, she has remained cancer-free. Remarkably, her medical records verify the physical devastation of her body that had taken place prior to coma, along with her complete recovery.

As to the miraculous nature of my own recovery, an independent objective medical review, headed by Dr. Bruce Greyson, noted the following:

"Three physicians not associated with Lynchburg General Hospital completed an independent review of the complete medical record of Dr. Alexander's hospitalization, and spoke with the hospital's two consulting neurologists to gather additional information. The records indicated that Dr. Alexander was brought to the emergency department unresponsive, with evidence of a bacterial infection, and he was assessed to have moderate brain injury, which rapidly progressed to severe brain injury over the next few hours. Brain scans showed that the membranes covering the brain as well as the grooves in his cerebral cortex were swollen with pus-filled liquid, compressing the cortical tissue. Laboratory examination showed evidence of a bacterial infection in his cerebrospinal fluid, due to an organism that very rarely causes meningitis in adults and, when it does, is almost always fatal or resulting in permanent neurological deficits. Nevertheless, after a profound near-death experience,

Dr. Alexander eventually awoke from his coma and within a few months had made what his surprised neurologists called a 'complete and remarkable recovery' from an illness they agreed might well have been fatal, without any residual neurological deficit."

Anita's experience helps to explain more clearly how I healed so totally from my near-lethal bout with bacterial meningoencephalitis. She credits her recovery to complete elimination of fear that had been ruling her life. From her higher soul's point of view, it was not so much a miracle as it was the natural flow expected from successfully learning the lesson to release all fear. Even though I had no conscious awareness of a choice to return in the same sense Anita had, my soul would forever be aware of the force and power of the unconditional love at the core of all existence, crucial to my own recovery.

As more profound capabilities for overall healing arise from attention to our spiritual nature, I expect more commonly to encounter examples of "miraculous healing" beyond the explanatory power of our current medical paradigm. This will allow for a shift in the dependence on formal brain death criteria (discussed in Chapter 7) toward one more aligned with the power of spiritual health. Notably, it's not only in the setting of NDEs that such dramatic physical healing can take place.

In *Radical Remission,* Dr. Kelly A. Turner identifies nine common factors that helped more than a thousand cancer patients achieve complete healing from their disease, but not necessarily from conventional medical treatment. While these cases are generally considered to be anomalies, it provides a worthy look at the body's ability to heal itself—without having to have a near-death experience. Among the identified factors are dietary changes, taking supplements (sometimes in concurrence with more traditional treatments), and taking charge of one's health. Remarkably, six of the nine factors are directly related to spiritual health, including following your intuition, releasing suppressed emotions, increasing positive emotions, embracing social support, deepening your spiritual connection, and having strong reasons for living. And unlike many external circumstances, these are *all* things we have the direct ability to enact and manage.

We are each unique, and specific results will vary based on our individual situation and the lessons we have chosen to address. Dr. Turner found it was never just one obvious cause that could be identified as the particular trigger for healing—it was a combination of these factors that contributed to the remission, and some patients focused more on one method than another. When faced with any disease, it is remarkable that attending to such matters as "deepening your spiritual connection" might contribute to improved health, but such mysteries are not new in medicine.

The placebo effect is the response to a sham procedure or an inert substance (i.e., a sugar pill) that suggests our minds have the power to alleviate symptoms or cure disease. The placebo does not actually cause any physiological effect—it is the patient's *belief* that they have received a therapeutic substance (medicine) or procedure that leads them toward healing (or, in some cases, the practitioner's belief in the healing method). The placebo effect is thus one of the purest forms of mind over matter.

Placebos have probably been used for millennia, but the modern medical discussion about them began with Henry Beecher's 1955 article "The Powerful Placebo" in the *Journal of the American Medical Association*. Beecher was an anesthesiologist who treated injured soldiers during World War II. When he ran out of morphine, he didn't tell the patients, but injected them with a saline solution instead. Much to his surprise, 40 percent of those soldiers reported their pain had been alleviated. He reviewed fifteen medical articles and estimated that the placebo effect played a role in an average of 35 percent of the total cases. He felt he was assessing the "reaction component of suffering" in conditions where subjective factors were important, such as wound pain, angina pectoris, headache, nausea, cough, anxiety, tension, and drug-induced mood changes.

Others claim that this "subject-expectancy effect" might be significantly greater. Herbert Benson of Harvard Medical School says that the placebo effect yields beneficial clinical results in 60 to 90 percent of diseases, including angina pectoris, bronchial asthma, herpes simplex, and duodenal ulcers.[1] Depending on the type of illness or symptom, the placebo effect is commonly assumed to apply roughly 30 to 35 percent of the time. But in some situations the effect might be as large as 90 percent. These are amazing results, seemingly due to the power of our mind to influence our health.

Since Beecher's initial paper, the placebo effect has come to dominate medical research because of the associated belief that approximately one-third of the benefit of therapeutic interventions might be due to the patient's own beliefs in getting better, not due to any other action of the treatment. In order to truly test the effectiveness of a particular substance, pharmaceutical companies must demonstrate that the drug in question is more effective than a placebo (a daunting challenge for any therapeutic intervention). When patients receiving the placebo report benefits similar to those of the drug being tested, the drug is considered to be ineffective. This demonstrates that belief in its ability to heal can be just as powerful as the drug itself. Or, perhaps in some cases, the drug itself is simply irrelevant.

Interestingly, in the last decade, it has become increasingly more difficult for clinical trials to demonstrate statistically that newly developed drugs are more effective than giving a patient an inert substance. This prompted an effort to investigate just how powerful our beliefs are.

In October 2015, Jeffrey Mogil, who directs the pain-genetics lab at McGill University in Montreal, was the lead investigator in a meta-analysis of eighty-four clinical drug trials performed between 1990 and 2013 for treating chronic pain that affects the nervous system. The results were startling. In 1996, the drug being tested outperformed the placebo control group by 27 percent, but by 2013, that difference was only 9 percent. Placebo pills had become 18 percent more effective than an actual drug over that seventeen-year interval.

There is wide speculation as to why this would be, but the authors noted several patterns. This effect has occurred only in the United States and is found more often in trials that last longer and involve more participants. A bigger trial would traditionally indicate the results should be considered more reliable than one with a smaller group of patients; however, Mogil speculates that perhaps the larger trial adds to expectations of the subjects, increasing their belief in the medicine being consumed. Some have pointed out that the prevalence of televised and magazine drug ads (which have been allowed in the United States since 1997, and also in New Zealand) have played a role in increasing the widespread belief of medicine as a cure.

Either way, these results suggest that something fascinating is at play and, considering the debilitating side effects that sometimes come with allopathic drugs, perhaps our research dollars would be better spent on the possible therapeutic effects of other types of health treatment related to the power of our minds to accomplish healing. Our minds seem to have tremendous ability to influence our health, thus becoming more consciously aware of our personal and societal beliefs is a good first step in learning how to harness this phenomenon to our benefit.

A common belief in Western culture is that our genetic makeup determines the likelihood of manifesting specific health issues. With the discovery of DNA and its attributes, by the middle of the 20th century it became standard to expect that if your father had diabetes, you would be more likely to contract the same diabetes because genes that cause such diseases are inherited from our parents.

As it turns out, this is another assumption that has been taken too far. DNA is so complex that if the DNA information contained in just one cell of the human body were printed out single-spaced in 12-point font (one letter for each DNA nucleotide) and made into a book, that book would be at least half the height of the Washington Monument (250 feet) in thickness. A major challenge to scientists in the 1940s had been how to pack that much information into one cell using just a minuscule amount of sugar molecules that are strung together to make up DNA. Everybody was amazed in 1953 when James Watson and Francis Crick were able to identify DNA's double-helix structure, which allowed for the efficient packing of so much information into such a tiny volume. Following this revelation, it was generally thought that we were on a direct pathway to discovering how all of inheritance works.

Subsequent research allowed for a complete sequencing of the human genome, making it much simpler to locate specific genes and mutations and correlate them to a particular disease. But researchers came to realize in the 1970s and '80s that more than 98 percent of DNA does not appear to function in this simplistic way (providing the template for transcription of proteins within the cell, its essential mechanism of heredity) and is thus labeled "junk" DNA. In fact, nobody yet knows the purpose of so-called junk DNA, although some of it is likely involved in the complex regulation of gene expression involved during embryogenesis, when all of the cells of a developing embryo transform into a fetus, then into an infant. Given the complexity of the human body, scientists initially postulated it would require 100,000 separate genes to fully explain human genetics. In fact, to their shock and chagrin, further work has shown that the human genome consists of only 20,000 protein-coding genes, similar to the number of genes in far simpler organisms, like fruit flies and roundworms.

The interpretation of how DNA information storage might be used to explain human heredity turns out to be not so simple. Many different disciplines have looked at humans as biological machines that are mechanistic and predictable, largely determined by our DNA.

However, the latest research is refuting such simplistic interpretations, as revealed in the book *Supergenes* by Dr. Rudolph Tanzi and Dr. Deepak Chopra. Tanzi is a professor of neurology at Harvard Medical School, with a focus on genetics and aging research, including pioneering studies related to Alzheimer's. In a startling about-face regarding the role of DNA, research reveals that only 5 percent of gene mutations assumed to commit one to having a given disease actually result in manifesting the disease. In the other 95 percent of cases where the presence of the gene might have resulted in the disease, it did not, thanks to environmental and behavioral influences. It turns out that we can actually modify our DNA by shifting our thoughts, beliefs, and behavior—we are not so much slave to our genetics, after all. This is a complete reversal from the conventional view of the science I was taught in medical school. When fully accepted and applied in clinical practice, this fact has the potential to overhaul our entire approach to health care.

Clearly, our underlying beliefs influence more than we might realize— they affect societal approaches to medical treatment, education, social policies, and more. Belief systems can be associated with a particular religion, culture, or spiritual tradition, or perhaps with being nonreligious (atheist or agnostic) or scientistic, the blind faith that the scientific method is the ultimate authority on truth, to the exclusion of all other channels of knowing.

Some of these traditions are rather rigid in their rules and dogma, while others are more open. Some of us readily accept the totality of a given belief system, while others adopt only particular elements or assemble a combination of teachings. Some societal beliefs come directly from the scientific community, such as "diabetes is likely if it runs in your family." Since our choices and behavior are influenced by such beliefs (whether actually true or not), they affect each moment of our lives. As long as we believe it, that belief has power in determining our course.

Stepping back to question our assumptions in order to see the bigger picture—starting from scratch, as I have done through deconstructing my former scientific belief system—helps to truly get to the heart of the matter. Following my coma, I came to realize that even though the scientific method allows for confirmation of certain facts about the world, much knowledge about reality must originate from outside of the simple and contrived use of such methodology. For example, scientific studies assessing the role of prayer in healing can become so distorted by the experimental setup as to obliterate any semblance of the experimental practice with the more natural real-world practice. Especially with materialism as the current dominant scientific model, the very worship of such science becomes its own trap. I am more of a scientist now than I've ever been, but through questioning my foundational assumptions back to the beginning, I have come to see materialism as a completely failed worldview (especially over the issue of consciousness and the brain-mind discussion).

Still other beliefs are based at the level of individual personal experience. None of us, especially as children, are immune to the well-meaning power of our parents, teachers, and other authority figures who instill limiting beliefs in us, such as "Women don't do well at math" or "You'll never amount to anything if you don't go to college." Of course, some imparted beliefs provide positive influence, such as "Be kind to others." The placebo effect demonstrates that our beliefs can strongly influence our health, along with every other aspect of life. But many beliefs stem from incorrect assumptions along with the unconscious thought patterns and negative inner voices that influence us in every moment.

Karen often remarks that my journey during coma was a gift of the ultimate objective state, given that I had complete amnesia for my life here on earth.

"Since he didn't remember his former beliefs, Eben's experience is a great example of how a completely blank slate can allow for a truly objective view, which often leads to new perspectives," she points out.

It is incumbent on each of us to examine where our beliefs came from, how they affect us, and, in some cases, after evaluating their veracity and applicability to our lives, make the choice to change them. Our beliefs are not always readily apparent—fully uncovering them can be challenging. Often, we are not aware of the underlying beliefs that might influence a given situation, and many of them limit our ability to succeed. Such limiting beliefs can become so ingrained that they often seem to be facts that cannot be altered. It is useful to identify habitual ways of thinking, which often involves sincere soul-searching. This is where developing the ability to sense the neutral inner observer becomes most useful. Paying close attention to the language you regularly use is an excellent task for your observer. This can be addressed in a contemplative or meditative state or as you interact and converse with others.

Begin to notice phrases you commonly use that support your limiting beliefs, whether spoken out loud or silently in your mind. Typical phrases might include, "I'm not smart enough" or "No one else does it that way" or "My boss makes my life miserable." Then look at those from a neutral viewpoint and ask yourself if it is a fact or an assumption. If you think it's a fact, would others completely agree with you? Or is it perhaps an assumption? If it's an assumption and not a fact, you have uncovered a belief. Is it possibly limiting you in achieving your goals in some way?

Once identified, changing one's underlying beliefs can be difficult, but addressing them can provide a useful key to making significant changes in life—and well worth the effort it takes. Imagining how your life might be affected after adopting a new belief can be quite useful. Envision yourself moving through life with that fresh outlook and project how it might impact different situations. Replacing your beliefs with new ones is like trying on clothes to see how they fit. Note also how you feel as you wear them. Consciously decide if you wish to change your belief and own that decision.

When Karen first attempted to meditate, she was accustomed to learning new skills with relative ease, but as previously revealed, meditation did not come easily. When she initially achieved less than desirable results, she assumed she was one of those people with a mind so active it couldn't be tamed. "I can't meditate" or "I'm not capable of meditating" were common thoughts that ran through her mind. But as she learned more about limiting beliefs, she came to realize that this might be holding her back. Like me, she had taken a course in Silva mind control, learning a technique used to interrupt undesirable thoughts by repeating the word *cancel* when they occur. She developed a habit of noticing when limiting or undesirable thoughts would occur, and when it happened, she consciously repeated "cancel—cancel" in her mind and then corrected her inner language to "I can meditate" or "I am capable of meditating." Over the course of several months, her meditation practice improved. This method, or a similar one, can be applied to all kinds of beliefs.

Dr. Lissa Rankin became especially interested in how beliefs affect personal health and has pursued a mission to demonstrate such a mechanism. As outlined in *Mind Over Medicine,* she reviewed studies on the placebo effect that revealed a wide variety of illnesses that benefited from sham treatments, such as asthma, depression, infertility, colitis, headaches, ulcers, high blood pressure, warts, and more. On the flip side, patients are often told they have just months to live, and there are cases where some have died at the exact time predicted, only to have an autopsy reveal no sign of the diagnosed condition.

Through interactions with her patients, Rankin attributes successful healing to the relaxation response, a lowering of stress that activates the parasympathetic nervous system, which is related to the body's natural ability to heal itself. This relaxation response is facilitated by many factors, including nurturing care, work-life balance, positive emotions, spiritual connection, community support, relationships, creative expression, and financial health. A habit of regular meditation alone has been shown to significantly contribute to overall relaxation and a reduction of stress. While these are among the important steps to address, the exact approach is different for each person. But applicable to all, belief is cited as the first of six steps to healing—the belief that one can be healed. She indicates that this is the underlying power of any treatment and boldly suggests that ultimately all healing might be attributable to the mind, whether through conventional Western medicine or through alternative approaches.

As a doctor, Rankin asks pointed questions of her patients, such as what they appreciate about their life, if they're fulfilled at work, if they feel like they're in touch with their life purpose, and if they feel financially healthy. Their answers often provide insights that lab tests cannot. When Rankin asks what's missing in their lives, many patients have long lists, or simply begin to cry. She was shocked when she began to ask, "What does your body need to heal?" People began to give answers such as, "I'm so lonely; I need to make more friends," "I have to quit my job," "I need to forgive myself," or "I need to meditate every day."

Many patients weren't ready to address such issues, but those who trusted their intuition and went on to make radical changes were often rewarded with astonishing results that medicine alone had not accomplished. Once becoming aware that you aren't a victim of circumstance and that your behavior, life situation, or perspective is the potential source of a problem, you can focus on making positive changes in your life. Rankin encourages each her patients to develop their own prescription for health by finding the ideal combination of lifestyle changes, treatments, and beneficial habits that bring the desired results.

Stacie Williams (a reader who shared her story), managed to do just that. During her twenties and thirties, she experienced cognitive fog, forgetfulness, difficulty with oral and written comprehension, difficulty finding words, anxiety, depression, issues with concentration and focus, some tinnitus, weakness in the extremities, and blurred vision. She tried both individual and group therapy to treat the depression and anxiety. She was prescribed various antidepressants, which didn't bring much relief, along with Depakote and lithium, and Adderall for attention-deficit issues. Eventually, a PhD professional diagnosed her with having cognitive disorder NOS (not otherwise specified), and another PhD's diagnosis was of mild atypical autism as the underlying concern.

Stacie was an avid reader and usually preferred mystery and romance novels when she could concentrate enough. But one day, when perusing a bookstore, she noticed a staff-recommended book, *The Power of Now* by Eckhart Tolle. At first she was nervous about buying it because it was completely different from anything she had ever read (or even thought about) and she was anxious about trying new things outside her comfort zone. But something about it called to her and she took the leap.

Tolle's words resonated with her as he described an essence of being, a presence that does not necessarily show up in terms of the personality and ego. Tolle defines the ego as a "false self" that develops as you grow up (through conditioning) into a mental image of who you think you are. He differentiated the presence of the watcher (the observer) and getting behind or underneath the pain and the ego to see what is really there—who you really are. Stacie's aha moment came when she read about remembering how you were as a child, because children by nature don't have the ego that adults generally have. Prior to establishing the ego, we are closer to a purer essence of lightness and being.

Meanwhile, her problems worsened to the point where she was sleeping twelve to sixteen hours per day and suffered from chronic fatigue, zinc deficiency, and suspected fibromyalgia. She ached most of the time and suffered from panic attacks and terrible gut pain. Doctors didn't know the cause and believed it to be autoimmune, but test after test, including MRIs, EKGs, EEGs, and bloodwork, came up within normal ranges. She continued to consult medical professionals, but eventually she was considered incurable. She was told that she had exhausted any potential benefit from modern medicine, other than its offering her some comfort by addressing the symptoms—and even that was rarely successful.

She recalled Tolle's book and remembered her own childhood, when she had that innocent joy and bliss. It was a state of being free and not having all the responsibilities, not having all the stress, not having all the pain. She knew that somehow she could get back to that feeling and was inspired to explore metaphysical topics and to try meditation. She began to search for various opportunities in the Chicago area (where she lived), including lectures, meditation groups, yoga, and alternative therapies. She found it vital to apply discernment because there were so many options and some were more effective than others. Meditation itself turned out to be quite valuable, although it was difficult in the beginning. There were a lot of times when she wondered, "Will I ever have a breakthrough?" But persistence and tenacity paid off.

A common practice noted by many teachers was simply to watch the breath (a form of mindfulness), and Stacie found this especially useful when she had a hard time staying focused. She followed Tolle's advice to notice the space between breathing in and breathing out. In conversations, she listened for the silence between the words she heard in order to *feel* the essence of the message, rather than what the person was speaking. This especially seemed to help with her verbal-comprehension issue.

"When you go deep and you can really see and feel that essence, that's comforting, even if you can't find it on the outside. You kind of get underneath all that pain and you feel that essence—that's the tremendous gift," Stacie explained.

Working with her doctor, Stacie chose to wean off medications and go the holistic and metaphysical route, including yoga, meditation, prayer, and maintaining a consistent schedule. Today, her cognitive functioning is back to normal. She works full-time, has reduced or eliminated most of her other symptoms, and now connects relatively easily with other people.

"Since I've been able to vocalize a lot better and be organized in terms of speech and all of that, I've found that it is tremendously helpful to be rebuilding community," Stacie explained. "There were times when I really needed to be alone, by myself, but friendships are just so important, I think for everyone, because they help to mirror our positive qualities and traits, and without them we don't always have perspective. When you have friends and people who you really trust, they can help direct and guide you and vice versa. Without that, you're navigating in the dark sometimes, and that's hard."

Developing a richer sense of our spiritual nature, along with a focus on our connectedness with others, and a broadening awareness of the beauty of our existence are all aspects of true health that we ignore at our peril. As a physician, I have come to see that any true vision of health must include not only the physical, mental, and emotional realms, but, most importantly, the spiritual. This principle applies not only to individual humans, but to families, soul groups, ethnic and national populations, humanity—indeed, to all of life on earth. Full health of any system demands acknowledging the spiritual aspects of our existence and our capacity as individuals to manage our health. Our beliefs are more powerful than we might imagine. Most important is the healing power of unconditional love—this profound force has infinite power to heal at all levels.

CHAPTER 16

THRIVING IN THE HEART OF CONSCIOUSNESS

> Everyone who is seriously involved in the pursuit
> of science becomes convinced that a spirit is
> manifest in the laws of the Universe–a spirit vastly
> superior to that of man, and one in the face of
> which we, with our modest powers, must feel
> humble.

> —ALBERT EINSTEIN (1879–1955),
> NOBEL PRIZE IN PHYSICS, 1921

Make no mistake—the imminent revolution in human thinking discussed throughout this book is already well under way. Our modern world, based on its foundational science, is in the midst of a paradigm shift, moving us from the empty materialist model toward discovering true meaning and purpose in our lives. As John Wheeler and Carl Friedrich von Weizsäcker postulated in their physics, pure information is at the core of all reality. That much is clearly acceptable to the general physics community. Of course, those physicists who postulated that pure information is at the core of all that exists also believed this pure information to have no "attitude" or "personality"—it was seen as neither benevolent nor malevolent in the interactions involving human beings; simply an ever-present, neutral field of information.

Albert Einstein actively wondered about the nature of such pure information. Toward the end of his life, an interviewer asked him if there were one question he could have answered, what would that question be? Einstein did not miss a beat. He wanted to know if the prime force at the very origins of the universe was a benevolent one, or not. Is this force indifferent (possibly the dominant belief among conventional scientists) or could it even be malevolent? Einstein did not presume to know the answer, and he felt this was, in fact, *the* most important question for all of humanity.

Based on the thousands of reported cases of those who have glimpsed more fully the workings of reality through NDEs and other mystical experiences, that informational substrate underlying our universe appears to be made of profound unconditional love. Those who have been to that brink and peered beyond, whose emotional state has been resonant with that infinite love, never forget the experience—they are forever changed. They know they are one with the universe. I have experienced this immersive love not only during my NDE, but have confirmed it repeatedly through my ongoing practice of going within.

A natural result of feeling the infinite love of the universe is to recognize that conscious awareness is the very same force at the core of all existence. Such oneness and dissolution of the sense of self, and complete identity with all of life and the source of all that is, is the pathway toward truth. Indeed, the deepest lesson of my journey was realizing that that unconditional love was the very fabric of the spiritual realm from which the totality of reality emerges.

Any discussion of the nature of reality, of the potential purpose of humanity, of any kind of meaning in our existence, is greatly enhanced by acknowledging the incredible power of that unconditional love and its infinite power to heal. The binding force of love reported by the vast majority of spiritual journeyers over millennia brings to mind the concept of "the ether," a substance that scientists in the late 19th century postulated might possibly exist to serve as the medium pervading the entire universe through which light waves might travel. Light fundamentally connects our entire universe with itself, pervading every bit of the physical universe throughout time.

In 1887, Albert Michelson and Edward Morley performed an experiment to investigate the ether, and they proved that the ether *as it was postulated* (as a classical medium, like air or water) did not exist. Yet in an amazing turn of events, the most recent work in physics demonstrates that the ether is how most modern physicists would describe the vacuum energy, the amazingly powerful source of energy that quantum physics has revealed to exist in the very fabric of space-time itself. Vacuum energy is a potentially endless source of energy that could revolutionize our society if we could just determine a way to harness it for our use here on earth. Ether has now resurged as an idea in physics, but it is a *relativistic ether* that is fully compatible with the ideas of relativity. But the concept of ether, which many would identify as the substance that acts as the binding force of our universe, is very much identical to that infinite binding force of love.

We can feel this force of the universe in expanded state of awareness, sometimes triggered by being out in nature. During a trip to Oregon, Karen and I found ourselves with unexpected free time when tickets to an event we planned to attend became unavailable. While I was still processing my disappointment, Karen quickly modified her attitude.

"Let's go to the beach!" she said with a wide, engaging smile and a twinkle in her eye.

It took me a few minutes to catch up with her shift of attention, but the seeming setback was an obvious opportunity in Karen's mind, one that hadn't been available to her for decades. The Oregon coast was just a 90-minute drive on Highway 26 from Portland, where Karen had earned her bachelor's degree at Lewis & Clark College.

It was a warm and beautiful day in May, which I have now ironically come to expect in the allegedly rainy and cloudy Pacific Northwest following several trips in recent years when each day was sunny and severely clear. Karen was excited to take advantage of the rain-free day, and I quickly realized this was a not-to-be-missed adventure. After a leisurely walk along the windy and unspoiled sands of Cannon Beach, where we collected shells and stones, Karen was inspired to revisit the church camp she had regularly attended in her youth. We drove south on Highway 101 as she attempted to recall its exact location.

"We would see a lake on the left just prior to the entrance. That was my landmark, so I'm not sure where to turn," Karen thought out loud. Following instinct, she suddenly turned right.

"Oh, my gosh, this is it!" she said with enthusiasm, as she pointed to the sign above us that read Camp Magruder. We toured the campgrounds on foot as Karen noted some changes, but was also pleased to see much of it was still the same.

"The ministers used to tell us to go into the woods alone to commune with God," Karen recalled. "I never really understood what that meant. I expected God would appear as a glowing light or I would hear a voice, but this never happened. Instead, I absolutely loved being alone out in nature with the trees, ferns, wind, insects, ocean waves, and driftwood— everything was so alive! I realized I could feel and sort of merge with the energy in every living thing. I would commune with nature, not God."

We came across a trail loop near the beach and followed the path along which information placards were posted. While Karen didn't recall these placards being present when she was a camper, one in particular was a clear reminder of a prime influence on her worldview.

"We can all learn valuable lessons from nature. Nature is an expression of God, or, if you prefer, of the creative force and intelligence in the universe. Since we are created by the same power as nature, we can use nature as a mirror in which to reflect on truths about ourselves," it read.

Looking back, Karen recalled, "I don't know if it was God or nature, but does it really matter what you call it?"

As we drove back to Portland, this time while admiring the Tilla-mook State Forest along Highway 6, we reflected on how the great out-doors is often a source of profound inspiration. Nature is a means for all of us to connect, not only with the beauty of our planet, but also with the vast energetic force behind it.

Feeling connected to a source greater than ourselves clearly brings great comfort, especially for one whose soul is journeying beyond our earthly consensus reality (such as in the depths of coma, or through any spiritually transformative experience). This observation is supported over millennia by the visions of prophets and mystics who have transcended the brain's filter and come into an intimate relationship with this energy.

Our concepts of a loving, merciful, and compassionate force operat-ing in the universe (whether from the Abrahamic faiths of Judaism,

Christianity, and Islam or from other traditions, such as Zoroastrianism, Shintoism, Hinduism, or Buddhism) have originated from human encounters in the spiritual realm. Most of those traditions emerged from individuals who had witnessed extraordinary features of the invisible realm that revealed a much deeper connection with the universe. In essence, this is the most basic definition of spirituality, that we have a connection with the universe that enables us to sense vital aspects of it and to have some influence in achieving our goals and desires. This connection suggests that emergence from conflict in our world will ultimately depend on acts of kindness and compassion, which we all can choose to demonstrate.

If you are fortunate, you might one day meet a person who appears to be the very embodiment of this spiritual energy—as we did during a visit in 2014 to Maui, Hawaii, hosted by our friend Chuck Blitz. We were honored to spend time with Ram Dass (formerly Richard Alpert), who began his career at Harvard University, where he researched hallucinogenic substances in the 1960s. After being relieved from his position at Harvard due to the surrounding controversy, he immersed himself in meditation practices during an extended time in India, wanting to explore a wide variety of spiritual methods and techniques (not involving drugs) as a means to interact with the nature of consciousness itself. He had suffered a stroke in February 1997 and was now confined to a wheelchair. As we approached him at our first meeting in a beachfront restaurant where we dined with Ram Dass and a small group of his close friends, Karen was struck by the reaction in her heart field.

"As I came closer to him, I was surprised to feel my heart swelling with pure love energy. It seemed as if it was coming from Ram Dass himself as he looked at me with clear, pure intent," she later told me.

Like Karen, I also felt a powerful energy coming from Ram Dass. His own mind had been widely opened during his robust experimentation with psychedelic drugs, investigations he had pursued with colleague Timothy Leary. But those experiences served mainly to whet his appetite for going deeply into consciousness in more revealing ways. He felt it was necessary to feel divine love directly, and to consistently live with joy throughout each moment of life. We enjoyed stimulating conversation as like-minded souls and our viewpoints had much in common, especially concerning the phenomenal mystery of consciousness and the power of love to heal at all levels.

So much of our discussion that soft, warm, breezy Hawaiian evening reflected the great wisdom he had crystallized in his remarkable 1971 book, *Be Here Now*, a compendium of Eastern wisdom, in a format easily understood by Westerners. I had purchased my still-owned copy of *Be Here Now* as a teenager in 1972 in San Francisco for $3.33. Back in the '70s when I first read it, the concepts of which he spoke were somewhat foreign to me, but now they made much more sense. Knowing we would be meeting him, I had brought my copy of his book along for him to sign.

"Through the journey inward, going deeper and deeper to meet Truth . . . we come to see the oneness we share, the oneness we are—together. No boundaries of separation," Ram Dass wrote in his book.

Aftereffects from his stroke still somewhat limited his verbiage, but the richness of his synthesis (which I supplemented by reviewing my worn copy of his book) offered a soothing bath in the purest of understanding. I heard his words, but I also *felt* his message. I was entranced in his presence.

"The guru is within us all. You *are* the guru. The guru is a perfect mirror because there's nobody here. The great teacher, beyond all duality, resides within."

He offered such astonishing revelation, such deep trust in our divine connection, our access to source, a trust so lacking in many of our orthodox religious teachings. To the extent that any religion promotes the basic tenets of oneness and connection with each other, with all life, and with the universe, those teachings are consistent with the myriad visions shared by spiritual journeyers. Thus, promotion of love, compassion, mercy, acceptance, and forgiveness are essential components of a spiritual worldview that honors the lessons of such experiences.

"When you know how to listen from within, everyone is the guru," I agreed.

"As you find the light in you, you begin to see the light in everyone else. . . . We're all just caught in the delusion, all of us caught in the illusion. Emerging from duality is being aware of it all as an illusion, and yet still being so much *in* it!"

He expressed deep fathoming of what we have described as the Supreme Illusion. The ultimate duality (being both in and outside the illusion, all at the same time) may sound paradoxical, but only from the viewpoint of duality. This way of being allows us to be aware of our connection to the tremendous love at the source of all existence while also going about our daily routines—the connection never ends! We simply become aware of it. We are more than our physical bodies, and knowing the vastness of our spiritual nature empowers us to see far beyond our material existence.

"You are pure spirit, eternal spirit. That very old being. Not physical matter!" None around the dinner table would differ with *that*. Ram Dass's entourage was quite aware that we are all spiritual beings, living in a spiritual universe.

"That inner place where you dwell, you just be. There is nothing to be done in that place. From that place then, it all happens, it manifests in perfect harmony with the universe."

Ram Dass's famous phrase "Be here now" speaks to the many spiritual practices that intend to bring you to the present moment—the stillness and calmness we find when we slow down and start paying attention. Staying in this space in every moment is the challenge he presents and one which we can all take to heart.

As we finished dinner and bade fond farewells, I elated in the sage wisdom Ram Dass had shared—a heartfelt knowing far beyond the simple truth of his words. All that he conveyed was aligned with what I was struggling to *know* in coming to grips with my coma experience. But his knowing (and I was coming to see *my* knowing) originated in very ancient teachings going back millennia, the deepest truth dripping from the mists of antiquity. These are not new lessons for humanity, but in today's world we need to *remember* them.

The magic of our trip to Maui didn't end there. We hiked through the Haleakala Crater in the center of the island guided by new friends Joel Friedman and Claudia Kirchmayr. Claudia began our 13-mile day trek with an Oli Aloha chant, a Hawaiian greeting that she sang with heartfilled gratitude to the spirit of the volcano. We drove along the spectacular Hana Road hugging the coastline, and snorkeled with colorful tropical fish in the crystal-clear water surrounding the island. From our hotel, about a mile from the oceanfront, we had a distant view of the sea and would occasionally see spouts of water indicating a whale was present. When spotting this telltale sign, from her practice with animal communication, Karen focused awareness on her heart energy and imagined it connecting with the distant whales.

"I expressed gratitude and appreciation for the whale's presence and acknowledged the connection from inside myself," she explained. "It's kind of like saying, 'Hello, whales,' and they say 'Hello' back."

This sentiment is similar to a Sanskrit greeting I have come to appreciate—namaste. Simply put, this means "the divinity in me acknowledges the divinity in you." Karen's greeting to the whales seemed perfectly appropriate.

It was a common activity to go out into the bay to get a much closer view of whales, either on a boat or paddleboard, but it was beyond the prime time for such an encounter and nearing the end of the whale-watching season in late April. Still, we agreed it might be fun to try.

Several days into our trip, Joyanna Cotter (a local new friend) shared that someone who worked at the rental facility at Four Seasons Resort Maui at Wailea owed her a favor and she could borrow two double-seated sea kayaks whenever she wished. She invited us and another friend, Michele Martin, to share in the excursion. We had only one mutually available window of opportunity among the four of us and together we made plans to paddle out to sea with the intention of sighting some whales.

As we left the shore in our two sea kayaks, our desire was to have a close-up sighting. Michele had shared with us a previous encounter with a mother and baby whale so this was foremost in our minds. It was at the very end of the time of year in Maui when mothers come to birth their babies and this particular area was a safe harbor for them to nurture and grow, but we were told not to get our hopes up since we were so late in the season.

As we began to paddle out to sea, we first encountered two magnificent sea turtles about 4 feet long. Their majestic presence was awe-inspiring as they swam gracefully, perhaps 5 to 10 feet from our kayaks. One swam right under my and Karen's kayak.

"Oh, gosh, look at the turtles," I exclaimed.

"Wow, that's incredible! I've never seen a sea turtle that large so close up. Amazing!" Karen agreed.

In the crystal-clear water, we had a perfect view of these magnificent creatures. We felt this was a good omen.

Joyanna and Karen were in the front seats of the two kayaks.

"Which way do you think we should go?" Joyanna asked Karen.

"How about that way?" Karen suggested, as she pointed out toward the bay northwest of our position.

We all agreed it felt right, so we began paddling in that direction. Many other board paddlers and boats were visible, but none were near to us.

"Hey, Karen, what sound would you make if you wanted to attract whales?" Joyanna asked as we paddled, knowing of Karen's work with sound.

Karen immediately thought of the sounds whales make, similar to the didgeridoo, an ancient instrument reported to be used for healing for many thousands of years. She and Kevin had experimented with listening to whale sounds incorporated into their sound recordings, finding them to be quite appealing. Whales create a deep and powerful resonant sound that has been shown to travel hundreds of miles under water. Whales and dolphins are known to communicate with each other this way.

"*Waaa-aaaah-oooooh-aaaah*," Karen warbled at a low pitch as she attempted to mimic a whale—booming, deep-toned pulsations. The rest of us joined in and we eventually settled into a low-frequency wavering om sound. Within a few minutes, Karen noticed something striking.

"Oh, gosh, my heart energy is growing tremendously. It's like a warm, swelling energy around my heart. I've never felt it this big," she shared with wide eyes.

Her heart's energy expanded to a rather large capacity surrounding her body, a sweet and compelling feeling she had learned to cultivate in recent years. As she described this feeling, her face revealed pure joy and wonder.

Within a few minutes, as Karen marveled over her growing heart field and we continued to chant out loud together, a whale suddenly appeared, perhaps 100 feet away from us. We were soon delighted to notice another smaller whale and realized it was a mother and baby who then proceeded to roll around, blow air and water out of their spouts, wave their tails above the water, and interact with us. We were filled with gratitude for such a magnificent display as Karen's heart energy grew still larger.

"I'm going to get closer," Michele said as she slipped into the water.

Michele got close, but the rolling waves and splash from a full breach of the baby whale (larger than a school bus!) as it fell back into the water sent her back to her kayak. She was safe, but she felt overwhelmed being so close to the frolicking of such large and impressive creatures.

"Hold my paddle, please," I asked Karen, as I donned mask, snorkel, and fins, and eased into the water to swim closer to these gentle behemoths. I reminded myself that these were fellow mammals, closely related to humans in the evolutionary tree, but I also realized that I was now in their world. In spite of their giant size, I felt a warm familiarity with them as I hovered beneath the surface, amazed at their awesome yet benevolent presence.

My evolving comprehension of the interrelationship of brain and mind acknowledges that the filter theory (which notes consciousness as primary and let in through the filtering mechanism of the brain) allows for bigger filters (brains) generally to be associated with grander conscious awareness (just as we presume our conscious awareness is grander than, say, that of a cat or dog, who have smaller brains).

I knew that their brains rivaled ours in size and plainly exceeded our own brains in some respects. One compelling example is the long-finned pilot whale (also known as the blackfish)—actually a species of dolphin found in the North Atlantic Ocean between Scotland and Iceland—which has about twice as many brain cells in the neocortex as humans do! If our large neocortex is as tightly linked with mental function as many neuroscientists believe, then we should expect some of these large-brained marine mammals to have quite sophisticated mental experience and awareness, and, potentially, even telepathy.[1]

We spotted a boat of whale watchers and several board paddlers coming our way, presumably to get a closer look at our new whale friends. Just then, the whales began a slow departure. There are restrictions in place to protect the whales, and we knew better than to follow after them. As they began to move away, their activity above water increased. They each waved their tails more vigorously and the baby whale stunned us with another full-breach jump out of the water. The friendly tail-waving seemed to us like a heartfelt farewell and we waved back with gratitude and delight.

Later that week, we returned to the same water, but with a different purpose. Ram Dass had always loved swimming in the ocean, but the stroke that had confined him to a wheelchair had left him unable to do so alone. In a beautiful display of communal support, Ram Dass's closest companions work together to make it possible for him to continue. Once a week, Ram Dass is transferred to a beach buggy made especially for traversing over sand to reach the beach. He is then lifted gently into the waves, equipped with specialized flotation devices that allow him to float and swim in the water out to about 40 feet while his companions maintain a close watch.

We joined a group of about two dozen people who gathered on a regular basis for this ritual. Ram Dass and the rest of us bobbed about in the water in roughly the same area with perhaps 3 to 6 feet between each of us, holding conversations and throwing a couple of balls around.

"Oh boy; oh boy; oh boy," Ram Dass began to slowly repeat, a complete surprise to us.

As he continued, the rest of us irresistibly joined in with childlike enthusiasm.

"Oh boy; oh boy; oh boy," we repeated together, getting louder.

Ram Dass clearly enjoyed his time in the water. He beamed with delight as he continued to lie back with the complete support of his flotation aids.

"Oh joy; oh joy; oh joy!" Ram Dass declared.

As his words changed, so did our energy. I could feel the love energy emanating out of Ram Dass. As each of us joined in the fray, we became a cohesive group of souls. Participating in this resonance with the others reminded me of the intricately coordinated and efficient movement of schools of fish or flocks of birds. We were becoming one conscious entity through the resonance of our heart connections, all deeply rooted in the pure joy shared with Ram Dass in that beautiful moment. Other beachgoers and swimmers looked over at our group curiously, but we paid them no mind.

"Oh joy; oh joy; oh joy!" we repeated in unison.

In his follow-up book, *Be Love Now*, Ram Dass illustrated his own path to the heart. He clearly radiates the love he holds within, a beautiful model for us all. On his *being* the love, identical to what Karen had first taught me, Ram Dass said, "Just love until you and the beloved become one."

Our Western culture stumbles a bit at the suggestion that we human beings can become one and identical with God. In our culture, such a disclosure can rapidly draw the ire of those who would accuse one of being an egomaniac or, worse yet, suffering from the affliction of a messiah complex or some mental illness of similar ilk. Yet the concrete reality of such true oneness is the exact opposite of any such egotistical interpretation,

"The enlightened can love that which is deeper than our personality or our body. They see beyond the illusion into the perfect divine essence that is at the core of each and every one of us. That binding of total love is not limited as are interpersonal love, or possessive love, or needful love. The enlightened one *is* love!" Ram Dass remarked in *Be Here Now*.

I had trod that arduous path of buying into the illusion before my coma. Ram Dass's teachings so perfectly aligned with the deepest messages of my NDE and with my recent processing of it all. So many assume that my perpetual gratitude is based in my miraculous healing, but the truth is that the lessons and understanding that have resulted from such a horrifically challenging experience as my week in coma due to meningoencephalitis have been a tremendous gift, no matter what the outcome of my illness. I am grateful for every facet of this gem called life, and know that my challenges and hardships have become close friends in this journey—without them, I would not have gained the privilege of striding along the brilliantly lit ridge far above the dark valley in which I first crawled as a disenfranchised soul, probing cautiously in the earliest stages of my coma journey. We can all come to see the hardships in life, illness, and injury as the stepping-stones on which our souls can grow and ascend toward that oneness with the Divine. It is through how we deal with such challenges, by recovering our sense of divinity and connectedness, that determines their ability to empower our growth.

As we ate lunch after our swim, I enjoyed further conversation with Ram Dass, nodding in hearty agreement as he explained, "You come to see that all you can know through your senses and all you can know through your thoughts are not going to be enough. It requires the falling away of worldliness, and a return of childlike innocence."

In that moment, I saw the youthful Richard Alpert, a young lad brimming with excitement and curiosity, with that perfect innocence that is the source of all true knowing. Yet such childlike innocence forever defies the egoistic "seeker."

"Got to be careful not to go through the door of enlightenment too fast; that would be going through the door with your ego on. Good way to get delusions of grandeur, a messianic complex, to wind up in a mental institution. You've got to be really pure. You can't just make believe you're pure."

That purity I was just beginning to glimpse, by going within, by cultivating the observer, the "I" within or "higher soul" that is purely aware of existence. Since awakening from coma nine years ago, I have gained enriched clarity around the notion of my "higher soul" as being intimately connected with all facets of this universe, including the higher souls of others, completely independent of my ego. I continue to develop increasing patience and trust that all is well. This journey of discovery unfolds through the grace of the Collective Mind (or God, for those comfortable with that term), and since I am an integral part of it, I trust that the same Mind has my best interest at heart. Of course, the highest and best good for all involved is the goal of that Collective Mind, and my higher soul honors that process completely.

In the end, Ram Dass reflected back on the original polarity that had energized his journey.

"I was still a Western rational man so I went and I looked and looked and looked, and as long as I looked like a rational man looking, I didn't find anything. I just found my own shadow. All the time, that's all you find: yourself. You're standing on a bridge, watching yourself go by. Be the observer, the I that exists. Be all that is, here, now."

Ram Dass followed his path from Harvard to India and back to the United States to teach others what he had learned. My journey since coma has brought pieces of the same wisdom—the universal truths. The greatest gift has been a complete reversal in my understanding of the workings of the universe, a journey that parallels recent shifts in the foundations of scientific thought. Such a reversal is cause for great optimism because this fundamental shift in worldview allows us to stake out a far grander role in determining the evolution of this universe, from selecting healing and completeness as individuals through a more harmonious existence of ethnic and national groups, through guidance into proper stewardship of our planet, and beyond. The gifts of this awakening appear limitless. As valuable as these lessons have been, it is important to realize that these gifts would have been bestowed upon me in my journey eventually, even if I had succumbed to my meningoencephalitis and departed this physical world.

As Einstein said, "The true value of a human being is determined primarily by the measure and the sense in which he has attained liberation from the self." Our self-focused world is a major part of the problems we currently face. Our little individual theater of consciousness appears at first glance to be ours alone, but the evidence emerging from quantum physics and from the deepest study of the nature of consciousness and the mind-body problem indicates that we are all truly part of one Collective Mind. We are all in this together, and are slowly awakening to a common goal—the evolution of conscious awareness.

As we each carve our unique passage through life, our collective destiny is to live in peace and harmony, one with all fellow beings, one with the universe, healing through the infinite power of unconditional love. This is not some pie-in-the-sky wishful thinking—it is the birthright of all sentient beings throughout all of existence. All of the seeming impediments to that destiny, especially the apparent evil and darkness in our world in the form of thoughtless homicide and suicide, conflict and warfare, and devastation of our ecosystem through the misguided application of modern science and technology—are all part of a greater plan, one that ultimately we devise together.

The imminent awakening in understanding will become the greatest revolution in human thought in recorded history, and it comes none too soon—we must awaken to take full stewardship of our planet because our blind and misguided actions to date have painted us into a very dangerous corner, with a third of the world's living species on the brink of extinction and too much of the world's population still exposed daily to the ravages of war and conflict.

This is a critical juncture in human history. Much like the "gift of desperation" faced by individuals circling the drain of addiction, we are all potentially in the midst of a collective gift of desperation.

Just as each person's soul grows through the hurdles and challenges of life, humanity is meant to face these challenges together, all to catalyze our growth to unprecedented levels. The human spirit has potential powers far beyond our wildest imagination. We have much cause for hope—that a brilliant and harmonious future can be ours. As we begin to realize our personal power over the events in our lives, we all will benefit. As more of us come to know that truly we are all eternal spiritual beings, the world will become far more harmonious and peaceful.

Of course, some are not yet ready to embrace this truth. Whenever we face a paradigm shift, there are those who leap across, those who wait for others to build a bridge, and those who plant their feet and refuse to budge. Centuries ago, some people trusted their own observations of the horizon to assert that the world was round, not flat. Some waited for astronomers and mathematicians to do experimental proofs showing that was the case. Others waited until there was complete scientific consensus, with satellite photos to back it up.

Truly, we all have the capacity to explore the vast well of consciousness that lies within and through us, and within and through the network of souls with which we are in a hidden but eternal pattern of connection. And we can each find out for ourselves.

At the entrance to the Temple of the Oracle at Delphi in Greece are inscribed the words "know thyself." This is the ultimate meaning and purpose of life, whether that be the life of an individual human being or of any larger assemblage of humans, life on earth, or of the far vaster collection of sentient life throughout the cosmos. Answering that ancient edict to "know thyself" thus becomes a far more ambitious and exciting journey as you come to realize that "thyself" includes the entire universe. As humanity comes more fully to know the reality of the Collective Mind, we will come to appreciate that our existence has far more meaning and importance than we might imagine. We are all part of a vast and creative consciousness, and the evolution of all of consciousness throughout the cosmos is nothing more than the individual journey of sentient beings in coming to understand their own role in this co-creative endeavor.

The most important feature of this understanding is that you, dear reader, are crucial to this process. The universe is evolving in vast and fascinating ways, and you are not only part of it—you *are* it. You *are* the universe. The mindful universe in which we live is self-aware, and learning, and evolving—your coming to know this fully, and living it, is the pathway toward perfect harmony with all that is. Each of us is a potential change agent that can help bring our collective vision to fruition. It is up to us individually to accept the invitation to break out of the illusion of the physical world as all that exists and to acknowledge our spiritual nature, and how it resonates with the fundamental nature of the universe. A brilliant, hopeful future is within our grasp—we must simply choose to *make it so*.

AUTHOR'S NOTE

Following my coma in 2008, I came to understand more and more the reality behind my experiences in other realms—and this, in turn, led me to focus on the critical flaws in our generally accepted scientific paradigm. My initial idea was to write a neuroscientific paper for a medical journal, but the reactions from those who heard my story made me realize a broader audience might greatly benefit from my message. Many books about near-death experiences had been published in recent years, including several by physicians. However, none of them had made much of a splash outside of a rather narrow group already interested in the topic. Nonetheless, publishers expressed interest and my story was published in October 2012.

Proof of Heaven spent more than forty weeks in the number-one position on the *New York Times* bestseller list for paperback nonfiction, and remained near the very top of that list for almost two years. Not just a North American phenomenon, *Proof of Heaven* has also been published in more than thirty countries worldwide. It clearly struck a chord with a large reading audience across many cultures. The book's rapid success came as a huge surprise to me, as I had thought it would take years to achieve such status. At the same time, though, it became clear in the feedback I received, from emails and letters and during my presentations, that I had not been as effective as I'd hoped in reaching those most like me—the true open-minded skeptics.

I suspect that is partially related to the book's title, which was suggested by my publisher. While my story certainly supports the reality of an afterlife, the book is far from being just a discourse on "heaven." The revelations of my message address the very fundamental nature of reality and human experience, and cover territory well beyond the question of whether or not some aspect of consciousness survives the death of the brain and body. Such knowledge is directly relevant to how we approach life in myriad ways. It is a mistake to assume that *Proof of Heaven* is a confirmation of the dogmatic teachings of modern-day Christianity (an accusation from close-minded skeptics who I'm convinced have not read the book, but rather are simply recoiling at the title). My books and talks have resulted in a deluge of communications from practitioners of some of the deep mystical traditions of many faiths (Kabbalah, Christianity, Islam, Sufism, Buddhism, Hinduism, Bahá'í Faith, among others) confirming the resonance of my journey and message with their own understandings. I can't stress enough that our message is for *all* humans.

Given the mostly favorable reception of *Proof of Heaven*, it is easy to forget the personal trials I went through when making the decision to publish my story. The risks to my career in academic neurosurgery were quite real—after all, I was rocking the boat in a major way, and the end result could have been a forced eviction from my tribe, that of neurosurgery and neuroscience. I knew my story dealt with the fundamental nature of consciousness and, indeed, of all reality. But the world might not recognize that, and I could wind up marginalized and ignored if the message was not plainly delivered. Nonetheless, I knew this message was far too important to bury.

My qualms were not altogether unreasonable. Following the publication of *Proof of Heaven*, I received invitations for countless media interviews and speaking engagements, most of which expressed sincere interest and shared the wonder and mystery my story presented. At the same time, I faced a backlash from the predictable mainstream scientific critics, including Sam Harris, Michael Shermer, and Oliver Sacks, who interpreted my experience as being an obvious confabulation with no evidence my brain was truly damaged beyond the capacity to have a hallucination. Most physicians I encountered seemed to realize the gargantuan task of trying to explain my experience in the context of my medical records, but those commenting most often in the press were either unaware of those medical details or failed to recognize the devastating picture that most physicians readily appreciated. I was eager to engage in a meaningful discussion of such interpretations, but this proved to be elusive. Most of the criticism simply ignored the facts of my experience or invented unfounded claims to discredit me personally.

I have had frustrating encounters, too, with Wikipedia in its treatment of the details of my story and its aftermath. While Wikipedia claims to be an objective source of information, its editors have a clear bias against (and very often edit out) submissions from those who trust the reality of spiritual experiences. Meanwhile, cynics who attack such experiences seem to have free rein to edit the site, rendering Wikipedia to be no more than a rampant source of misinformation regarding certain topics.

My co-author, Karen Newell, is a spiritual mentor, co-creator, and, most important, my loving life partner in this effort. We have become deep soul mates through our profound connections at all levels. I have come to experience the true Oneness of the self-aware universe through the evolution of my relationship with Karen. Much of my thinking and representation of it in both *Proof of Heaven* (2012) and *The Map of Heaven* (2014) were due to her clarifications and insights, and this book had no way of moving forward without Karen's extensive involvement at all levels. Far more than my "muse," she has become the sine qua non (indispensable) for my ongoing learning and teaching efforts—indeed, for my fundamental understanding of consciousness and reality. We developed these concepts together, over countless hours of conversation, combining my proficiencies in neurosurgery, astronomy, physics, cosmology, consciousness, and the lessons of my near-death experience with Karen's depth of knowledge in metaphysics, ancient wisdom, technology, the heart, and interpersonal communications. She has personally experimented with and evaluated innumerable practical tools for accessing nonlocal consciousness. Any impact I have for good is in no small part a reflection of her passionate, lifelong quest to uncover the truths of our existence through direct knowing and experience.

While my collective understanding is still evolving, I believe we are on the verge of the greatest revolution in human thought in all of recorded history, a true synthesis of science and spirituality. I wrote *Proof of Heaven* and *The Map of Heaven* to help the modern intelligent reader, the truly open-minded skeptic (like I was before my coma), come to a richer worldview that fully embraces both the scientific and spiritual nature within each of us.

Living in a Mindful Universe is the next step in this ongoing effort to help the open-minded, discerning, skeptical reader discover their own path to this refreshing, liberating worldview—one that fully embraces modern spirituality within the leading edges of physics, cosmology, and consciousness studies.

The message itself is imperative. The status quo is not working. Humanity is long overdue to enter an era that is free of the barbaric tribal conflicts and wars that have devastated so much of humanity over millennia, for no good reason whatsoever. We can stop this madness.

This awakening will foster a far gentler and kinder world, one much more harmonious and peaceful for all beings on earth. It will also inspire a far grander sense of human potentialities only dreamed of today, and of a deeper knowing of the profound nature of the human spirit—who we are, why we are here, and where we are headed.

It is time for humanity to wake up. Our very survival depends on it.

Eben Alexander, MD
Charlottesville, Virginia
June 12, 2017

ACKNOWLEDGMENTS

Karen and I are appreciative of the countless souls who have played integral roles throughout our individual and common journeys along the pathway to writing this book. We have benefited from the love and sharing of thousands of individuals, all of them teachers in their own way. There are far too many to name here, but we would like to acknowledge a few for their specific contributions.

We are grateful for the many pioneering physicians, scientists, and philosophers who have courageously confronted the dominant paradigm and who fully acknowledge and appreciate the deep mystery of consciousness. Their contributions continue to advance human knowledge in this imminent and profound awakening. We wish to specifically recognize Julie Beischel, Margaret Christensen, Larry Dossey, Bruce Greyson, Allan and Janey Hamilton, Charlie Joseph, Bernardo Kastrup, Ed Kelly, Edgar Mitchell, Raymond and Cheryl Moody, Dean Radin, Gary and Rhonda Schwartz, Jim Tucker, and Pim van Lommel.

We are eminently thankful to our friends, colleagues, and readers who generously offered their personal stories or who shared direct experiences with us: PMH Atwater, John Audette, Paul Aurand, Chuck Blitz, Sophia Cody and Osha Reader, Caroline Cook, Joyanna Cotter, Ram Dass, Joel Friedman and Claudia Kirchmayr, Bill Guggenheim, His Holiness the fourteenth Dalai Lama, Laura Lynne Jackson, Kevin and Catherine Kossi, Brian Maness, Michele Martin, Anita and Danny Moorjani, William Peters, Michael and Jennifer Shermer, Alison Sugg, Michael and Page Sullivan, Stacie Williams, and Gary Zukav and Linda Francis.

Several early readers provided invaluable guidance in the development of our manuscript, including Suzanne and Michael Ainsley, Bill Beaman, Neal Grossman, Judson Newbern, and Jan Pipkin.

Special thanks to our literary agent, Gail Ross, Howard Yoon, Dara Kaye, Anna Sproul-Latimer, and all of their colleagues at Ross Yoon Agency in Washington, DC, as well as to our editors Leah Miller, Allison

Janice, and publisher, Gail Gonzales, at Rodale Books. Thank you for supporting and believing in the grander aspects of our message.

We appreciate the support offered by IANDS researchers Robert and Suzanne Mays in elaborating the deep truth underlying the story first told in *Proof of Heaven*.

Abundant appreciation goes to Elizabeth Hare for her stalwart and efficient daily support in helping us to manage the many aspects of our mutual endeavors.

We are eternally grateful to our families, with special thanks to Karen's mother and daughter, Diane and Jamie, for agreeing to share their intimate stories of challenge and struggle; to her parents Clayton and Gwen; and to Eben's family, Betty and Eben Jr., Eben IV, Bond, Holley, Jean, Betsy, Phyllis, and his entire birth family.

APPENDIX A

FAILURE TO FIND MEMORY LOCALIZED IN THE BRAIN

Dr. Wilder Penfield, a renowned Canadian neurosurgeon, spent much of his career electrically stimulating the brain in awake patients to guide the removal of damaged brain that caused their seizures. Over three productive decades, he greatly expanded our knowledge of the function and anatomy of the neocortex, including some major revelations about memory.

Given that brain tissue feels no pain, he performed these procedures in awake patients, using local anesthesia in the scalp. Memories elicited through such precise electrical stimulation included movement, colors, emotions, dreams, smells, déjà vu, "strangeness," and visual and auditory experiences. He noted that these stimulated memories were much more distinct than usual memory, and often concerned material quite different from things remembered under ordinary circumstances. In some cases, repeat stimulation gave a replay of the same memory, although many locations offered no such reproducibility. In cases of repeat operation, he found that such stimulation points were not generally consistent over time intervals between operations.

Such a putative physical basis for memory was termed an engram. Penfield found that only by stimulating the temporal lobes (the parts of the brain directly underneath the ears) could he trigger meaningful recollections of memory—no other regions of neocortex were found to be related to such memories. In spite of his perfection of the technique, such memories could only be triggered in 5 percent of his surgical cases, and the memories only occurred during the passage of electrical current.

Dr. Penfield made many observations that are profoundly relevant to the mind-body discussion based on the experiences, perceptions, and memories engendered in his awake patients by such stimulation. Interestingly, he considered the main sensory lobe of the brain, the parietal lobe, to be silent in the face of such cortical stimulation. Only stimulation of the temporal lobes (which are generally viewed as more dispensable than other lobes by neurosurgeons) involved an association with reported memories and perceptions, and this only in the setting of patients "whose temporal region may be said to have been conditioned by habitual local epileptic discharge"—patients without such epileptic conditioning failed to respond to stimulation over the temporal lobes.[1] He continued, "Such stimulation may produce in the patient an auditory experience as a buzzing sound, an equilibratory sensation of dizziness, or a rather complicated hallucination or dream."

Penfield noted that these stimulation points had "been somehow conditioned by years of electrical discharges from a neighbouring epileptogenic focus,"[2] suggesting that they were a pathological consequence of the abnormal region of brain causing their seizures.

So although occasionally such memories could be elicited through electrical stimulation, much more often no such locations could be found in a patient, and those identified were restricted to the area of brain abnormality.

Although in the early years, his research suggested the possibility of such localization of memory in the temporal neocortex, further investigation and reflection led him to believe that there was no such thing as local memory storage in the brain.

Barbara Milner disclosed her interactions with Penfield concerning memory in an article in the *Canadian Medical Association Journal* in 1977: "Of course this is not memory as you psychologists understand the term when you refer to the variability of memory, with its abstractions, generalizations, and distortions. In ordinary remembering we do not have direct access to the record of past experience in our brain," Penfield told Milner.

Milner went on to write: "Where was this record? For a time he [Penfield] toyed with the idea that it might be laid down bilaterally in the neocortex of the temporal lobes but he gave up this idea in his later writings and suggested that the record must be located somewhere in the higher brain stem. The lateral temporal cortex would then have what he called an interpretive function rather than being itself the storehouse of memory traces."[3]

Although his initial experience suggested that memory engrams could be found in the temporal neocortex, over the years he came to believe that memory was not stored in any localizable brain region, a finding that is consistent with the work of other neurosurgeons.

Short-term, or working, memory (less than a minute or so) involves connections between the dorsolateral prefrontal cortex (frontal lobes) and the parietal lobes, but the mechanism and location of long-term memory storage remains a complete mystery. Certain anatomic structures, notably the hippocampus and entorhinal cortex of the medial temporal lobes, are crucial for the consolidation of short-term into long-term memories. However, long-term memories are not actively stored in that region.

Neurosurgeons must proceed with great caution when operating near the medial temporal lobe due to long-term memory formation mechanisms that are intimately involved with the integrity of the hippocampus (small regions on the medial surface of the temporal lobes). Although significant damage to the dominant hippocampus or adjacent entorhinal cortex (and especially bilateral damage) leads to a shocking deficit in which the patient is unable to form new long-term memories, no other brain regions are so strongly involved in memory.

The general idea in conventional neuroscience is that memories are diffusely stored throughout the neocortex. Yet the overall experience of neurosurgeons who have resected large regions of neocortex from every lobe of the brain in countless patients over the last century for myriad pathological conditions (brain tumors, epilepsy, aneurysms, malformations of the brain's blood vessels, and infections, among others), without encountering patterns of broad swaths of memory loss in their patients, belies the notion of the general cortical storage of specific memories as false.

Current neuroscientific hypotheses about the possible biochemical nature of memory are all over the map, with nothing remotely resembling a consensus in sight. Recent viable hypotheses include primitive proteins known as prions,[4] specific chemical methylation of critical regions of DNA,[5] the interplay between a neuron's synaptic activity and its nuclear DNA transcription,[6] memory linkage through synaptic co-clustering within the dendrites of common neurons,[7] and the possibility that quantum calculations in microtubules within neurons are involved (the Penrose-Hameroff Orchestrated OR hypothesis discussed further in Appendix B).[8]

APPENDIX B

FURTHER COMMENTARY ON THE MEASUREMENT PARADOX OF QUANTUM PHYSICS

Although the field of quantum physics arguably began with Max Planck's 1900 hypothesis describing the discrete "energy elements" of any energy-radiating atomic systems and Albert Einstein's 1905 paper on the photoelectron effect (that light stimulates the emission of electrons from the surface of a metal dependent on the frequency of the incoming light), it was Erwin Schrödinger's introduction of his famous wave equation in 1925 (leading to Schrödinger's receiving the Nobel Prize in Physics in 1933) that allowed for the robust application of experiment to assess the reality of quantum physics in our world. His linear partial differential wave-equation describes the deterministic evolution over time of the state function of any quantum system, no matter what size (including up to that of the entire universe).

Schrödinger's wave function describes a *superposition* of possible results, i.e., an electron demonstrating wavelike behavior can be described as going through both the left and right slits of a double-slit experiment with various assigned probabilities (its location is "superposed" between the two options, the wave function being unitary or all-inclusive).

The mathematics and the physics of Schrödinger's wave equation have been fully corroborated not only through decades of scientific refinement, but also through the practical successes that have driven roughly a third of the world's economic growth over the last few decades. The problem arises in trying to interpret the actual implications (scientific, philosophical, and metaphysical) of such math and physics if we pay attention to the underlying reality revealed by the experimental results themselves.

American mathematical physicist Henry Stapp summarized the dilemma thus: "In short, orthodox quantum mechanics is Cartesian dualistic at the pragmatic/operational level, but mentalistic on the ontological level." In other words, the standard accepted interpretation of quantum mechanics is one that honors both brain and mind from a practical viewpoint, but that insists on the primacy of mind at the most fundamental level of explaining reality. This is why modern materialist science is so violently conflicted on trying to grok the deeper lessons of quantum physics: Those lessons are fundamentally at odds with the materialist position that continually tries to remove mind and consciousness from having any basis in the underlying reality when, in fact, through the primordial mind hypothesis, it is clear that consciousness might well be at the very core of all of reality. Denying the obvious can only proceed to a certain breaking point, which I believe we are fast approaching.

Interestingly, even arranging a quantum mechanical experiment such that neither measurement can be claimed to have occurred first, measurements of the two entangled particles remain tightly correlated. Given that the choice of reference frames can be such that event A occurs first in its inertial reference frame and event B occurs first in its reference frame, one cannot conclude that one measurement caused the other due to the fact that neither event can claim priority of its reference frame—they are equally valid. Observers based in either reference frame could claim their measurement to be the cause of the other's measurement effect, yet both have the same valid claim to priority.

Note that the measurement paradox is a challenge that goes far beyond simply presenting difficulties in the overall interpretation of quantum physics: It seems to point to some logical inconsistencies within the very foundations of quantum theory. This problem is rooted in the dynamics of the measurement process itself, the very rules that describe the trajectories of quantum systems through the mathematical space in which they are described. Within quantum mechanics, there are facts about whole systems that don't result simply from the facts about their constituent parts and the spatial arrangement of those parts, contributing to the deep mystery underlying quantum physics and our comprehending the implications of such experimental findings for our conceptualization of the world.

Einstein remained deeply troubled by quantum entanglement. His concern had to do with one of the bedrock premises of physical science, notably the concept of local realism, which involves two assumptions:

In the subatomic world, all interactions, including the light rays coming from an object that enter my eye, involve information transfer that cannot be instantaneous because the light photons must move from the object to my eye to register the information (and thus are local, that is, the photon must be local to the receiving pigments in my retina). That information transfer is limited by the speed of light (a consequence of Einstein's special theory of relativity).

Realism is the notion that nature exists independently of the human mind. Subatomic particles must possess the measurable property prior to the conscious decision of the observing mind to make the measurement. Realism, in this sense, would be a direct rebuttal of metaphysical idealism, which posits that all of reality is contained within consciousness. What troubled Einstein was the fact that quantum experiments indicate that reality *does* behave as if mind is intimately involved (i.e., that metaphysical idealism is the correct answer!).

Physicists paid scant attention to the Einstein-Podolsky-Rosen paper (EPR, referred to in Chapter 5), viewing it as a philosophical curiosity, until Irish physicist John Bell recognized that the EPR argument could actually be assessed through experiments. He published his paper on Bell's theorem (or Bell's inequality) in 1964, opening the door to the experimental assessment of the instantaneous connectedness throughout the universe suggested by quantum physics.

The results of experiments inspired by Bell's brilliant paper continue to affirm quantum entanglement as a real phenomenon that defies Einstein's assumptions of local realism. They continue to imply that there is no fundamental objective physical reality—that it is best envisioned as an information field that requires an overarching structure, or a conscious observer, for its existence. In addressing Bell's theorem, physicists often discuss various loopholes, or hypotheses that attempt to clarify nature's message to us about reality, as assessed through experiments addressing Bell's concepts.

In 1982, Alain Aspect strengthened Stuart Freedman and John Clauser's findings (see Chapter 5) by further closing a loophole concerning possible communication between the two photon detectors. The most sophisticated recent experiments in quantum physics continue to strengthen the conclusion that there is no underlying objective reality independent of the mind of the conscious observer.[1]

Interestingly, one of the last possible loopholes in assessing Bell's inequality is that of conscious free will itself: In a superdeterministic universe (defined as a block universe in which *all* of past and future history has already happened in a frozen crystal of actuality throughout all of eternity), such "spooky action at a distance" occurs because all outcomes of any such measurements have already been determined by the universe. In such a system, sentient beings could be fooled into believing they have free will through some mechanism (such as an organizing principle that presents remembered "past" events and wide-open possibilities for "unre-membered" events that are thus considered to be "future"), even though the actual events have "always" been determined from the very beginning in this assumed superdeterministic universe. I, for one, believe that we truly have free will, and that this loophole will never be applicable, because in the primordial mind hypothesis, consciousness is what creates all of emerging reality. The Collective Mind influences all of unfolding reality through the free will of sentient beings, like humans.

Renowned physicist John Wheeler proposed a thought experiment in the late 1970s to further probe the mysterious nature of quantum physics through the double-slit experiment. This experiment examines the behavior of photons to assess the level at which they "sense" and "adapt" to an experimental setup, using very fast switching of various detectors to isolate the specific factors involved in the photon's behavior.

The general approach in this "delayed choice quantum eraser" type of experiment is to make each photon "decide" whether it is to demonstrate either particle or wave behavior. Even as the photon is still en route to the detection device, a second change in the experimental setup uses a quantum random number generator to serve as the choice of the observer. This would make it seem as if the photon had "changed its mind," or "chosen" to behave in the opposite way.

Placing two aligned polarizers at each of the two slits cancels out any wavelike behavior by providing the "which path" information, thus "collapsing the wave function." However, placing the photon detectors so that the photons encounter them only *after* passing through the slits allows the photons to delay their choice as to whether to behave as particles or waves, i.e., whether to traverse one or both slits. This is most peculiar!

Even stranger is the fact that one can "erase" the past for these photons through an adjustment to the experimental apparatus. By using a third polarizer that erases the effect of forcing the photons' decisions about behavior as wave or particle, one finds you can restore the photons to their original state of behaving as waves, as demonstrated by their display of an interference pattern after passage through the third polarizer.

In a version of Wheeler's delayed choice quantum eraser experiment reported in 2015, Andrew G. Manning and his colleagues used a single helium atom in a special interferometer to create an atomic analogue of Wheeler's original proposal. They replaced the physical beam splitters and mirrors of the original experiment with optical Bragg pulses to assess the atom's quantum state. In some ways, the fact that this experiment, using a slow-moving helium atom at very cold temperature, still shows the erasure of its quantum past by a future event (determination of the method of detection by a quantum random number generator choice made *after* the atom has passed the pi-pulse, that replaces the slit[s] of the original experiment), is even more shocking than similar demonstrations with fast-moving photons because this experiment more closely resembles our classical world. Manning and team concluded, in agreement with generations of physicists similarly shocked by the "spooky" findings of quantum experiments, that it does not make sense to ascribe the wave or particle behavior to a massive particle before the measurement takes place. The act of observation determines emergent reality.

Berkeley's conclusion that "to be is to be perceived" (from Chapter 5) was invoked by physicist Wheeler in explaining the astonishing results of his delayed choice quantum eraser experiments:

> The thing that causes people to argue about when and how the photon learns that the experimental apparatus is in a certain configuration and then changes from wave to particle to fit the demands of the experiment's configuration is the assumption that a photon had some physical form before the astronomers observed it. Either it was a wave or a particle; either it went both ways around the galaxy or only one way. Actually, quantum phenomena are neither waves nor particles but are intrinsically undefined until the moment they are measured. In a sense, the British philosopher Bishop [George] Berkeley was right when he asserted two centuries ago "to be is to be perceived."

—*John Wheeler (1911–2008)*

Clarification requires a thought experiment in which, for the moment, we assume not only that the brain is a quantum computer, but we go so far as to admit that the mysterious nature of results in quantum physics is actually the smoking gun revealing that *all* of reality is quantum—in other words, all is contained within consciousness itself.

Princeton philosopher of logic Hal Halvorson offers an interesting perspective in his recent writings.[2] By combining the concepts of superposition and entanglement with the way quantum systems evolve over time (especially that changes of quantum state always preserve superpositions, i.e., "linear dynamics" or "unitarity" prevails), when we make observations, we become entangled with physical objects so that *we* end up having no determinate properties.

The measurement paradox reveals the apparent incoherence of quantum mechanics, which quantum physicists have attempted to resolve in three main ways.

One can reject the superposition principle by invoking hidden variables, as occurs in David Bohm's interpretation. This requires an empirically undetectable guiding field that does not carry any energy-momentum and is not associated with any specific region of space-time (unlike all other fields in physics—note that as much as Einstein sought such a deterministic interpretation, the mysterious nature of Bohm's guiding field was too much of a stretch for him to accept). Note that Bohm viewed such a guiding field as having a quasi-mental nature, in that the guiding field contains "objective and active information . . . similar in certain key ways to the activity of information in our ordinary subjective experience," leading to a close analogy between matter and mind, resulting in "a new theory of mind, matter, and their relationship, in which the basic notion is participation rather than interaction."[3]

Alternatively, one can deny that observation actually occurs, as in the popular Hugh Everett's many-worlds interpretation (MWI) of quantum physics. In Everett's view, the act of measurement leads to the observer becoming entangled with both the object being observed and the measurement device, such that, at the end of measurement, one has not been required to have a definite observation because all possible observations lead to a new parallel universe in which only that one result occurs. The price paid is the most nonparsimonious invocation of infinite parallel universes, to avoid any actual measurement or observation.

Simply put, Everett wished to fully satisfy the mathematical formulations of quantum physics and found that he could readily do so by assuming that every possible subatomic interaction actually occurred, but each such instance branched into a new universe. Decoherence—or destruction of quantum-state information through interaction with the physical environment—is the postulated mechanism replacing wave-function collapse. In effect, this removes the observer from the system. Thus there is no need to postulate wave-function collapse by the observing mind. This is the driving goal of Everett's interpretation of infinite parallel universes arising at every instant in space-time, each reflecting the perfection of the evolving wave function and its determination of subatomic actuality. The observed universe is thus only one superposition of possible quantum states among an infinity of possible universes.

Of course, parsimony is not one of MWI's virtues, but at least it keeps the mathematics and predictability of quantum physics intact. To be fair, proponents of Everett's MWI argue that Occam's razor would best be satisfied by their interpretation: The complexity of the model is less than that of opposing interpretations, even though the apparent multiplicity of universes might seem objectionable. Note that conservation of energy continues to apply within a given observable universe to avoid the extreme violation of conservation of energy that would be unleashed if such were not the case (given the explosion of novel universes, all to satisfy the MWI).

In a third possibility, dynamical reduction theories allow one to reject the dynamical laws of quantum mechanics, especially the notion that superpositions are preserved over time. This third option, in my mind, makes the most sense in invoking metaphysical (or ontological) idealism. It involves the presupposition that human (and all sentient) beings are crucial to evolving reality, i.e., that our very consciousness elevates us above the status of mere physical matter. In a sense, I see all of our conscious awareness of experience, and all memory of such experience, as occurring in the realm of the Collective Mind, outside of the four-dimensional space-time of the physical universe. Here, I am stipulating that "the More" of William James is the soul or spirit that influences all of evolving reality. It is also "the More" because it is that which is required to fully explain causality, which cannot be accomplished within the physical universe alone.

Superpositions occur among the various constituents of the microscopic physical world, but such a concept does not apply to the realm of consciousness and the Collective Mind. As Erwin Schrödinger first pointed out, and others (such as physicists Roger Penrose, David Albert, and Barry Loewer, among others) have remarked in support, it makes no sense to say that mental states can exist in superposition; they are simply that which is observed—the perception in the mind of the percipient. Even though superposed physical states are not something we actually observe, their consequences—such as the interference pattern in the double-slit experiment—are observed. Thus, the notion of superposition of physical states has direct empirical implications.

The most popular of such dynamical reduction theories is that of Italian theoretical physicists Giancarlo Ghirardi, Alberto Rimini, and Tullio Weber, or GRW theory (named for the initials of their surnames, originally published in 1985). This theory utilizes the fact that collapse of a component of a quantum system is "contagious" and perpetuates throughout the entire quantum system through entanglement. Thus the very rare (about once per one hundred million years) but random and spontaneous collapse of the wave function of a particle in, say, a measuring device (containing more than a million quadrillion such particles), will lead to the collapse of the wave function throughout the entire system, all through the entangled nature of the assemblage of all particles involved.

Halvorson makes sense of the measurement paradox by arguing (as would most psychologists) that mental states are unlike physical states in that they *cannot be superposed,* and thus cannot become entangled with physical states. He then proceeds to elaborate a psychophysical interaction in which mental states reliably track the states of the physical world. He invokes a form of what is known as the logical independence hypothesis by noting the conceptual distinction that a physical state is a different sort of thing than a mental state, and that "physical states do not logically or conceptually necessitate mental states, and vice versa." He compares mental and physical states with the complementary conjugates of quantum physics, such as position and momentum, or of time and energy.

Returning to the GRW collapse theory, Halvorson explains, "If a physical thing (e.g., a brain) is joined to a nonphysical thing (e.g., a mind) in such a way that their states are correlated in a lawlike way, then the physical thing cannot exactly and without exception obey the laws of quantum mechanics. The nonexistence of superpositions of mental states entails that the joint physical-mental object cannot obey the laws of quantum mechanics. . . . If the physical part in isolation would follow the rules of quantum mechanics but is *constrained by the nature of its mental counterpart*, then the GRW laws would provide a highly natural and harmonious way for these two sorts of objects to interact with each other and with other physical objects." (Italics are mine.)

Halvorson concludes that this position, which outlines a process by which the soul could interact with the brain and body, should please a mind-body dualist by underwriting this argument with the metaphysics assuming the mental aspect of dualism, thus of mind influencing matter through this mechanism. What I would add to this argument is that this reasoning also applies to our chosen assumption of metaphysical idealism and the mind's influence on the physical world, given that all that exists originates in that mental realm. In fact, metaphysical idealism is preferable to any dualistic arrangements by eliminating any thorny issues around dualistic interactions, such as violations of the law of conservation of energy in attempts to describe the mechanism by which mind would influence matter.

It is too early to be committing to any one of the current interpretations as "the answer," although I believe that various features of the GRW collapse hypothesis lend it certain appeal. Another interpretation that has garnered significant interest is the orchestrated objective reduction ("Orchestrated OR") interpretation proposed by British mathematical physicist Roger Penrose and American anesthesiologist Stuart Hameroff.

In his remarkable 1989 book *The Emperor's New Mind* (and expanded upon in his 1997 book *The Large, the Small and the Human Mind*), Penrose observed that human thought is noncomputable in that mathematicians can know the truth of certain statements that are unprovable in a fundamental sense. This "fundamental sense" had been expressed by the towering genius of the great 20th-century philosopher Kurt Gödel. Gödel, through his renowned incompleteness theorems, addressed the impossibility of proving both the *consistency* and *completeness* of any mathematical system from within itself without reference to rules completely outside of itself. I believe that, in many ways, this same limitation applies to achieving any understanding of consciousness from "within itself," which I would refine to mean from within the temporally and spatially bound forms of limited conscious awareness generally available to humans only surveying the physical realm. Thus, only through the states of transcendent conscious awareness that we sense in reuniting with the Collective Mind do we gain sufficient perspective to help us better realize the underpinnings of the mind-body relationship, and the resultant grokking of the nature of underlying reality.

In particular, Penrose and Hameroff's elucidation of the microtubules in neurons as an environment that can actually preserve quantum information long enough for it to play a role in the generation of human consciousness is a valuable addition to our understanding. In their model, wave-function collapse occurs through an objective process dependent on the yet-to-be-defined effects of quantum gravity (itself related to the difference in space-time curvature between various candidate states of actualities, with an objective threshold for such collapses to occur). Briefly, as the energy difference between two distinct quantum states approaches Penrose's "1 graviton" level (approximately equal to a Planck mass, or about 0.022 milligram, roughly that of a flea's egg), then the quantum state collapses to one actual value.

Penrose and Hameroff are not approaching such wave-function collapse as the result of primordial consciousness influencing emergent reality, but I believe that much of their mechanistic concepts could be linked to such metaphysical idealism to reveal a means by which consciousness influences all of the physical realm into our perceptions of it.

Quantum physics clearly opens the door to a much richer role for consciousness itself in determining the nature of unfolding reality, in spite of the sometimes vehement opposition from those still seduced by the cunning, baffling, and powerful nature of the Supreme Illusion concerning the "reality" of the material world. I do not feel that we are far enough along to be deciding on the "correct" interpretation of the measurement paradox in quantum physics, but I strongly suspect we can only make sense of the measurement paradox as we come to refine the mechanism by which consciousness influences the apparent evolving reality we experience.

BIBLIOGRAPHY

Alexander, Eben. *The Map of Heaven: How Science, Religion, and Ordinary People Are Proving the Afterlife.* New York: Simon & Schuster, 2014.

———. *Proof of Heaven: A Neurosurgeon's Journey into the Afterlife.* New York: Simon & Schuster, 2012.

Bair, Puran, and Susanna Bair. *Living from the Heart: Heart Rhythm Meditation for Energy, Clarity, Peace, and Inner Power,* 2nd ed. Tucson, AZ: Living Heart Media, 2010.

Baker, Mark C., and Stewart Goetz, eds. *The Soul Hypothesis: Investigations into the Existence of the Soul.* New York: Continuum International Publishing Group, 2011.

Beischel, Julie. *Investigating Mediums: A Windbridge Institute Collection.* Tucson, AZ: The Windbridge Institute, 2015.

Capra, Fritjof. *The Tao of Physics: An Exploration of the Parallels Between Modern Physics and Eastern Mysticism.* Berkeley, CA: Shambhala, 1975.

Chalmers, David J. *The Conscious Mind: In Search of a Fundamental Theory.* Oxford, UK: Oxford University Press, 1996.

Chopra, Deepak, and Rudolph E. Tanzi. *Super Genes: Unlock the Astonishing Power of Your DNA for Optimum Health and Well-Being.* New York: Penguin Random House, 2015.

Dalai Lama XIV. *The Universe in a Single Atom: The Convergence of Science and Spirituality.* New York: Random House, 2005.

Dass, Ram. *Be Here Now.* San Cristobal, NM: Lama Foundation, 1971.

———. *Be Love Now: The Path of the Heart.* New York: HarperCollins Publishers, 2011.

Dossey, Larry. *Healing Words: The Power of Prayer and the Practice of Medicine.* New York: HarperCollins Publishers, 1993.

———. *One Mind: How Our Individual Mind Is Part of a Greater Consciousness and Why It Matters.* New York: Hay House, 2013.

Dupré, Louis, and James A. Wiseman, eds. *Light from Light: An Anthology of Christian Mysticism.* New York: Paulist Press, 2001.

Grof, Stanislav. *Psychology of the Future: Lessons from Modern Consciousness Research.* Albany, NY: State University of New York Press, 2000.

Grossman, Neal. *The Spirit of Spinoza: Healing the Mind.* Princeton, NJ: ICRL Press, 2003.

Guggenheim, Bill, and Judy Guggenheim. *Hello from Heaven!* New York: Bantam Books, 1995.

Hagan, John C. III. *The Science of Near-Death Experiences.* Columbia, MO: University of Missouri Press, 2017.

Hamilton, Allan. *The Scalpel and the Soul: Encounters with Surgery, the Supernatural, and the Healing Power of Hope.* New York: Penguin Group, 2008.

Hancock, Graham. *Fingerprints of the Gods: The Evidence of Earth's Lost Civilization.* New York: Crown Publishers, Inc., 1995.

Holden, Jan, Bruce Greyson, and Debbie James, eds. *The Handbook of Near-Death Experiences: Thirty Years of Investigation.* Santa Barbara, CA: ABC-CLIO, 2009.

Jackson, Laura Lynne. *The Light Between Us: Stories from Heaven, Lessons for the Living.* New York: Random House, 2016.

Jahn, Robert, and Brenda Dunne. *Margins of Reality: The Role of Consciousness in the Physical World.* Orlando, FL: Harcourt Brace Jovanovich, 1987.

Kak, Subhash, Sir Roger Penrose, Stuart Hameroff, eds. *Quantum Physics of Consciousness.* Cambridge, MA: Cosmology Science Publishers, 2011.

Kastrup, Bernardo. *Brief Peeks Beyond: Critical Essays on Metaphysics, Neuroscience, Free Will, Skepticism, and Culture.* Winchester, UK: Iff books, 2015.

———. *More Than Allegory: On Religious Myth, Truth, and Belief.* Winchester, UK: Iff books, 2016.

Kelly, Edward F., Adam Crabtree, and Paul Marshall, eds. *Beyond Physicalism: Toward Reconciliation of Science and Spirituality.* Lanham, MD: Rowman & Littlefield, 2015.

Kelly, Edward F., Emily Williams Kelly, Adam Crabtree, Alan Gauld, Michael Grosso, and Bruce Greyson. *Irreducible Mind: Toward a Psychology for the 21st Century.* Lanham, MD: Rowman & Littlefield, 2007.

McFadden, Johnjoe, and Jim Al-Khalili. *Life on the Edge: The Coming of Age of Quantum Biology.* New York: Crown Publishers, 2014.

Mitchell, Edgar D. *The Way of the Explorer: An Apollo Astronaut's Journey through the Material and Mystical Worlds.* Norwalk, CT: The Easton Press, 1996.

Mitchell, Edgar D., et al. *Psychic Exploration: A Challenge for Science.* New York: G.P. Putnam's Sons, 1974.

Monroe, Robert. *Journeys Out of the Body.* New York: Doubleday, 1971.

Moody, Raymond. *Life after Life: The Investigation of a Phenomenon—Survival of Bodily Death.* MBB Inc., 1975.

Moody, Raymond, with Paul Perry. *Glimpses of Eternity: Sharing a Loved One's Passage from This Life to the Next.* New York: Guideposts, 2010.

Moorjani, Anita. *Dying to Be Me: My Journey from Cancer, to Near Death, to True Healing.* New York: Hay House, 2012.

Newton, Michael. *Journey of Souls: Case Studies of Life Between Lives.* Woodbury, MN: Llewellyn Publications, 1994.

Olsen, Scott. *The Golden Section: Nature's Greatest Secret.* New York: Walker & Company, 2006.

O'Neill, John J. *Prodigal Genius: The Life of Nikola Tesla.* New York: Ives Washburn, Inc. 1944.

Pearce, Joseph Chilton. *The Biology of Transcendence: A Blueprint of the Human Spirit.* Rochester, NY: Park Street Press, 2002.

Penfield, Wilder. *The Mystery of the Mind*. Princeton, NJ: Princeton University Press, 1975.

Penrose, Roger. *The Emperor's New Mind: Concerning Computers, Minds, and the Laws of Physics*. New York: Oxford University Press, 1989.

———. *The Large, the Small and the Human Mind*. Cambridge, UK: Cambridge University Press, 1997.

Plato. *Gorgias and Timaeus*. Translated by Benjamin Jowett. Mineola, NY: Dover Publications, 2003.

Radin, Dean. *Conscious Universe: The Scientific Truth of Psychic Phenomena*. New York: HarperCollins Publishers, 1997.

———. *Entangled Minds: Extrasensory Experiences in a Quantum Reality*. New York: Simon & Schuster, 2006.

———. *Supernormal: Science, Yoga, and the Evidence for Extraordinary Psychic Abilities*. New York: Random House, 2013.

Rankin, Lissa. *Mind Over Medicine: Scientific Proof That You Can Heal Yourself*. New York: Hay House, 2013.

Ritchie, George C. *Return from Tomorrow*. Grand Rapids, MI: Revell Books, 1978.

Rivas, Titus, Anny Dirven, and Rudolf H. Smit. *The Self Does Not Die: Verified Paranormal Phenomena from Near-Death Experiences*. Durham, NC: IANDS Publications, 2016.

Schwartz, Gary. *The Afterlife Experiments: Breakthrough Scientific Evidence of Life After Death*. New York: Simon & Schuster, 2002.

Schwartz, Robert. *Your Soul's Plan: Discovering the Real Meaning of the Life You Planned Before You Were Born*. Berkeley, CA: Frog Books, 2007.

Singer, Michael A. *The Untethered Soul: The Journey Beyond Yourself*. Oakland, CA: New Harbinger Publications, Inc., 2007.

Stapp, Henry P. *Mindful Universe: Quantum Mechanics and the Participating Observer*. Heidelberg: Springer, 2007.

Teilhard de Chardin, Pierre. *The Phenomenon of Man*. New York: Harper & Row, 1959.

Tolle, Eckhart. *The Power of Now: A Guide to Spiritual Enlightenment*. Novato, CA: New World Library, 1999.

Tucker, Jim B. *Return to Life: Extraordinary Cases of Children Who Remember Past Lives*. New York: St. Martin's Griffin, 2013.

Turner, Kelly A. *Radical Remission: Surviving Cancer Against All Odds*. New York: HarperCollins Publishers, 2014.

van Lommel, Pim. *Consciousness Beyond Life: The Science of the Near-Death Experience*. HarperCollins Publishers, 2010.

Zukav, Gary. *The Dancing Wu Li Masters: An Overview of the New Physics*. New York: William Morrow and Company, 1979.

———. *The Seat of the Soul*. New York: Simon & Schuster, 1989.

ENDNOTES

CHAPTER 2

1   M. Thonnard, et al., "Characteristics of Near-Death Experiences Memories as Compared to Real and Imagined Events Memories," *PLOS ONE* 8 (2013), 3, doi:10.1371/journal.pone.0057620.

2   A. Palmieri et al., "'Reality' of Near-Death-Experience Memories: Evidence from a Psychodynamic and Electrophysiological Integrated Study," *Frontiers in Human Neuroscience* 8 (2014), doi.org/10.3389/fnhum.2014.00429.

3   James William. *Human Immortality: Two Supposed Objections to the Doctrine,* 2nd ed. (Boston: Houghton, Mifflin, 1900). Original work published in 1898.

CHAPTER 3

1   Pim van Lommel et al., "Near-Death Experience in Survivors of Cardiac Arrest: A Prospective Study in the Netherlands," *Lancet* 358, no. 9298 (2001), 2039–45.

CHAPTER 4

1   Wilder Penfield and Theodore C. Erickson, *Epilepsy and Cerebral Localization: A Study of the Mechanism, Treatment and Prevention of Epileptic Seizures* (Springfield, IL: Charles C. Thomas, 1941), 127–30.

2   Wilder Penfield, *Mystery of the Mind* (Princeton, NJ: Princeton University Press, 1975), 113–14.

3   Daryl J. Bem, "Feeling the Future: Experimental Evidence for Anomalous Retroactive Influences on Cognition and Affect," *Journal of Personality and Social Psychology* 100, no. 3 (2011): 407–25.

4   D. Bem et al., "Feeling the Future: A Meta-Analysis of 90 Experiments on the Anomalous Anticipation of Random Future Events," *F1000Research* 4 (2015), 1188, doi:10.12688/f1000research.7177.1.

5   Michael Nahm et al., "Terminal Lucidity: A Review and a Case Collection," *Archives of Gerontology and Geriatrics* 55, no. 1 (2012): 138–42, doi:10.1016 /j.archger.2011.06.03.

CHAPTER 5

1   Daryl J. Bem, "Feeling the Future: Experimental Evidence for Anomalous Retroactive Influences on Cognition and Affect," *Journal of Personality and Social Psychology* 100, no. 3 (2011), 407–25.

2   M. Ringbauer et al., "Measurements on the Reality of the Wavefunction," *arXiv*: 1412.6213v2 [qaunt-ph], January 20, 2015.

3   Bernardo Kastrup, *Brief Peeks Beyond: Critical Essays on Metaphysics, Neuroscience, Free Will, Skepticism and Culture* (Winchester, UK: Iff Books, 2015), 157–64.

4   Bernardo Kastrup, "Transcending the Brain: At Least Some Cases of Physical Damage Are Associated with Enriched Consciousness or Cognitive Skill," *Scientific American* (blog), March 29, 2017, https://blogs.scientificamerican.com/guest-blog /transcending-the-brain/.

5   D. Radin, L. Michel, and A. Delorme, "Psychophysical Modulation of Fringe Visibility in a Distant Double-Slit Optical System," *Physics Essays* 29, no. 1 (2016), 14–22.

CHAPTER 6

1   John J. O'Neill, *Prodigal Genius: The Life of Nikola Tesla* (New York: Ives Washburn, Inc., 1944), 265–67.

CHAPTER 8

1   R. L. Carhart-Harris et al., "Neural Correlates of the Psychedelic State Determined by fMRI Studies with Psilocybin," *Proceedings of the National Academy of Sciences of the United States of America* 109, no. 6 (February 2012), 2138–43.

2   F. Palhano-Fontes et al., "The Psychedelic State Induced by Ayahuasca Modulates the Activity and Connectivity of the Default Mode Network," *PLOS ONE* (February 2015), https://doi.org/10.1371/journal.pone.0118143.

3   M. Ullman, S. Krippner, and A. Vaughan, *Dream Telepathy: Experiments in Nocturnal ESP,* 2nd ed. (Jefferson, NC: McFarland, 1989).

CHAPTER 11

1   A. J. Rock et al., "Discarnate Readings by Claimant Mediums: Assessing Phenomenology and Accuracy Under Beyond Double-Blind Conditions," *Journal of Parapsychology* 78, no. 2 (2014), 183–94, http://windbridge.org/papers /JP2014v78n2RockBeischel.pdf.

CHAPTER 15

1   H. Benson and R Friedman, "Harnessing the Power of the Placebo Effect and Renaming It 'Remembered Wellness,'" *Annual Review of Medicine* 47 (February 1996), 193–99, doi:10.1146/annurev.med.47.1.193.

CHAPTER 16

1   Heidi S. Mortensen et al., "Quantitative Relationships in Delphinid Neocortex," *Frontiers in Neuroanatomy* 8, no. 132 (2014), 1–10, http://journal .frontiersin.org/article/10.3389/fnana.2014.00132/abstract.

APPENDIX A

1   Wilder Penfield and Theodore C. Erickson, *Epilepsy and Cerebral Localization: A Study of the Mechanism, Treatment and Prevention of Epileptic Seizures* (Springfield, IL: Charles C. Thomas, 1941), 52–56.

2   Wilder Penfield, "The Role of the Temporal Cortex in Certain Psychical Phenomena," *Journal of Mental Science* 101, no. 424 (1955), 453.

3   Brenda Milner, "Memory Mechanisms," *Canadian Medical Association Journal* 116 (1977), 1374–76.

4   Andreas Papassotiropoulos et al., "The Prion Gene Is Associated with Human Long-Term Memory," *Human Molecular Genetics* (Oxford Journals) 14, no. 15 (2005), 2241–46, doi:10.1093/hmg/ddi228. PMID 15987701.

5   C. Miller and J. Sweatt, "Covalent Modification of DNA Regulates Memory Formation," *Neuron* 53, no. 6 (March 5, 2007), 857–69, doi:10.1016/j.neuron .2007.02.022. PMID 17359920.

6   M. Hendricks, "Reducing Memory to a Molecule: A Researcher Explores the Molecular Essence of Memory," *Johns Hopkins Medicine,* Institute for Basic Biomedical Sciences (2009), http://www.hopkinsmedicine.org/institute_basic _biomedical_sciences/news_events/articles_and_stories/learning_memory/200906 _reducing_memory_molecule.html.

7   G. Kastellakis, A. J. Silva, and P. Poirazi, "Linking Memories across Time via Neuronal and Dendritic Overlaps in Model Neurons with Active Dendrites," *Cell Reports* 17, no. 6 (2016): 1491–1504, http://dx.doi.org/10.1016/j.celrep.2016.10.015.

8   T. J. A. Craddock, J. A. Tuszynski, and S. Hameroff, "Cytoskeletal Signaling: Is Memory Encoded in Microtubule Lattices by a CaMKII Phosphorylation?" *PLOS Computational Biology* 8, no. 3 (2012), e1002421.

APPENDIX B

1   M. Ringbauer et al., "Measurements on the Reality of the Wavefunction," *arXiv:* 1412.6213v2 [qaunt-ph], January 20, 2015.

2   Hans Halvorson, "The Measure of All Things," in *The Soul Hypothesis: Investigations into the Existence of the Soul,* ed. Mark C. Baker and Stewart Goetz (New York: Continuum International Books, 2011), 138–63.

3   David Bohm, "A New Theory of the Relationship of Mind and Matter," *Philosophical Psychology* 3, no. 2 (1990), 271–86.

INDEX